FEDERAL ROLE IN FUNDING RESEARCH AND DEVELOPMENT

CONGRESSIONAL POLICIES, PRACTICES AND PROCEDURES

Additional books in this series can be found on Nova's website at:

https://www.novapublishers.com/catalog/index.php?cPath=23_29&seriesp=
Congressional+Policies%2C+Practices+and+Procedures

Additional E-books in this series can be found on Nova's website at:

https://www.novapublishers.com/catalog/index.php?cPath=23_29&seriespe=
Congressional+Policies%2C+Practices+and+Procedures

CONGRESSIONAL POLICIES, PRACTICES AND PROCEDURES

FEDERAL ROLE IN FUNDING RESEARCH AND DEVELOPMENT

PIPER B. COLLINS
EDITOR

Nova
Nova Science Publishers, Inc.
New York

NOTICE TO THE READER

LIBRARY OF CONGRESS CATALOGING-IN-PUBLICATION DATA

Available upon request.
ISBN : 978-1-60741-486-5

Published by Nova Science Publishers, Inc. † *New York*

CONTENTS

PREFACE

The United States government supports a broad range of scientific and engineering research and development R&D. Its purposes include addressing specific concerns such as national defense, health, safety, the environment, and energy security, as well as advancing knowledge generally, developing the scientific and engineering workforce and strengthening U.S. innovation and competitiveness in the global economy. The federal government has played an important role in supporting R&D efforts that have led to scientific breakthroughs and new technologies. This book examines the federal role in funding research and development in such areas as energy technology, colleges and universities, and others.

Chapter 1 - Some policymakers have concluded that the energy challenges facing the United States are so critical that a concentrated investment in energy research and development (R&D) should be undertaken. The Manhattan project, which produced the atomic bomb, and the Apollo program, which landed American men on the moon, have been cited as examples of the success such R&D investments can yield. Investment in federal energy technology R&D programs of the 1970s, in response to two energy crises, have generally been viewed as less successful than the earlier two efforts. This report compares and contrasts the three initiatives.

In 2007 dollars, the cumulative cost of the Manhattan project over 5 fiscal years was approximately $21 billion; of the Apollo program over 14 fiscal years, approximately $96 billion; of post-oil shock energy R&D efforts over 35 fiscal years, $115 billion. A measure of the nation's commitments to the programs is their relative shares of the federal outlays during the years of peak funding: for the Manhattan program, the peak year funding was 1% of federal outlays; for the Apollo program, 2.2%; and for energy technology R&D programs, 0.5%. Another measure of the commitment is their relative shares of the nation's gross domestic product (GDP) during the peak years of funding: for the Manhattan project and the Apollo program, the peak year funding reached 0.4% of GDP, and for the energy technology R&D programs, 0.1%.

Besides funding, several criteria might be used to compare these three initiatives including perception of the program or threat, goal clarity, and the customer of the technology being developed. By these criteria, while the Manhattan project and the Apollo program may provide some useful analogies for thinking about an energy technology R&D initiative, there are fundamental differences between the forces that drove these historical R&D success stories and the forces driving energy technology R&D today. Critical differences include (1) the ability to transform the program or threat into a concrete goal, and (2) the use to which the technology would be put. On the issue of goal setting, for the Manhattan project, the response to the threat ofenemy development of a nuclear bomb was the goal to construct a bomb; for the Apollo program, the threat of Soviet space dominance was translated into a specific goal of landing on the moon. For energy, the response to the problems of insecure oil sources and high prices has resulted in multiple, sometimes conflicting, goals. Regarding use, both the Manhattan project and the Apollo program goals pointed to technologies primarily for governmental use with little concern about their environmental impact; for energy, in contrast, the hoped-for outcome depends on commercial viability and mitigation of environmental impacts from energy use.

Although the Manhattan project and the Apollo program may provide some useful analogies for funding, these differences may limit their utility regarding energy policy. Rather, energy technology R&D has been driven by at least three not always commensurate goals — resource and technological diversity, commercial viability, and environmental protection — which were not goals of the historical programs.

Some policymakers have concluded that the energy challenges facing the United States are so critical that a concentrated investment in energy research and development (R&D) should be undertaken.[1] The Manhattan project, which produced the atomic bomb, and the Apollo program, which landed American men on the moon, have been cited as examples of the success such R&D investments can yield. Investment in federal energy technology R&D programs of the 1970s, in response to two energy crises, have generally been viewed as less successful than the earlier two efforts. This report compares and contrasts the goals of, and the investments in, the three initiatives, which may provide useful insights for Congress as it assesses and debates the nation's energy policy.

Chapter 2 - In the early 1990s, Congress recognized that several federal agencies had ongoing high-performance computing programs, but no central coordinating body existed to ensure long-term coordination and planning. To provide such a framework, Congress passed the High-Performance Computing and Communications Program Act of 1991 (P.L. 102-194) to enhance the effectiveness of the various programs. In conjunction with the passage of the act, the White House Office of Science and Technology Policy (OSTP) released *Grand Challenges: High-Performance Computing and Communications*. That document outlined a research and development (R&D) strategy for high-performance computing and a framework for a multiagency program, the High-Performance Computing and Communications (HPCC) Program. The HPCC Program has evolved over time and is now called the Networking and Information Technology Research and Development (NITRD) Program, to better reflect its expanded mission.

Proponents assert that federal support of information technology (IT) R&D has produced positive outcomes for the country and played a crucial role in supporting long-term research into fundamental aspects of computing. Such fundamentals provide broad practical benefits, but generally take years to realize. Additionally, the unanticipated results of research are often as important as the anticipated results. Another aspect of government-funded IT research is that it often leads to open standards, something that many perceive as beneficial, encouraging deployment and further investment. Industry, on the other hand, is more inclined to invest in proprietary products and will diverge from a common standard when there is a potential competitive or financial advantage to do so. Finally, proponents of government support believe that the outcomes achieved through the various funding programs create a synergistic environment in which both fundamental and application-driven research are conducted, benefitting government, industry, academia, and the public. Supporters also believe that such outcomes justify government's role in funding IT R&D, as well as the growing budget for the NITRD Program. Critics assert that the government, through its funding mechanisms, may be picking "winners and losers" in technological development, a role more properly residing with the private sector. For example, the size of the NITRD Program may encourage industry to follow the government's lead on research directions rather than selecting those directions itself.

The FY2009 budget calls for $3.548 billion for the NITRD Program, an increase from the FY2008 projected budget of $3.341 billion. Because the NITRD Program "budget" consists of the budgets allocated to the 13 participating agencies, final budget figures are not available for FY2008.

Chapter 3 - The historically black colleges and universities (HBCUs), which have traditionally educated a significant number of the nation's blacks, have faced, and continue to face, substantial challenges in attempting to enhance their academic and research capabilities. Some of these institutions have a myriad of problems — aging infrastructures, limited access to digital and wireless networking technology, absence of state-of-the-art equipment, low salary structures, small endowments, and limited funds for faculty development and new academic programs for students. While many of these problems exist in other institutions, they appear to be considerably more serious in HBCUs. In addition, those HBCUs damaged by Hurricane Katrina have the added costs in the millions of replacing facilities, research equipment, and rebuilding their infrastructure. This is an issue for Congress because the distribution of federal funding for HBCUs is one of the critical issues facing these institutions.

HBCUs comprise approximately 2.3% of all institutions of higher education, and enroll approximately 11.6% of all black students attending post-secondary institutions. Approximately 33.0% of the undergraduate degrees in science and engineering earned by blacks were awarded at HBCUs. Some of the most successful programs designed to attract and retain underrepresented minorities into the sciences and in research careers have been initiated at HBCUs. Data indicate that in 2004, HBCUs provided the education for approximately 20.2% of blacks earning bachelor degrees in engineering, 39.5% in the physical sciences, 26.3% in computer science, 37.0% in mathematics, 36.1% in the biological sciences, 47.0% in agricultural sciences, 16.4% in social sciences, and 21.4% in psychology.

On August 14, 2008, the President signed into law P.L. 110-315, the Higher Education Opportunity Act (HEOA). The HEOA provides authority for loans for repair and renovation of academic research facilities, among other facilities. Language in Title III, Part B, provides formula grants to eligible institutions. The percentage of funds allocated to each institution is based on several factors, and no institution can receive less that $250,000. Title III, Part D of the HEOA establishes a bonding authority to raise capital to be lent to HBCUs for repair and renovation of facilities. The total amount that would be available for financing is $1.1 billion. The aggregate authority principal and unpaid accrued interest on these loans cannot be more than $733.3 million for private HBCUs and no more than $366.7 million for public HBCUs. Title III, Part E of the HEOA provides funding for two new minority science and engineering improvement programs. A partnership grant program is directed at increasing the participation of underrepresented minority youth or low- income youth in science, mathematics, engineering, and technology education. Activities to be supported include outreach, hands-on, and experiential-based learning projects. Another program will focus on encouraging minorities to pursue careers in the scientific and technical disciplines.

Chapter 4 - President Bush proposed total research and development (R&D) funding of $147.0 billion in his FY2009 budget request to Congress, a $3.9 billion (2.7%) increase over the estimated FY2008 level of $143.1 billion. The President's request included $29.3 billion for basic research, up $847 million (3.0%) from FY2008; $27.1 billion for applied research, down $1.0 billion (-3.6%); $84.0 billion for development, up 1.6 billion (1.9%); and $6.5 billion for R&D facilities and equipment, up $2.5 billion (61.7%). Congress is to play a central role in defining the nation's R&D priorities, especially with respect to two overarching issues: the extent to which the Federal R&D investment can grow in the context of increased pressure on discretionary spending and how available funding will be prioritized and allocated. A low or negative growth rate in the overall R&D investment may require movement of resources across disciplines, programs, or agencies to address priorities.

The Administration requested significantly larger percentage increases in the R&D budgets of the three agencies that are part of its American Competitiveness Initiative: the Department of Energy's Office of Science, the National Science Foundation, and the National Institute of Standards and Technology. In 2007, Congress authorized substantial R&D increases for these agencies under the America COMPETES Act (P.L. 110-69). The President's budget would reduce R&D funding for the Department of Agriculture, down $357 million; Department of Veterans Affairs, down $76 million; Department of the Interior, down $59 million; and Environmental Protection Agency, down $7 million. The FY2009 request included increases for three multiagency R&D initiatives: the National Nanotechnology Initiative, up $35 million; Networking and Information Technology R&D program, up $194 million; and Climate Change Science Program, up $177 million.

On September 30, 2008, President Bush signed into law H.R. 2638, the Consolidated Security, Disaster Assistance, and Continuing Appropriations Act, 2009 (P.L. 110-329). This act provides FY2009 appropriations for the Department of Defense, Department of Homeland Security, and Military Construction and Veterans Affairs; continued funding for all other agencies not covered under these provisions at their FY2008 funding levels through March 6, 2009; and supplemental funding for disaster relief. Under this act, FY2009 R&D funding is approximately $147.2 billion. None of the FY2008 regular appropriations bills has been passed by both the House and Senate.

For the past two years, federal R&D funding and execution has been affected by mechanisms used to complete the annual appropriations process — the year-long continuing resolution for FY2007 (P.L. 110-5) and the combining of 11 appropriations bills into the Consolidated Appropriations Act, 2008 for FY2008 (P.L. 110-161). For example, FY2008 R&D funding for some agencies and programs is below the level requested by the President and passed by the House of Representatives and the Senate. Completion of appropriations after the beginning of each fiscal year has also resulted in delays or cancellation of planned R&D and equipment acquisition.

Chapter 5 - New knowledge and continuing innovation have been major factors in increasing economic well-being. Private businesses are the largest sponsors of research and development (R&D) in the United States, producing the discoveries that in turn lead to new products and services and the growth of productivity; however, the federal government has long provided significant support for R&D activities to both supplement and encourage private efforts. The government finances research and development through spending—fiscal year 2007 appropriations for R&D activities total $137 billion—and tax benefits that give businesses an incentive to increase their R&D spending.

Studies of federally supported research and development provide multifaceted but incomplete answers to questions about those governmental activities: whether the current level of spending is appropriate, what returns taxpayers receive for public investment in R&D, and whether funds are allocated to areas of inquiry and projects that will provide the highest return on that investment. Results of the Congressional Budget Office's (CBO's) economic analysis of federal support for R&D and its review of trends in the data over time indicate the following:

- Over the 1953–2004 period as a whole, federal spending for R&D has grown, on average, as fast as the overall economy. Spending rose rapidly in the 1950s and early 1960s, reaching almost 2 percent of gross domestic product (GDP) in 1964, a peak that coincided with the acceleration of the U.S. space program. Since then, with the exception of a period in the 1980s—when an expansion of national defense activities prompted more funding for research and development—federal R&D spending has generally declined as a share of GDP.

- Distinguishing between research and development is important in evaluating the effectiveness of the government's R&D spending and the benefits it may provide. Research (particularly basic research) may be conducted without a specific commercial purpose in mind, but it may nevertheless have large "spillovers" in the economy because the knowledge it produces may be useful not only to researchers in other fields but also to businesses seeking to develop new products and production processes. Development occurs closer to a product's introduction so that its benefits go more directly to innovating firms and their customers. The federal government funds about half of all research in the United States but only 17 percent of development. Since the early 1 980s, federal spending for research has grown more steadily and more quickly than federal spending for development.

- Federal funding of research—particularly of basic research—is generally viewed favorably because of its large potential for spillovers and the corresponding economic benefits. Nonetheless, the economic returns to basic research are difficult to measure because the progress that results from research may be hard to identify or to value and the interval between the research and its application to a product or process is sometimes long.

- Studies of federal spending for basic research in the past, particularly studies of research conducted at academic institutions, have estimated that the average returns from that spending exceed the returns that might have been gained had those resources been put to other uses. Additional federal spending could generate comparable benefits, although the returns to individual projects are likely to vary. Also, the gains from large increases in spending might be constrained if sufficient scientific and technical workers and facilities were not available.

- In recent years, the share of federal research funding allocated to the life sciences has expanded, an emphasis supported by the high rates of returns to life sciences research that some studies have reported. But other studies indicate that researchers reach across disciplines for new ideas and tools, which would suggest that supporting research over a wide range of scientific fields is an important element in generating an economic return from federal research funding.

Federal spending for development has generally focused on accomplishing public missions, most prominently that of national defense. Although in the past that spending has generated some commercially viable spin-off technologies, such by-products are largely unpredictable. A consideration of how supported projects would contribute to their stated mission therefore provides the best guidance to policymakers who are responsible for deciding whether to spend public funds for those activities.

In 2004, the research and experimentation (R&E) tax credit drew claims of $5.6 billion from firms, a small amount compared with the funds that lawmakers have appropriated for R&D activities. Studies have found that the credit has the desired effect of boosting R&D spending by businesses; however, those studies do not compare the benefits derived from the increase in research and development with the potential benefits from other uses of the forgone revenues. In addition, the results of those studies may be overstated because firms have an incentive to classify as many expenses as possible as credit-eligible research, even if those expenses are not associated with new R&D activities.

Chapter 6 - In 2006, the federal government spent $13 billion—14 percent of its research and development (R&D) expenditures—to enable 38 federally funded R&D centers (FFRDCs) to meet special research needs. FFRDCs—including laboratories, studies and analyses centers, and systems engineering centers—conduct research in military space programs, nanotechnology, microelectronics, nuclear warfare, and biodefense countermeasures, among other areas. GAO was asked to identify (1) how federal agencies contract with organizations operating FFRDCs and (2) agency oversight processes used to ensure that FFRDCs are well-managed.

GAO's work is based on a review of documents and interviews with officials from eight FFRDCs sponsored by the departments of Defense (DOD), Energy (DOE), Health and Human Services (HHS), and Homeland Security (DHS).

Chapter 7 - Energy research and development (R&D) intended to advance technology played an important role in the successful outcome of World War II. In the post-war era, the federal government conducted R&D on fossil fuel and nuclear energy sources to support peacetime economic growth. The energy crises of the 1970s spurred the government to broaden the focus to include renewable energy and energy efficiency. Over the 30-year period from the Department of Energy's inception at the beginning of fiscal Year (FY) 1978 through FY2007, federal spending for renewable energy R&D amounted to about 16% of the energy R&D total, compared with 15% for energy efficiency, 25% for fossil, and 41% for nuclear. For the 60-year period from 1948 through 2007, nearly 11% went to renewables, compared with 9% for efficiency, 25% for fossil, and 54% for nuclear.

In: Federal Role in Funding Research and Development   ISBN: 978-1-60741-486-5
Editor: Piper B. Collins   © 2010 Nova Science Publishers, Inc.

Chapter 1

THE MANHATTAN PROJECT, THE APOLLO PROGRAM, AND FEDERAL ENERGY TECHNOLOGY R&D PROGRAMS: A COMPARATIVE ANALYSIS

Deborah D. Stine

SUMMARY

Some policymakers have concluded that the energy challenges facing the United States are so critical that a concentrated investment in energy research and development (R&D) should be undertaken. The Manhattan project, which produced the atomic bomb, and the Apollo program, which landed American men on the moon, have been cited as examples of the success such R&D investments can yield. Investment in federal energy technology R&D programs of the 1970s, in response to two energy crises, have generally been viewed as less successful than the earlier two efforts. This report compares and contrasts the three initiatives.

In 2007 dollars, the cumulative cost of the Manhattan project over 5 fiscal years was approximately $21 billion; of the Apollo program over 14 fiscal years, approximately $96 billion; of post-oil shock energy R&D efforts over 35 fiscal years, $115 billion. A measure of the nation's commitments to the programs is their relative shares of the federal outlays during the years of peak funding: for the Manhattan program, the peak year funding was 1% of federal outlays; for the Apollo program, 2.2%; and for energy technology R&D programs, 0.5%. Another measure of the commitment is their relative shares of the nation's gross domestic product (GDP) during the peak years of funding: for the Manhattan project and the Apollo program, the peak year funding reached 0.4% of GDP, and for the energy technology R&D programs, 0.1%.

Besides funding, several criteria might be used to compare these three initiatives including perception of the program or threat, goal clarity, and the customer of the technology being developed. By these criteria, while the Manhattan project and the Apollo program may provide some useful analogies for thinking about an energy technology R&D initiative, there are fundamental differences between the forces that drove these historical R&D success stories and the forces driving energy technology R&D today. Critical differences include (1) the ability to transform the program or threat into a concrete goal, and (2) the use to which the technology would be put. On the issue of goal setting, for the Manhattan project, the response to the threat of enemy development of a nuclear bomb was the goal to construct a bomb; for the Apollo program, the threat of Soviet space dominance was translated into a specific goal of landing on the moon. For energy, the response to the problems of insecure oil sources and high prices has resulted in multiple, sometimes conflicting, goals. Regarding use, both the Manhattan project and the Apollo program goals pointed to technologies primarily for governmental use with little concern about their environmental impact; for energy, in contrast, the hoped-for outcome depends on commercial viability and mitigation of environmental impacts from energy use.

Although the Manhattan project and the Apollo program may provide some useful analogies for funding, these differences may limit their utility regarding energy policy. Rather, energy technology R&D has been driven by at least three not always commensurate goals — resource and technological diversity, commercial viability, and environmental protection — which were not goals of the historical programs.

Some policymakers have concluded that the energy challenges facing the United States are so critical that a concentrated investment in energy research and development (R&D) should be undertaken.[1] The Manhattan project, which produced the atomic bomb, and the Apollo program, which landed American men on the moon, have been cited as examples of the success such R&D investments can yield. Investment in federal energy technology R&D programs of the 1970s, in response to two energy crises, have generally been viewed as less successful than the earlier two efforts. This report compares and contrasts the goals of, and the investments in, the three initiatives, which may provide useful insights for Congress as it assesses and debates the nation's energy policy.

THE MANHATTAN PROJECT

The Manhattan project took place from 1942 to 1946.[2] Beginning in 1939, some key scientists expressed concern that Germany might be building an atomic weapon and proposed that the United States accelerate atomic research in response. Following the Pearl Harbor attack in December 1941, the United States entered World War II. In January 1942, President Franklin D. Roosevelt gave secret, tentative approval for the development of an atomic bomb. The Army Corps of Engineers was assigned the task and set up the Manhattan Engineer District to manage the project. A bomb research and design laboratory was built at Los Alamos, New Mexico. Due to uncertainties regarding production effectiveness, two possible fuels for the reactors were produced with uranium enrichment facilities at Oak Ridge, Tennessee, and plutonium production facilities at Hanford, Washington. In December 1942, Roosevelt gave final approval to construct a nuclear bomb. A bomb using plutonium as fuel was successfully tested south of Los Alamos in July 1945. In August 1945, President Truman decided to use the bomb against Japan at two locations. Japan surrendered a few days after the second bomb attack. At that point, the Manhattan project was deemed to have fulfilled its mission, although some additional nuclear weapons were still assembled. In 1946, the civilian

Atomic Energy Commission was established to manage the nation's future atomic activities, and the Manhattan project officially ended.

According to one estimate, the Manhattan project cost $2.2 billion from 1942 to 1946 ($21 billion in 2007 dollars), which is much greater than the original cost and time estimate of approximately $148 million for 1942 to 1944.[3] General Leslie Groves, who managed the Manhattan project, has written that Members of Congress who inquired about the project were discouraged by the Secretary of War from asking questions or visiting sites.[4] After the project was under way for over a year, in February 1944, War Department officials received essentially a "blank check" for the project from Congressional leadership who "remained completely in the dark" about the Manhattan project, according to Groves and other experts.[5]

THE APOLLO PROGRAM

The Apollo program, FY1960 to FY1973, encompassed 17 missions, including six lunar landings.[6] NASA was created in response to the Soviet launch of Sputnik in 1958 and began operation in 1959.[7] Although preliminary discussions regarding the Apollo program began in 1960, Congress did not decide to fund it until 1961 after the Soviet Union became the first nation to launch a human into space. The goals of the Apollo program were

To land Americans on the Moon and return them safely to Earth;
To establish the technology to meet other national interests in space;
To achieve preeminence in space for the United States;
To carry out a program of scientific exploration of the Moon; and
To develop man's capability to work in the lunar environment.[8]

The program included a three-part spacecraft to take two astronauts to the Moon surface, support them while on the Moon, and return them to Earth.[9] Saturn rockets were used to launch this equipment. In July 1969, Apollo 11 achieved the goal of landing Americans on the Moon and returning them safely to Earth. The last lunar landing took place in December 1972.

The Apollo program was only one part of NASA's activities during this period. NASA's peak funding during the Apollo program occurred in FY1966 when its total funding was $4.5 billion (in current dollars), of which $3.0 billion went to the Apollo program.[10] According to NASA, the total cost of the Apollo program for FY1960-FY1973 was $19.4 billion ($95.7 billion in 2007 dollars).[11] The activities with the greatest cost were the Saturn V rockets ($6.4 billion) followed by the Command and Service Modules ($3.7 billion), the Lunar Modules ($2.2 billion), and Manned Space Flight Operations ($1.6 billion).

ENERGY TECHNOLOGY RESEARCH AND DEVELOPMENT

The Arab oil embargo of 1973 (the "first" energy crisis) put energy policy on the national "agenda." At that time, Americans began to experience rapidly rising prices for fuel and related goods and services.[12] Until then, energy R&D had been focused on the development of nuclear power under the Atomic Energy Commission (AEC). After the Manhattan project ended, Congress had established the AEC to manage both civilian and military projects in the Atomic Energy Act of 1946 (P.L. 79-585).[13] In response to the energy crisis, Congress subsumed the AEC, including the Manhattan project facilities, and other energy programs, into the Energy Research and Development Administration (ERDA), which became the focus for federal energy technology R&D, and the Nuclear Regulatory Commission (NRC) as part of the Energy Reorganization Act of 1974 (P.L. 93-438).[14]

In the Department of Energy Organization Act of 1977 (P.L. 95-91), Congress decided to combine the activities of ERDA with approximately 50 other energy offices and programs in a new Department of Energy (DOE), which began operations on October 1, 1977.[15] In 1979, the Iranian Revolution precipitated the "second" energy crisis that took place from 1978-1981. High oil prices and inflation lasted for several years. An ensuing recession curbed demand and oil prices fell markedly by 1986. The scale of funding for most of DOE's energy R&D programs dropped steadily during the 1980s (see **Figure 1**).

The large energy technology demonstration projects funded during the late 1970s and early 1980s were viewed by some as too elaborate and insufficiently linked to either existing energy research or the marketplace.[16] A well known example is the Synthetic Fuels Corporation (SFC).[17] The goal of SFC was to support largescale projects that industry was unwilling to support due to the technical, environmental, or financial uncertainties. The program ended in 1986 due to a combination of lower energy prices, environmental issues, lack of support by the Reagan Administration, and administrative challenges.[18]

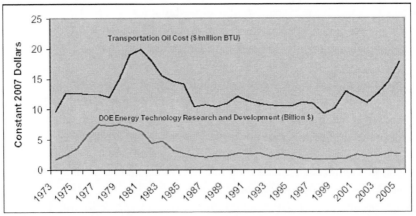

Source: Congressional Research Service. Transportation oil costs are from transportation/petroleum column of Table 3.4 Consumer Price Estimates for Energy by End-Use Sector, 1970-2005 in Energy Information Administration, Annual Energy Review 2007, Report No. DOE/EIA-0384(2007), Posted: June 23, 2008, at [http://www.eia.doe.gov/aer/finan.html]. DOE data is from CRS Report RS22858, *Renewable Energy R&D Funding History: A Comparison with Funding for Nuclear Energy, Fossil Energy, and Energy Efficiency R&D*, by Fred Sissine. Dollars for both transportation oil costs and DOE energy R&D were adjusted to 2007 dollars using the information from Bureau of Economic Analysis, Table 1.1.4. Price Indexes for Gross Domestic Product at [http://www.bea.gov/bea/dn/nipaweb/index.asp].

Figure 1. Comparison of Consumer Transportation Oil Cost and DOE Energy Technology R&D Funding, 1973-2005

Oil prices began to rise substantially in 2004, but funding for energy technology R&D has not increased as it did during the energy crisis of the late 1970s to early 1980s. With oil prices reaching nearly $150 per barrel in July 2008, some believe that the nation is in another energy crisis, while others believe that oil prices will moderate.[19] In the 110th Congress, the policy debate regarding the magnitude and priorities for energy R&D continues — in response both to oil prices and to concerns about climate change, as energy-related activities are a major source of greenhouse gas emissions.[20]

COMPARATIVE ANALYSIS OF THE MANHATTAN PROJECT, THE APOLLO PROGRAM, AND FEDERAL ENERGY TECHNOLOGY R&D

A general understanding of driving forces of and funding histories for the Manhattan project and Apollo program, and a comparison of these two initiatives to Department of Energy (DOE) energy technology R&D programs, may provide useful insights for Congress as it assesses and determines the nation's energy R&D policy. Four criteria that might be used to compare these programs are funding, perception of threat, goal clarity, and technology customer. Each is discussed in more depth below.

Funding

Table 1 provides a comparison of the total and annual average program costs for the Manhattan project, Apollo program, and federal energy technology R&D program since the first energy crisis. Annual average long-term (1974-2008) DOE energy technology R&D funding was approximately $3 billion (in 2007 constant dollars) as is the FY2008 budget and the FY2009 budget request.[21] In comparison, the annual average funding (in 2007 constant dollars) for the Manhattan project was $4 billion and for the Apollo program and the DOE energy technology program at its peak (1975-1980) was $7 billion.

At the time of peak funding, the percentage of federal spending devoted to DOE energy technology R&D was half that of the Manhattan project, and one-fifth that of the Apollo program. From an overall economy standpoint, the percentage of the gross domestic product (GDP) spent on DOE energy technology R&D in the peak funding year was one-fourth that spent on either the Manhattan project or the Apollo program.

As shown in **Figure 2,** although cumulative funding for the DOE energy technology R&D program is greater than for the Manhattan project or the Apollo program, the annual funding for each of the historical programs was higher than that for energy technology R&D which occurred over a greater number of years. This is an important distinction: the Manhattan project and the Apollo program were specific and distinct funding efforts whereas the national energy R&D effort has been ongoing over a longer period of time. In all three cases, a rapid increase in funding was followed by a rapid decline.

Table 1. Cumulative and Annual Average Program Year Funding for the Manhattan Project, the Apollo Program, and DOE Energy Technology R&D Program

	Cumulative Funding (in billions of 2007 dollars)	Number of Fiscal Years	Annual Average Funding Per Program Year (in billions of 2007 dollars)	Percent of Federal Outlays During Year of Peak Funding	Percent of GDP During Year of Peak Funding
The Manhattan Project (1942-1946)	$21	5	$4	1.0	0.4
The Apollo Program (1960-1973)	$96	14	$7	2.2	0.4
DOE Energy Technology Programs (1975-1980) [Peak Funding]	$41	6	$7	0.5	0.1
DOE Energy Technology Program (1974-2008) [Long-Term Funding]	$115	35	$3	0.5	0.1

Source: Congressional Research Service. Manhattan Project data: Richard G. Hewlett and Oscar E. Anderson, Jr., A *History of the United States Atomic Energy Commission: The New World,1939/1946,Volume I.* Apollo program data: Richard Orloff, *Apollo By The Numbers: A Statistical Reference*, NASA SP-2000-4029, 2004 web update. DOE data: CRS Report RS22858, *Renewable Energy R&D Funding History: A Comparison with Funding for Nuclear Energy, Fossil Energy, and Energy Efficiency R&D*, by Fred Sissine. Federal Outlay and Gross Domestic Product (GDP) data: Office of Management and Budget, *Historical Tables, Budget of the United States Government* FY2009. Peak year of funding (in current dollars) for Manhattan project was 1946, for Apollo program, 1966, and for DOE Energy Technology R&D programs, 1980. The greatest annual funding (in constant dollars) for DOE energy technology programs took place from 1975-1980.

Threat Perception

The Manhattan project and Apollo project were both responses to perceived threats, which compelled policymaker support for these initiatives. The Manhattan project took place during World War II. Although the public might have been unaware of the potential threat of Germany's use of nuclear weapons and the Manhattan project, the President and Members of Congress could feel confident about public support for the war effort of which the Manhattan project was a part. Similarly, the Apollo program took place during the Cold War with the Union of Soviet Socialist Republics (USSR). When the USSR launched the Sputnik satellite and first man into space, the U.S. public felt threatened by the potential that the USSR might take leadership in the development of space flight technology, and potentially greater control of outer space. President Jimmy Carter said that

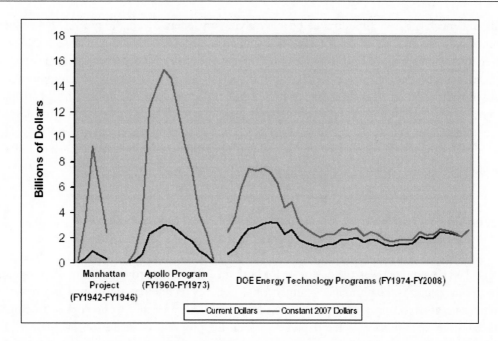

Source: Congressional Research Service. Manhattan Project data: Richard G. Hewlett and Oscar E. Anderson, Jr., A *History of the United States Atomic Energy Commission: The New World, 1939/1946,Volume I.* Apollo program data: Richard Orloff, *Apollo By The Numbers: A Statistical Reference*, NASA SP-2000-4029, 2004 web update. DOE data: CRS Report RS22858, *Renewable Energy R&D Funding History: A Comparison with Funding for Nuclear Energy, Fossil Energy, and Energy Efficiency R&D*, by Fred Sissine.

Figure 2. Annual Funding for Manhattan Project, Apollo Program, and DOE Energy Technology R&D Program

> With the exception of preventing war, this [energy crisis] is the greatest challenge that our country will face during our lifetime ... our decision about energy will test the character of the American people and the ability of the President and the Congress to govern this Nation. This difficult effort will be the 'moral equivalent of war,' except that we will be uniting our efforts to build and not to destroy."[22]

The threat to which investment in energy technology R&D responds, however, is largely economic rather than military. In addition, the threat posed by climate change, which is related to energy consumption, will likely be gradual and longterm.[23]

Goal Clarity

Another issue is the degree to which there is clarity and consensus on the program goal. The Manhattan project had a clear and singular goal — the creation of a nuclear bomb. For the Apollo program, the goal was also clear and singular — land American astronauts on the moon and return them safely to Earth. In the case of energy technology R&D, however, the overall goal of clean, affordable, and reliable energy is multi-faceted. While "energy independence" has from time to time been a rallying cry, energy technology R&D has in fact, been driven by at least three not always commensurate goals: resource and technological diversity, commercial viability, and environmental protection. To help reduce the risk of dependence on a single energy source, diversity of resources and energy technologies have always been seen as a goal of the energy R&D program. Second, unlike the Manhattan project or the Apollo program, the DOE energy technology R&D program seeks ultimately to be commercially viable. Third, the energy R&D program must meet environmental goals, including reducing the impact of energy-related activities on land, water, air, and climate change.

Technology Customer

Another comparison criterion is the customer for technologies that may result from the R&D. The government was the customer for both the Manhattan project and Apollo program. The private sector is the ultimate customer for any energy technology developed as a result of federal energy R&D programs. Therefore, the marketability of any technologies developed will be a key determinant of the degree to which the program is successful. Moreover, the inherent involvement of the private sector raises a number of issues related to the appropriateness of different government roles. Some believe that focusing R&D on one particular technology versus another may result in government, instead of the marketplace, picking "winners and losers."[24] Some experts believe that the most important driver for private sector deployment or commercialization is not the need for new technologies, but regulation or economic incentives.[25] Others, however, believe that without government support and intervention, the private sector is unlikely to conduct the R&D necessary to achieve the public goal of clean, affordable, and reliable energy, and that current technologies are insufficient to achieve this goal.[26]

IMPLICATIONS FOR CONGRESS

When the Manhattan project and the Apollo program are used as analogies for future DOE energy technology R&D, the following points may be important to consider:

To be equivalent in annual average funding, DOE energy technology R&D funding would need to increase from approximately $3 billion in FY2008 to at least $4 billion per program year to match the Manhattan project funding, or $7 billion per program year to match Apollo program funding levels or DOE energy technology R&D funding at its peak. To be equivalent of peak year funding would require even greater increases. In terms of federal outlays, energy technology R&D funding would need to increase from 0.5% to 1% (Manhattan project) or 2.2 % (Apollo program) of federal outlays. As a percentage of GDP, this funding would need to increase from 0.1% to 0.4% of GDP (for both the Manhattan project and the Apollo program).

Both the Manhattan project and the Apollo program had a singular and specific goal. For the Manhattan project, the response to the threat of enemy development of a nuclear bomb was the goal to construct a bomb; for the Apollo program, the threat of Soviet space dominance was translated into a specific goal of landing on the moon. For energy, however, the response to the problems of insecure oil sources and high prices has resulted in multiple, sometimes conflicting goals.

Both the Manhattan project and the Apollo program goals pointed to technologies primarily for governmental use with little concern about their environmental impact; for energy, in contrast, the hoped for outcome depends on commercial viability and mitigation of the environmental impacts of the energy technologies developed.

Although the Manhattan project and the Apollo program may provide some useful analogies for funding, these differences may limit their utility regarding energy policy. Rather, energy technology R&D has been driven by at least three not always commensurate goals — resource and technological diversity, commercial viability, and environmental protection — which were not goals of the historical programs.

End Notes

[1] Examples in the 110th Congress include bills such as the New Manhattan Project for Energy Independence (H.R. 6260); the PROGRESS Act (H.R. 1300); the Gas Price Reduction Act of 2008 (S. 3202); the Apollo Energy Independence Act of 2008 (H.R. 6385); the Comprehensive Energy Exploration, Price Reduction, and Renewable Energy Investment Act of 2008 (H.R. 6412); and the New Apollo Energy Act of 2007 (H.R. 2809). For a further discussion of this issue, see CRS Report RL34621, *Capturing CO2 from Coal-Fire Power Plants: Challenges for a Comprehensive Strategy*, by Larry Parker, Peter Folger, and Deborah D. Stine.

[2] U.S. Department of Energy, Office of History and Heritage Resources, "The Manhattan Project: An Interactive History," [http://www.cfo.doe.gov/me70/manhattan/1939-1942.htm]. F.G. Gosling, *The Manhattan Project: Making the Atomic Bomb*, January 1999 edition (Oak Ridge, TN: Department of Energy).

[3] Richard G. Hewlett and Oscar E. Anderson, Jr., A *History of the United States Atomic Energy Commission: The New World, 1939/1946, Volume I,* (University Park, PA: The Pennsylvania State University Press, 1962). Appendix 2 provides the annual Manhattan project expenditures. These costs were adjusted to 2007 dollars using the price index for gross domestic product (GDP), available from the Bureau of Economic Affairs, National Income and Product Accounts Table webpage, Table 1.1.4, at [http://www.bea.gov/bea/dn/nipaweb/].

[4] Leslie R. Groves, *Now it Can be Told: The Story of the Manhattan Project* (New York: Harper & Brothers, 1962).

[5] Ibid., Kevin O'Neil, "Building the Bomb," Chapter 1 in Stephen I. Schwartz (ed.), *Atomic Audit: The Costs and Consequences of U.S. Nuclear Weapons Since 1940* (Washington, DC: Brookings Institution Press, 1998), pp. 58-59.

[6] Richard Orloff, National Aeronautics and Space Administration (NASA), *Apollo By The Numbers: A Statistical Reference,* NASA SP-2000-4029, 2004 web update at [http://history.nasa.gov/SP-4029/Apollo_00_Welcome.htm]. There is some difference of opinion regarding what activities comprised the Apollo program, and thus when it began and ended. For example, two different cost figures are provided on NASA's website. This is probably because some analysts include the first studies for Apollo, Skylab, and the use of Apollo spacecraft in the Apollo-Soyuz Test Project. The Orloff analysis includes the first studies of Apollo, but not Skylab (1973-74) or Soyuz (1975) activities. Another NASA analysis provides the cost as $25.4 billion, but provides no details as to how the cost were determined. See Roger D. Launius, NASA, *The Legacy of Project Apollo* at [http://history.nasa.gov/ap11-35ann/legacy.html].

[7] For more information, see CRS Report RL34263, *U.S. Civilian Space Policy Priorities: Reflections 50 Years After Sputnik*, by Deborah D. Stine.

[8] NASA, Kennedy Space Center, "Project Apollo," webpage, at [http://www-pao.ksc.nasa.gov/kscpao/history/apollo/apollo.htm]. A list of the top ten Apollo scientific discoveries as determined by the Smithsonian Institution is at [http://www.nasm.si.edu/collections/imagery/apollo/apollotop10.htm].

[9] NASA, Kennedy Space Center, "Project Apollo," webpage, at [http://www-pao.ksc.nasa.gov/kscpao/history/apollo/apollo.htm]. The three parts were the command module (CM), the crew's quarters and flight control section; the service module (SM) for the propulsion and spacecraft support systems (when together, the two modules are called CSM); and the lunar module (LM).

[10] The funding data is available at [http://history.nasa.gov/SP-4214/app2.html#1965]. It is based on information in NASA, *The Apollo Spacecraft - A Chronology*, NASA Special Publication-4009, at [http://www.hq.nasa.gov/office/pao/History/SP-4009/contents.htm]. This data is from Volume 4, Appendix 7, at [http://www.hq.nasa.gov/office/pao/History/SP-4009/v4app7.htm].

[11] Richard Orloff, *Apollo By The Numbers: A Statistical Reference*, NASA SP-2000-4029, 2004 web update, at [http://history.nasa.gov/SP-4029/Apollo_00_Welcome.htm]. The funding data is available at [http://history.nasa.gov/SP-4029/Apollo_18-16_Apollo_Program_Budget_Appropriations.htm]. It is based on information in NASA, *The Apollo Spacecraft - A Chronology*, NASA Special Publication-4009, at [http://www.hq.nasa.gov/office/pao/History/SP-4009/contents.htm].

[12] Energy Information Administration, "25th Anniversary of the 1973 Oil Embargo," at [http://www.eia.doe.gov/emeu/25opec/anniversary.html].

[13] U.S. Department of Energy, Office of History and Heritage Resources, "The Manhattan Project: An Interactive History," "Civilian Control of Atomic Energy" webpage at [http://www.cfo.doe.gov/me70/manhattan/civilian_control.htm].

[14] Department of Energy, "Energy Research and Development Administration," webpage at [http://www.ch.doe.gov/html/site_info/energy_research.htm].

[15] Although DOE did not begin operating until 1977, the term "DOE Energy Technology R&D Program" in this report is defined as encompassing DOE programs funded beginning in 1977 as well as energy R&D activities that occurred prior to 1977 that were managed by the organizations it subsumed.

[16] See, for example, Bruce L.R. Smith, *American Science Policy Since World War II* (Washington, DC: Brookings Institution, 1990).

[17] The Synthetic Fuels corporation was established by the United States Synthetic Fuels Corporation Act of 1980 (P.L. 96-294), and its operation was discontinued by the Synthetic Fuels Corporation Act of 1985 (P.L. 99-272).

[18] National Academy of Sciences, *The Government Role in Civilian Technology: Building a New Alliance* (Washington, DC: National Academy Press 1992).

[19] See CRS Report RL33521, *Gasoline Prices: Causes of Increases and Congressional Response*, by Carl E. Behrens.

[20] For more information, see CRS Report RL34513, *Climate Change: Current Issues and Policy Tools*, by Jane A. Leggett.

[21] For information on the DOE energy technology R&D budget, see CRS Report RL34448, *Federal Research and Development Funding: FY2009*, coordinated by John F. Sargent.

[22] President Jimmy Carter, "Address to the Nation on Energy," speech, April 18, 1977. A video and text is at [http://millercenter.org/scripps/archive/speeches/detail/3398].

[23] CRS Report RL34513, *Climate Change: Current Issues and Policy Tools*, by Jane A. Leggett.

[24] For more discussion of this issue, see CRS Report RL33528, *Industrial Competitiveness and Technological Advancement: Debate Over Government Policy*, by Wendy H. Schacht.

[25] See for example, David Goldston, "Misspent Energy," *Nature*, 447:130, May 10, 2007 at [http://www.nature.com/nature/journal/v447/n7141/pdf/447130a.pdf].

[26] See, for example, The National Academies, *Rising Above the Gathering Storm: Energizing and Employing America for a Brighter Economic Future* (Washington, DC: National Academy Press, 2007).

In: Federal Role in Funding Research and Development   ISBN: 978-1-60741-486-5
Editor: Piper B. Collins   © 2010 Nova Science Publishers, Inc.

Chapter 2

THE FEDERAL NETWORKING AND INFORMATION TECHNOLOGY RESEARCH AND DEVELOPMENT PROGRAM: FUNDING ISSUES AND ACTIVITIES

Patricia Moloney Figliola

SUMMARY

In the early 1990s, Congress recognized that several federal agencies had ongoing high-performance computing programs, but no central coordinating body existed to ensure long-term coordination and planning. To provide such a framework, Congress passed the High-Performance Computing and Communications Program Act of 1991 (P.L. 102-194) to enhance the effectiveness of the various programs. In conjunction with the passage of the act, the White House Office of Science and Technology Policy (OSTP) released *Grand Challenges: High-Performance Computing and Communications*. That document outlined a research and development (R&D) strategy for high-performance computing and a framework for a multiagency program, the High-Performance Computing and Communications (HPCC) Program. The HPCC Program has evolved over time and is now called the Networking and Information Technology Research and Development (NITRD) Program, to better reflect its expanded mission.

Proponents assert that federal support of information technology (IT) R&D has produced positive outcomes for the country and played a crucial role in supporting long-term research into fundamental aspects of computing. Such fundamentals provide broad practical benefits, but generally take years to realize. Additionally, the unanticipated results of research are often as important as the anticipated results. Another aspect of government-funded IT research is that it often leads to open standards, something that many perceive as beneficial, encouraging deployment and further investment. Industry, on the other hand, is more inclined to invest in proprietary products and will diverge from a common standard when there is a potential competitive or financial advantage to do so. Finally, proponents of government support believe that the outcomes achieved through the various funding programs create a synergistic environment in which both fundamental and application-driven research are conducted, benefitting government, industry, academia, and the public. Supporters also believe that such outcomes justify government's role in funding IT R&D, as well as the growing budget for the NITRD Program. Critics assert that the government, through its funding mechanisms, may be picking "winners and losers" in technological development, a role more properly residing with the private sector. For example, the size of the NITRD Program may encourage industry to follow the government's lead on research directions rather than selecting those directions itself.

The FY2009 budget calls for $3.548 billion for the NITRD Program, an increase from the FY2008 projected budget of $3.341 billion. Because the NITRD Program "budget" consists of the budgets allocated to the 13 participating agencies, final budget figures are not available for FY2008.

OVERVIEW OF THE FEDERAL NITRD PROGRAM

The federal government has long played a key role in the country's information technology (IT) research and development (R&D) activities. The government's support of IT R&D began because it had an important interest in creating computers that would be capable of addressing the problems and issues the government needed to solve and study. One of the first such problems was planning the trajectories of artillery and bombs; more recently, such problems include simulations of nuclear testing, cryptanalysis, and weather modeling. That interest continues today. Such complexity requires there be adequate coordination to ensure the government's evolving needs (e.g., homeland security) will continue to be met in the most effective manner possible.

NITRD Structure

The Networking and Information Technology Research and Development (NITRD) Program is a collaborative effort in which 13 agencies coordinate and cooperate to help increase the overall effectiveness and productivity of federal IT R&D.[1] Of those 13 members, the majority of funding, in descending order, goes to the National Science Foundation, National Institutes of Health, Department of Energy (DOE) Office of Science, Defense Advanced Research Projects Agency (DARPA), and DOE National Nuclear Security Administration. Dr. Christopher Greer was named as the director of the NITRD Program in October 2007. **Figure 1** illustrates the organizational structure of the NITRD Program.

The National Coordinating Office (NCO) coordinates the activities of the NITRD Program. On July 1, 2005, the NCO became the "National Coordination Office for Networking and Information Technology Research and Development." The Director of the NCO reports to the Director of OSTP. The NCO supports the Subcommittee on NITRD (also called the NITRD Subcommittee)[2] and the President's Information Technology Advisory Committee (PITAC).[3]

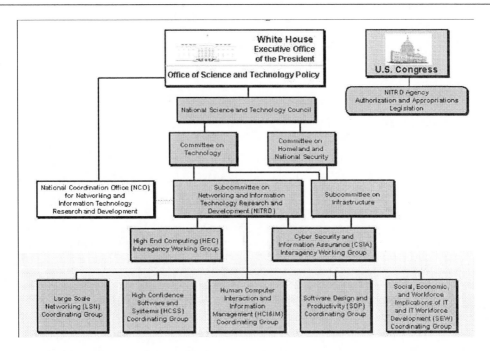

Source: NITRD Program website, [http://www.nitrd.gov].

Figure 1. Management Structure of the NITRD Program

- The NITRD Subcommittee provides policy, program, and budget planning for the NITRD Program and is composed of representatives from each of the participating agencies, OSTP, Office of Management and Budget, and the NCO. Two Interagency Working Groups and five Coordination Groups reporting to the NITRD Subcommittee focus their work in eight Program Component Areas (PCAs).[4]
- The PITAC is composed of representatives of private industry and academia who are appointed by the President. The group provides expert independent advice to the President on the federal role in maintaining U.S. preeminence in advanced IT and works with the NITRD Program agencies and the NITRD Subcommittee.
- The NITRD Program is funded out of each member agency's individual budget, rather than in a single appropriations bill (e.g., NITRD Program activities conducted by the National Institutes of Health (NIH) are funded through the NIH appropriations bill). The program's NCO is not explicitly funded; rather, the NITRD member agencies contribute toward NCO operations.

The NITRD Program has undergone a series of structural changes since its inception in 1991 and both it and the NCO have had a number of different names over the years. When the Program was created in December 1991, it was named the High Performance Computing and Communications (HPCC) Program, and when the NCO was created in September 1992, it was named the NCO for HPCC. The name was changed to the National Coordination Office for Computing, Information, and Communications per the FY1 997 Supplement to the President's Budget (also known at that time as the "Blue Book"). The name was changed to the National Coordination Office for Information Technology Research and Development per the FY2001 Blue Book.[5] Most recently, on July 1, 2005, the name was changed to the

National Coordination Office for Networking and Information Technology Research and Development. These changes were made to reflect the evolution of the program as it came to encompass a broader range of related topics.

NITRD Funding

The FY2009 budget calls for $3 .548 billion for the NITRD Program, an increase from the FY2008 projected budget of $3.341 billion. Because the NITRD Program "budget" consists of the budgets allocated to the 13 participating agencies, final budget figures are not available for FY2008. The chronology of NITRD funding is detailed in **Table 1**.[6]

The Administration's American Competitiveness Initiative has increased the NITRD budgets of agencies that are part of the Initiative. The Initiative calls for a doubling over 10 years of the investment in three federal agencies that support basic research programs in the physical sciences and engineering: the National Science Foundation (NSF), the Department of Energy's Office of Science (DOE/SC), and the National Institute of Science and Technology (NIST) — are NITRD Program member agencies. All three received FY2007 NITRD budget increases that exceed the percentage increase in the overall Program budget, as follows: NSF, 12%; DOE/SC, 35%; and NIST, 10%. The aggregated NITRD budget increase for these three agencies from 2006 estimates to 2007 request is $186 million (17% above 2006 estimates), which accounts for over 85% of the overall NITRD Program budget increase for 2007.[7]

NCO, PITAC, and Related Reports

As explained earlier, the NCO provides technical and administrative support to the NITRD Program, the NITRD Subcommittee, and the PITAC. This includes supporting meetings and workshops and preparing reports. The NCO interacts with OSTP and OMB on NITRD Program and PITAC matters.

Federal Plan for Advanced Networking Research and Development
This plan was developed by the Interagency Task Force on Advanced Networking, established under the NITRD National Science and Technology Council by the Director of the OSTP to provide a strategic vision for future networked environments.[8] The overall conclusions of the Task Force can be summarized as follows:

Improved networking security and reliability are strategic national priorities;
New paths to advanced networking are required;
Federal R&D efforts will support a spectrum of advanced networking capabilities;
Close cooperation is needed to integrate Federal R&D efforts with the full technology development cycle—this cycle includes basic and applied research, and partnerships with researchers, application developers, users, and other stakeholders; and
Testbeds and prototype networks enable research on network challenges in realistic environments.

Table 1. NITRD Funding Chronology FY1991-FY2009 ($ in millions)

Fiscal Year	Budget	Fiscal Year	Budget
FY1991	489	FY2001	1,929
FY1992	655	FY2002	1,830
FY1993	795	FY2003	1,976
FY1994	938	FY2004	2,115
FY1995	1,038	FY2005	2,256
FY1996	1,043	FY2006	2,855
FY1997	1,009	FY2007	2,967
FY1998	1,070	FY2008[*]	3,341
FY1999	1,312	FY2009[**]	3,548
FY2000	1,546		

[*]Final figure not yet available
[**]Requested

The report notes that

The Internet's phenomenal growth and elasticity have exceeded all expectations. At the same time, we have become captive to the limitations and vulnerabilities of the current generation of networking technologies. Because vital U.S. interests — for example, national defense communications, financial markets, and the operation of critical infrastructures such as power grids — now depend on secure, reliable, highspeed network connectivity, these limitations and vulnerabilities can threaten our national security and economic competitiveness. Research and development to create the next generation of networking technologies is needed to address these threats.

The plan is centered on a vision for advanced networking based on a design and architecture for security and reliability that provides for heterogeneous, anytime- anywhere networking with capabilities such as federation of networks across domains and widely differing technologies; dynamic mobile networking with autonomous management; effective quality of service (QoS) management; support for sensornets; near-realtime autonomous discovery, configuration, and management of resources; and end-to-end security tailored to the application and user.

The report outlines four goal for realizing this vision:

Provide secure network services anytime, anywhere;
Make secure global federated networks possible;
Manage network complexity and heterogeneity; and
Foster innovation among the Federal, research, commercial, and other sectors through development of advanced network systems and technologies.

Leadership under Challenge: Information Technology R&D in a Competitive World

This report assesses global U.S. competitiveness in networking and information technology and provides recommendations aimed at ensuring that the NITRD Program is appropriately focused and implemented. The report makes specific recommendations for Federal R&D that would enhance U.S. competitiveness in this economically critical area. In developing the report, the PCAST consulted extensively with experts from industry and academia. The PCAST concluded that while the United States is still in a leadership position, other nations are challenging that lead in a number of areas and that the NITRD Program must focus on visionary research and work with universities to keep the United States at the cutting edge. Some of the report recommendation areas follows:

Both the U.S. federal government and the private sector need to address the demand for skilled IT professionals, including such steps as updating curricula, increasing fellowships, and simplifying visa processes.

With respect to the federally-funded research portfolio, the NITRD Program should emphasize larger-scale and longer-term, multidisciplinary IT R&D and innovative, higher-risk projects.

The United States should give priority to R&D in economically important areas, including IT systems connected with and embedded in the physical world, software, use and management of digital data, and advanced Internet capabilities. The PCAST noted that with an annual federal investment of over $3 billion in the NITRD Program, changes in the Program's interagency process to strengthen assessment and planning are needed.[9]

Federal Plan for Cyber Security and Information Assurance Research and Development

In April 2006, the NITRD Subcommittee released its "Federal Plan for Cyber Security and Information Assurance Research and Development."[10] This report sets out a framework for multi-agency coordination of federal R&D investments in technologies that can better secure the interconnected computing systems, networks, and information that together make up the U.S. IT infrastructure. The plan outlines strategic objectives for coordinated federal R&D in cyber security and information assurance (CSIA) and presents a broad range of CSIA R&D technical topics, identifying those topics that are multi-agency technical and funding priorities. The plan's findings and recommendations address R&D priority setting, coordination, fundamental R&D, emerging technologies, roadmapping, and metrics.

NSA Superconducting Technology Assessment

In August 2005, NSA released its "Superconducting Technology Assessment"[11] as part of its participation in the High-End Computing PCA of the NITRD Program. NSA had been concerned about projected limitations of conventional technology and wanted to explore possible alternatives to meet its future mission-critical computational needs. This report presented the results of the technology assessment, which found the following.

Government investment is necessary, because private industry currently has no compelling financial reason to develop alternative technologies for mainstream commercial applications.

With aggressive federal investment (estimated between $372 and $437 million over five years), by 2010 next generation technologies would be sufficiently mature to allow the initiation of the design and construction of an operational petaflops[12]-scale system.

Although significant risks exist, the panel has developed a roadmap that identifies the needed technology developments with milestones and demonstration vehicles.

Computational Science: Ensuring America's Competitiveness

In June 2005, the PITAC released "Computational Science: Ensuring America's Competitiveness."[13] The report identified obstacles to progress in this field, including "rigid disciplinary silos in academia that are mirrored in federal research and development agency organizational structures." According to the report, these "silos stifle the development of multi-disciplinary research and educational approaches essential to computational science." The report recommends the following.

- Both academia and government fundamentally change their organizational structures so that they promote and reward collaborative research.
- The National Science and Technology Council commission the National Academies to convene one or more task forces to develop and maintain a multi-decade roadmap for computational science, with a goal of assuring continuing U.S. leadership in science, engineering, and the humanities.
- The federal government establish national software sustainability centers to harden, document, support, and maintain long-term vital computational science software.
- The federal government provide long-term support for computational science community data repositories. These should include defined frameworks, metadata structures, algorithms, data sets, applications, and review and validation infrastructure. It should also require funded researchers to deposit their data and research software in these repositories or with other approved access providers.
- The federal government provide long-term funding for national high-end computing centers at levels sufficient to ensure the regularly scheduled deployment and operation of the fastest and most capable high-end computing systems that address the most demanding computational problems.
- The federal government implement coordinated, long-term computational science programs that include funding for interconnecting the software sustainability centers, national data and software repositories, and national high-end leadership centers with the researchers who use those resources.
- The federal government should rebalance its R&D investments to: (a) create a new generation of well-engineered, scalable, easy-to-use software suitable for computational science that can reduce the complexity and time to solution for today's challenging scientific applications and can create accurate simulations that answer new questions; (b) design, prototype, and evaluate new hardware architectures that can deliver larger fractions of peak hardware performance on scientific applications; and (c) focus on sensor- and data-intensive computational science applications in light of the explosive growth of data.

Cyber Security: A Crisis of Prioritization

In February 2005, the PITAC released "Cyber Security: A Crisis of Prioritization."[14] That report outlined four key findings and recommendations on how the federal government could "foster new architectures and technologies to secure the Nation's IT infrastructure." Specifically, the PITAC urged the government to

significantly increase support for fundamental research in civilian cyber security in 10 priority areas;

intensify federal efforts to promote the recruitment and retention of cyber security researchers and students at research universities;

increase support for the rapid transfer of federally-developed cybersecurity technologies to the private sector; and

strengthen the coordination of federal cybersecurity R&D activities.

Also in February 2005, the NCO released the FY2006 Supplement to the President's Budget.[15] The supplement provides a brief technical outline of the FY2006 budget request for the NITRD Program. The FY2007 Supplement has not yet been released.

NITRD Enabling and Governing Legislation

The NITRD Program is governed by two laws. The first, the High-Performance Computing Act of 1991, P.L. 102-194,[16] expanded federal support for high- performance computing R&D and called for increased interagency planning and coordination. The second, the Next Generation Internet Research Act of 1998, P.L. 105-305,[17] amended the original law to expand the mission of the NITRD Program to cover Internet-related research, among other goals.

High-Performance Computing Act of 1991

This law was the original enabling legislation for what is now the NITRD Program. Among other requirements, it called for the following.

Setting goals and priorities for federal high-performance computing research, development, and networking.

Providing for the technical support and research and development of high-performance computing software and hardware needed to address fundamental problems in science and engineering.

Educating undergraduate and graduate students.

Fostering and maintaining competition and private sector investment in high-speed data networking within the telecommunications industry.

Promoting the development of commercial data communications and telecommunications standards.

Providing security, including protecting intellectual property rights,

Developing accounting mechanisms allowing users to be charged for the use of copyrighted materials.

This law also requires an annual report to Congress on grants and cooperative R&D agreements and procurements involving foreign entities.[18]

Next Generation Internet Research Act of 1998

This law amended the High-Performance Computing Act of 1991. The act had two overarching purposes. The first was to authorize research programs related to high-end computing and computation, human-centered systems, high confidence systems, and education, training, and human resources. The second was to provide for the development and coordination of a comprehensive and integrated U.S. research program to focus on (1) computer network infrastructure that would promote interoperability among advanced federal computer networks, (2) economic high-speed data access that does not impose a "geographic penalty." and (3) flexible and extensible networking technology.

CONTEXT OF FEDERAL TECHNOLOGY FUNDING

In the early 1990s, Congress recognized that several federal agencies had ongoing high-performance computing programs,[19] but no central coordinating body existed to ensure long-term coordination and planning. To provide such a framework, Congress passed the High-Performance Computing Program Act of 1991 to improve the interagency coordination, cooperation, and planning of agencies with high performance computing programs.

In conjunction with the passage of the act, OSTP released, "Grand Challenges: High-Performance Computing and Communications." That document outlined an R&D strategy for high-performance computing and communications and a framework for a multi-agency program, the HPCC Program.

The NITRD Program is part of the larger federal effort to promote fundamental and applied IT R&D. The government sponsors such research through a number of channels, including

  federally funded research and development laboratories, such as Lawrence Livermore National Laboratory;
  single-agency programs;
  multi-agency programs, including the NITRD Program, but also programs focusing on nanotechnology R&D and combating terrorism;
  funding grants to academic institutions; and
  funding grants to industry.

In general, supporters contend that federal funding of IT R&D has produced positive results. In 2003, the Computer Science and Telecommunications Board (CSTB) of the National Research Council (NRC) released a "synthesis report" based on eight previously released reports that examined "how innovation occurs in IT, what the most promising research directions are, and what impacts such innovation might have on society."[20] One of the most significant of the CSTB's observations was that the unanticipated results of research are often as important as the anticipated results. For example, electronic mail and instant messaging were by-products of [government-funded] research in the 1 960s that was aimed at making it possible to share expensive computing resources among multiple simultaneous interactive users.

Additionally, the report noted that federally funded programs have played a crucial role in supporting long-term research into fundamental aspects of computing. Such "fundamentals" provide broad practical benefits, but generally take years to realize. Furthermore, supporters state that the nature and underlying importance of fundamental research makes it less likely that industry would invest in and conduct more fundamental research on its own. As noted by the CSTB, "companies have little incentive to invest significantly in activities whose benefits will spread quickly to their rivals."[21] Further, in the Board's opinion:

> government sponsorship of research, especially in universities, helps develop the IT talent used by industry, universities, and other parts of the economy. When companies create products using the ideas and workforce that result from federally-sponsored research, they repay the nation in jobs, tax revenues, productivity increases, and world leadership.[22]

Another aspect of government-funded IT R&D is that it often leads to open standards, something that many perceive as beneficial, encouraging deployment and further investment. Industry, on the other hand, is more likely to invest in proprietary products and will diverge from a common standard if it sees a potential competitive or financial advantage; this has happened, for example with standards for instant messaging.[23]

Finally, proponents of government R&D support believe that the outcomes achieved through the various funding programs create a synergistic environment in which both fundamental and application-driven research are conducted, benefitting government, industry, academia, and the public. Supporters also believe that such outcomes justify government's role in funding IT R&D, as well as the growing budget for the NITRD Program.

Critics assert that the government, through its funding mechanisms, may be setting itself up to pick "winners and losers" in technological development, a role more properly residing with the private sector.[24] For example, the size of the NITRD Program may encourage industry to follow the government's lead on research directions rather than selecting those directions itself.

Overall, CSTB states that, government funding appears to have allowed research on a larger scale and with greater diversity, vision, and flexibility than would have been possible without government involvement.[25]

ACTIVITY IN THE 110TH AND 109TH CONGRESS

There has been no NITRD-specific activity in the 110th Congress. The 109th Congress introduced one bill and held three hearings related to the NITRD Program.

Major Legislation, 109th Congress

Representative Judy Biggert introduced H.R. 28, the High-Performance Computing Revitalization Act on January 4, 2005. The bill would have amended the High-Performance Computing Act of 1991 and further delineate the responsibilities of the NITRD Program, including setting the goals and priorities for federal high- performance computing research, development, networking, and other activities and providing more specific definitions for the responsibilities of the PCAs. The bill was referred to the House Committee on Science, which reported the bill on April 12, 2005.[26] The committee also approved, by voice vote, an amendment that stated that the results and benefits of federal supercomputing research should be shared with the private sector. The committee rejected, by a vote of 17-19, an amendment offered by Representative Brad Sherman that would have directed the National Science Foundation to investigate the societal, ethical, legal, and economic implications of computers that one day might be capable of mimicking human abilities to learn, reason, and make decisions. H.R. 28 was agreed to by voice vote in the House on April 26, 2005, and received in the Senate, where it was read twice and referred to the Committee on Commerce, Science, and Transportation, on April 27, 2005.[27] No further action was taken.

Hearings, 109th Congress

On July 17, 2006, the Senate Committee on Commerce, Science and Transportation's Subcommittee on Technology, Innovation, and Competitiveness, held a hearing to discuss issues related to supercomputing research. In particular, the witnesses expressed concern that although supercomputers are now faster than ever, U.S. government investment in supercomputers had decreased significantly over the past decade, leaving such investment to the private sector. However, a number of witnesses noted that the Bush Administration's FY2007 budget calls for increased supercomputing research investment and that a consistent investment over the next few years would prompt industry and academia to invest more steadily as well.

On February 16, 2005, the House Committee on Science held a hearing to discuss the federal R&D Budget for FY2006.[28] This hearing covered the entire R&D budget and included an overview of NITRD activities by Dr. John Marburger, the Director of OSTP.

On May 12, 2005, the House Committee on Science held a hearing entitled, "The Future of Computer Science Research in the U.S."[29] That hearing focused on three primary areas of investigation.

What effects are shifts in federal support for computer science (e.g., shifts in the balance between short- and long-term research, shifts in the roles of different agencies) having on academic and industrial computer science research and development?

What impacts will these changes have on the future of the U.S. information technology industry and on innovation in this field?

Are the federal government's current priorities related to computer science research appropriate? If not, how should they be changed?

What should the federal government be doing to implement the recommendations of the recent PITAC report on cybersecurity?

At this hearing, the committee heard testimony from Dr. Marburger, OSTP; Dr. Anthony J. Tether; DARPA; Dr. William A. Wulf, National Academy of Engineering; and Dr. Tom Leighton, Akamai Technologies and member of the PITAC. Testimony from Drs. Marburger and Tether stressed the growing budget of computer research and their belief that the overall health of the U.S. science and technology research community remains strong. However, Doctors Wulf and Leighton, representing the research community, stated that they believed government needed to provide even more funding, as industry was not willing to fund the levels of fundamental research they believed necessary to sustain the United States' research needs.

ISSUES FOR CONGRESS

Federal IT R&D is a multi-dimensional issue, involving many government agencies working together towards shared and complementary goals. Most observers believe that success in this arena requires ongoing coordination among government, academia, and industry.

Through hearings, the House Committee on Science has been investigating issues related to U.S. competitiveness in high-performance computing and the direction the IT R&D community has been taking. Those issues and others remain salient and may merit further investigation if the United States is to maintain a comprehensive IT R&D policy. Included among the possible issues Congress may wish to pursue are: the United States' status as the global leader in high-performance computing research; the apparent bifurcation of the federal IT R&D research agenda between grid computing and supercomputing capabilities; the possible over-reliance on commercially available hardware to satisfy U.S. research needs; and the potential impact of deficit cutting on IT R&D funding.

Many Members of Congress as well as those in the research community have expressed concern over whether the United States is maintaining its position as the global leader in high-performance computing R&D. That concern was highlighted in 2003 when Japan briefly surpassed the United States in possessing the fastest and most efficient supercomputer in the world.[30] While this was a reason for some concern, it was also viewed by some as an indicator of how the United States' research agenda had become bifurcated, with some in the R&D community focusing on traditional supercomputing capabilities, and others focusing more on cluster computing or grid computing. Each type of computing has its advantages, based on its application. Stand-alone supercomputers are often faster and are generally used to work on a specific problem. For example, cryptanalysis and climate modeling applications require significant computing power and are best accomplished using specialized, stand-alone computers. Cluster computing, however, allows the use of commercially available hardware, which helps contain costs. The cluster configuration is useful for applications in which a problem can be broken into smaller independent components.[31] Therefore, one possible course for Congress could be to monitor closely the work that was begun by the High-End Computing Revitalization Task Force and is now being performed by the NITRD Program's High-End Computing Interagency Working Group and provide ongoing feedback and guidance.

Without a clear plan as to how to proceed, pursuing two disparate research agendas (with goals that could be viewed as being at odds with each other) could split the research community further, damaging its ability to provide leadership in either area. The NITRD Program already is working on a "roadmap" for future directions in supercomputing;

therefore, one possible course for Congress at this time would be to monitor closely the work of the High-End Computing Revitalization Task Force and provide input or a more visible forum for discussion (i.e., additional hearings involving task force participants). Congress may wish to conduct its own inquiry into the debate over grid versus stand-alone computing. For example, at a July 2003 hearing, one of the overarching questions the panelists were asked to address was whether federal agencies were pursuing conflicting R&D goals and, if so, what should and could be done to ensure they moved toward a more coordinated, unified goal.

Another issue is whether the United States is relying too heavily on commercially available hardware to satisfy its R&D needs. While use of computers designed for mass-market commercial applications can certainly be a part of a successful high-end computing R&D plan, Congress may wish to monitor how this reliance may be driving the new emphasis on grid computing.

As noted earlier, critics of IT R&D funding often state that industry should conduct more fundamental R&D on their own, without government backing, and that fiscal restraint dictates that less funding should be made available. Conversely, supporters of government funding would point out that IT R&D has a very long cycle from inception to application and that any reductions in funding now could have a significant negative impact for many years to come in terms of innovation and training of researchers. Therefore, Congress may monitor and assess the potential impact of deficit-cutting plans on progress in IT R&D.

End Notes

[1] The members of the NITRD Program, as listed in the FY2006 Supplement to the President's Budget, are: Agency for Healthcare Research and Quality (AHRQ); Defense Advanced Research Projects Agency (DARPA); Office of the Secretary of Defense, Defense Research & Engineering, and the DOD service research organizations; Department of Energy, National Nuclear Security Administration (DOE/NNSA); Department of Energy, Office of Science (DOE/SC); Department of Homeland Security (DHS); Environmental Protection Agency (EPA); National Aeronautics and Space Administration (NASA); National Institutes of Health (NIH); National Institute of Standards and Technology (NIST); National Oceanic and Atmospheric Administration (NOAA); National Security Agency (NSA); and National Science Foundation (NSF). The history of agency participation can be found at [http://www.nitrd.gov/about/history/agency-participants.pdf].

[2] The NITRD Subcommittee was previously called the Interagency Working Group for IT R&D (IWG/IT R&D).

[3] The PITAC was established on February 11, 1997, to provide the President, OSTP, and the federal agencies involved in IT R&D with guidance and advice on all areas of high performance computing, communications, and information technologies. Representing the research, education, and library communities and including network providers and representatives from critical industries, the committee advises the Administration's effort to accelerate development and adoption of information technologies. Additional information about the PITAC is available at [http://www.nitrd.gov/pitac]. The most recent PITAC Executive Order expired on June 1, 2005.

[4] The eight PCAs are (1) *High-End Computing Infrastructure and Applications (HEC I&A)* — to extend the state of the art in high-end computing systems, applications, and infrastructure; (2) *High-End Computing R&D (HEC R&D)* — to optimize the performance of today's high-end computing systems and develop future generations of high-end computing systems; (3) *Cyber Security and Information Assurance* — to perform fundamental and applied R&D to improve the security and assurance of information systems; (4) *Human Computer Interaction and Information Management (HCI&IM)* — to develop new user interaction technologies, cognitive systems, information systems, and robotics that benefit humans; (5) *Large Scale Networking (LSN)* — to develop leading-edge network technologies, services, and techniques to enhance performance, security, and scalability; (6) *Software Design and Productivity (SDP)* — to advance concepts, methods, techniques, and tools that improve software design, development, and maintenance to produce more usable, dependable and cost-effective software-based systems; (7) *High Confidence Software and Systems (HCSS)* — to develop the scientific foundations and IT to achieve affordable and predictable high levels of safety, security, reliability,

and survivability, especially in U.S. national security and safety-critical systems; and **(8)** *Social, Economic, and Workforce Implications of IT and IT Workforce Development (SEW)* — to study the impact of IT on people and social and economic systems; develop the IT workforce; and develop innovative IT applications in education and training. Additional information about the program component areas is available at [http://www.nitrd.gov/subcommittee/index.html]. HEC R&D and HEC I&A are both covered by the HEC Interagency Working Group. A diagram illustrating the evolution of the PCAs, 1992-present, is available at [http://www.nitrd.gov/about/history/new -pca-names.pdf].

[5] That change was effective October 2000.

[6] The FY2008 budget request is available at [http://www.nitrd.gov/pubs/2008supplement/08-Supp-Web/TOC%20Pages/08supp-Budget.pdf]

[7] The FY2007 NITRD Budget request is at [http://www.nitrd.gov/pubs/2007supplement/].

[8] This report is available at [http://www.nitrd.gov/pubs/ITFAN-FINAL.pdf].

[9] This report responds to reporting requirements of the High-Performance Computing Act of 1991 (Public Law 102-194) and the Next Generation Internet Research Act of 1998 (Public Law 105-305). The laws call for a President's Information Technology Advisory Committee (PITAC) to assess periodically what is now known as the NITRD Program. Executive Order 13385, signed on September 29, 2005, assigned the PITAC's responsibilities to PCAST. This report is available at [http://www.nitrd.gov/pcast/ reports/PCAST-NIT-FINAL.pdf].

[10] This report is available at [http://www.nitrd.gov/pubs/csia/csia_federal_plan.pdf].

[11] This report is available at [http://www.nitrd.gov/pubs/nsa/sta.pdf].

[12] In computing, "flops" or "FLOPS" is an abbreviation of Floating Point Operations Per Second. This is used as a measure of a computer's performance, especially in fields of scientific calculations that make heavy use of floating point calculations. A petaflops-scale machine operates at 10^{15} flops.

[13] This report is available at [http://www.nitrd.gov/pitac/reports/20050609_computational/ computational.pdf].

[14] This report is available at [http://www.nitrd.gov/pitac/reports/20050301_cyber security/cybersecurity.pdf].

[15] This report is available at [http://www.nitrd.gov/pubs/2006supplement].

[16] High Performance Computing Act of 1991, P.L. 102-194, 15 U.S.C. 5501, 105 Stat. 1595, December 9, 1991. The full text of this law is available at [http://www.nitrd.gov/ congressional/laws/pl_1 02-1 94.html].

[17] Next Generation Internet Research Act of 1998, P.L. 105-305, 15 U.S.C. 5501, 112 Stat. 2919, October 28, 1998. The full text of this law is available at [http://www.nitrd.gov/ congressional/laws/pl_h_1 05-305 .html].

[18] The first report mandated information on the "Supercomputer Agreement" between the United States and Japan be included in this report. A separate one-time only report was required on network funding, including user fees, industry support, and federal investment.

[19] "High-performance" computing is a term that encompasses both "supercomputing" and "grid computing." In general, high-performance computers are defined as stand-alone or networked computers that can perform "very complex computations very quickly." Supercomputing involves a single, stand-alone computer located in a single location. Grid computing involves a group of computers, in either the same location or spread over a number of locations, that are networked together (e.g., via the Internet or a local network). House of Representatives, Committee on Science, *Supercomputing: Is the United States on the Right Path* (Hearing Transcript), [http://commdocs.house.gov/committees/science/ hsy8823 1 .000/hsy8823 1_0f.htm], 2003, pp. 5-6.

[20] National Research Council, *Innovation in Information Technology*, 2003, p. 1. This report discusses all federal funding for R&D, not only the NITRD Program.

[21] Ibid, p. 4.

[22] Ibid, p. 4.

[23] Ibid, p. 18.

[24] Cato Institute, *Encouraging Research: Taking Politics Out of R&D*, September 13, 1999, [http://www.cato.org/pubs/wtpapers/990913catord.html].

[25] National Research Council, *Innovation in Information Technology*, 2003, p. 22.

[26] See H.Rept. 109-36.

[27] See H.Rept. 109-36.

[28] The charter and submitted testimony for this hearing is available at [http://www.house.gov/science/hearings/full05/index.htm].

[29] The charter and submitted testimony for this hearing is available at [http://www.house.gov/science/press/109/109-71 .htm].

[30] House of Representatives, Committee on Science, *Supercomputing: Is the United States on the Right Path?* (Hearing Transcript), [http://commdocs.house.gov/committees/science/ hsy88231.000/hsy88231_0f.htm], 2003, p. 13.

[31] Ibid, p. 6-7.

In: Federal Role in Funding Research and Development   ISBN: 978-1-60741-486-5
Editor: Piper B. Collins   © 2010 Nova Science Publishers, Inc.

Chapter 3

FEDERAL RESEARCH AND DEVELOPMENT FUNDING AT HISTORICALLY BLACK COLLEGES AND UNIVERSITIES

Christine M. Matthews

SUMMARY

The historically black colleges and universities (HBCUs), which have traditionally educated a significant number of the nation's blacks, have faced, and continue to face, substantial challenges in attempting to enhance their academic and research capabilities. Some of these institutions have a myriad of problems — aging infrastructures, limited access to digital and wireless networking technology, absence of state-of-the-art equipment, low salary structures, small endowments, and limited funds for faculty development and new academic programs for students. While many of these problems exist in other institutions, they appear to be considerably more serious in HBCUs. In addition, those HBCUs damaged by Hurricane Katrina have the added costs in the millions of replacing facilities, research equipment, and rebuilding their infrastructure. This is an issue for Congress because the distribution of federal funding for HBCUs is one of the critical issues facing these institutions.

HBCUs comprise approximately 2.3% of all institutions of higher education, and enroll approximately 11.6% of all black students attending post-secondary institutions. Approximately 33.0% of the undergraduate degrees in science and engineering earned by blacks were awarded at HBCUs. Some of the most successful programs designed to attract and retain underrepresented minorities into the sciences and in research careers have been initiated at HBCUs. Data indicate that in 2004, HBCUs provided the education for approximately 20.2% of blacks earning bachelor degrees in engineering, 39.5% in the physical sciences, 26.3% in computer science, 37.0% in mathematics, 36.1% in the biological sciences, 47.0% in agricultural sciences, 16.4% in social sciences, and 21.4% in psychology.

On August 14, 2008, the President signed into law P.L. 110-315, the Higher Education Opportunity Act (HEOA). The HEOA provides authority for loans for repair and renovation of academic research facilities, among other facilities. Language in Title III, Part B, provides formula grants to eligible institutions. The percentage of funds allocated to each institution is based on several factors, and no institution can receive less that $250,000. Title III, Part D of the HEOA establishes a bonding authority to raise capital to be lent to HBCUs for repair and renovation of facilities. The total amount that would be available for financing is $1.1 billion. The aggregate authority principal and unpaid accrued interest on these loans cannot be more than $733.3 million for private HBCUs and no more than $366.7 million for public HBCUs. Title III, Part E of the HEOA provides funding for two new minority science and engineering improvement programs. A partnership grant program is directed at increasing the participation of underrepresented minority youth or low- income youth in science, mathematics, engineering, and technology education. Activities to be supported include outreach, hands-on, and experiential-based learning projects. Another program will focus on encouraging minorities to pursue careers in the scientific and technical disciplines.

INTRODUCTION

The historically black colleges and universities (HBCUs), which have traditionally educated a significant number of the nation's blacks, have faced and continue to face substantial challenges in attempting to enhance their academic and research capabilities and develop programs to compete with other institutions of higher education. Some of these black institutions have a myriad of problems — aging infrastructures, limited access to computer resources and digital network technology, absence of state-of-the-art equipment, low salary structures, small endowments, and limited funds for faculty development and new academic programs for students.[1] While many of these problems exist in other institutions, they appear to be considerably more serious in HBCUs.[2] In addition, those HBCUs damaged by Hurricane Katrina have the added costs in the millions for replacing facilities, research equipment, and rebuilding their infrastructure.[3]

The changing external environment (increasing public demand for institutional accountability and effectiveness) and new competitive conditions in higher education (varying levels of state support coupled with spiraling costs of research) have made it increasingly harder for HBCUs to develop and expand their research programs.[4] Because of their level of financial support (federal, state, and private), some believe many HBCUs are unable to engage in the level of cutting-edge scientific research conducted by many non-HBCUs.[5] Many HBCUs face difficulty competing for federal research dollars with other research-performing universities.[6] Coupled with limited federal support, HBCUs have very small endowments. A 2005 report of the Southern Education Foundation found that HBCUs have received attention and support from only a few foundations.[7]

Amid criticism by officials and representatives of HBCUs concerning the disparity in their receipt of federal science and engineering support, several executive orders were issued between 1980 to 2002, designed to strengthen and increase the participation of the HBCUs in federally sponsored programs and to improve the administrative infrastructure of the institutions.[8] The most recent executive order was released on February 12, 2002, and states that:

In developing its annual plan, each executive department and agency identified by the Secretary shall emphasize programs and activities that develop the capacity of historically black colleges and universities to contribute to the development of human capital and to strengthen America's economic and technological base through: (1) infrastructure development and acquisitions for instruction and research; (2) student and faculty doctoral fellowships and faculty development: (3) domestic and international faculty and student exchanges and study-abroad opportunities; (4) undergraduate and graduate student internships; and (5) summer, part-time, and permanent employment opportunities.[9]

An August 2008 report of the NSF reveals that for the academic year 2006, approximately 3 3.0% of the black science and engineering doctorate recipients had earned their bachelor degrees at an HBCU.[10] While HBCUs have played an important role in providing the undergraduate preparation for many of those black students entering highly specialized science and engineering disciplines, forecasts indicate that their efforts at attracting, retaining, preparing, and graduating students in the sciences and engineering may need to be expanded in order to respond to changing demographics.[11] A September 2006 report of the Department of Education (ED) states that between 2004 and 2015, enrollment in degree-granting institutions is projected to increase 27% for black, non-Hispanic students, 42% for Hispanic students, 30% for Native American/Alaskan Natives, 28% for Asian/Pacific Islanders, and 6% for white, non-Hispanic students.[12] These groups, the "new majority,"[13] on which the economy must increasingly rely, have traditionally been underrepresented in the sciences compared to their fraction of the total population.[14]

There are those observers who believe that the problem of underrepresented minorities in science, mathematics, engineering, and technology could compromise the United States' ability to develop and advance its traditional industrial base and to compete in international marketplaces.[15] Freeman A. Hrabowski, President, University of Maryland, Baltimore County, states that : "... [T]he paucity of minority scientists is not simply a minority issue; it is an American issue."[16]

HISTORICAL BACKGROUND[17]

HBCUs are defined as those institutions that were established prior to 1964, with the principal mission of educating black Americans.[18] While three HBCUs were established prior to the Civil War, the majority of these institutions were established after the War, several with the public support of land grants through the Freedman's Bureau.[19] The National Land-Grant Colleges Act of 1862 (P.L. 37-108), otherwise known as the 1862 Morrill Act, provided public lands to various states for the purpose of constructing educational institutions.[20] Funds appropriated under this act were distributed to the states "with the intention that they would foster equal educational opportunities for all students, especially newly freed Blacks."[21] However, the land-grant higher education system resulting from the 1862 Morrill Act failed to provide equal educational opportunities. Black students were excluded from enrolling in traditionally white institutions.

Funds from the Morrill Act began to flow systemically to schools offering only all-white education. Congress attempted by various legislation to force racial equality, including equality of educational opportunity. However, the U.S. Supreme Court initiated a series of interpretations of the post-Civil War constitutional amendments which ultimately defeated these various legislative efforts. Culminating with its landmark 1882 decision finding the first Civil Rights Act [1866] unconstitutional, the Supreme Court held that the 14th amendment only protected against direct discriminatory action by a State government.[22]

A Second Morrill Act was passed in 1890, which included language mandating States with dual systems of higher education to provide land-grant institutions for both systems. As a result, 19 institutions were established as black land-grant institutions, enrolling those black students who had been excluded under the 1862 legislation. While there was the creation of two land-grant systems — one established under the 1862 Land-Grant Act (1862 Morrill Act) and the other under the 1890 Land-Grant Act (Second Morrill Act) — the level of support for the 1890 institutions (both federal and state) never approximated the level received by the 1862 land-grant institutions.[23] In particular, during the expansion of program offerings and disciplines at the 1890 institutions, the disparity in funding for research infrastructure between them and the earlier established institutions severely limited their efforts to support basic and applied research.[24] In written testimony before the House Committee on Agriculture in support of legislation providing assistance to 1890 institutions, the Honorable Harold E. Ford noted that:

> The 1890 institutions were never adequately funded the way they should have been by the various states. With assistance from the various states and Federal Government, the 1862 institutions were permitted to thrive and expand, while the 1890 institutions received meager funding from both their respective state and Federal Government.
>
> Furthermore, the 1890 institutions were not eligible to participate in the facilities programs provided in the late 1960s and early 1970s by the Federal Government. Under the Research Facilities Act of 1963, only the 1862 land-grant institutions were permitted to participate in this program. Not until 1967 did the Federal Government start to provide research funds to the 1890 programs. These funds were for research projects, and not for constructing research facilities.[25]

CLASSIFICATION OF HBCUS

The diversity of HBCUs parallels that of other institutions of higher education. HBCUs are composed of public and private institutions, single-sex and coeducational, predominantly black and predominantly white,[26] two-year and four-year institutions, research universities, liberal arts colleges, professional schools, and community colleges. A March 2008 report of ED provides statistical data on 100 HBCUs — 41 public four-year colleges, 11 public two-year colleges, 46 private four-year colleges, and 2 private two-year colleges.[27]

HBCUs comprise almost 2.3% of all institutions of higher education and enroll approximately 11.6% of black students attending post-secondary institutions.[28] Approximately 3 3.0%, on average, of the undergraduate degrees in science and engineering earned by blacks were awarded by HBCUs. In addition, some of the most successful programs designed to attract underrepresented minorities into the sciences and in research careers have been initiated at HBCUs.[29] An analysis of ED 2006-2007 preliminary data shows that Xavier University, an HBCU, ranks first nationally in the number of blacks earning undergraduate degrees in the biological and biomedical sciences.[30] The institution has received national recognition for its model science program and has participated in NSF's Model Institutions for Excellence program. North Carolina A&T State University, also an HBCU, ranks first in the number of blacks earning undergraduate degrees in engineering.[31] Data compiled by the NSF reveal that in 2004, HBCUs provided the education for approximately 20.2% of blacks earning bachelor degrees in engineering, 39.5% in the physical sciences, 26.3% in computer sciences, 37.0% in mathematics, 36.1% in the biological sciences, 42.0% in agricultural sciences, 16.4% in social sciences, and 21.4% in psychology.[32]

FEDERAL RESEARCH AND DEVELOPMENT SUPPORT AT HBCUS

The National Science Foundation (NSF) provides data on federal academic science and engineering support to colleges and universities in six categories: research and development (R&D); fellowships, traineeships, and training grants; R&D plant; facilities and equipment for instruction; general support for science and engineering; and other science and engineering activities.[33] An important issue in the academic community, and in science and technology policy in general, is the distribution of federal R&D funds to colleges and universities. A major criticism of federal R&D funding patterns is that there is concentration in certain colleges and universities, restricting the development and expansion of scientific and technical capabilities in other institutions. In an analysis of 650 research-performing institutions, NSF found that the top 100 institutions accounted for approximately 80% of all academic R&D funding in FY2006. Those institutions falling in the top 100 category showed only minimal changes in more than 20 years.[34] The charge is that the elite institutions ("haves") continue in their status, and the less-prestigious research institutions ("have-nots") continue to struggle for research funding.[35] While various measures of equity can be calculated based on the number of institutions, geographic distribution, student enrollments, science and engineering students, graduate students, and so forth — the following analysis will examine federal obligations for R&D to HBCUs as a percentage of all institutions receiving R&D expenditures.

An October 2007 report of the NSF reveals that in FY2005, 908 U.S. colleges and universities received R&D support.[36] Of that total, 72 are HBCUs.[37] Trend data reveal that these research-performing HBCUs have not shared proportionately in the distribution of federal R&D obligations to colleges and universities.[38] Although funding to HBCUs has increased in the past 10 years in absolute terms, it remains only a small fraction of the total awarded to all U.S. colleges and universities. A 2007 report of the NSF, *Federal Science and Engineering Support to Universities, Colleges, and Nonprofit Institutions: Fiscal Year 2005,* reveals that for FY2005, HBCUs received approximately $294.2 million for R&D, an increase of $19.4 million (7.1%) over the FY2004 level of $274.8 million.[39] Data from FY1996-FY2005 show that while research-performing HBCUs are approximately 5.9% of all U.S. institutions conducting R&D, they receive approximately 1.2%, on average, of all federal academic R&D support.[40]

RESEARCH FUNDING AT HBCUs

An analysis of federal academic R&D support finds that funding is concentrated at selected institutions. Funding for non-HBCUs also is concentrated at selected institutions.[41] In FY2005, the top 10 HBCUs (in terms of receipt of federal R&D to HBCUs) accounted for approximately 52.7% of total federal R&D support, and the top 20 HBCUs accounted for approximately 72.3% of total R&D support. (In FY1 996, the top 10 HBCUs received 61.2% of funding to these institutions, and the top 20 institutions received 82.7% of funding.)

Table 1 below provides a listing of the top 20 HBCUs and their level of total academic science and engineering support.[42] The rankings (by R&D amounts received in FY2005) reveal that there has been only relative change in the concentration of federal R&D support among the top 20 HBCUs since FY1 996. Eight of the top 10 HBCUs in FY2005 for R&D support also were ranked in the top 10 for FY1996 (in different ordinal positions). In addition, 15 of the top 20 institutions for R&D support in FY2005, also were among the top 20 institutions in FY1996. However, a few institutions have received increased support so as to change their ranking. In FY2005, Jackson State University ranked sixth in R&D support; in FY1 996, it had ranked fifteenth. Lincoln University (Jefferson City) ranked fifteenth in FY2005. It had ranked twenty-fifth in FY1996. South Carolina State University, which ranked sixteenth in FY2005, ranked twenty-third in FY1 996. North Carolina Central University ranked nineteenth in FY2005, and had ranked forty-fourth in FY1996. The Hampton University ranked first in R&D support for FY2005; it had ranked eighth in FY1996.[43]

RESEARCH FACILITIES AT HBCUs

Facility construction/modernization/maintenance probably represents the largest capital investment for institutions of higher education. Many in academia contend that the quality of an institution's facilities is directly linked to the quality of education offered. While estimates vary on the level of deferred research facilities expenditures at all institutions of higher education, the amount of deteriorating physical plant and backlog of maintenance at HBCUs may be more pronounced.[44] Approximately 70% of the HBCUs were established prior to 1900 (55% date from before 1890). Some have aging facilities with electrical systems that are inadequate for the loads that complex computer systems and other state-of-the-art equipment (if available) would require.

In the mid-1980s, hearings were held in both the House and the Senate to examine the condition of the nation's scientific and engineering research facilities.[45] In addition to congressional interest, there was particular concern by those in the academic and scientific community about the quantity and quality of research space at nondoctorate-granting institutions, minority-serving institutions, and biomedical institutions. As a result of the hearings, NSF was directed to collect and analyze data on a range of academic research facilities issues (How much space is there for conducting scientific research?, What is the condition of the existing space?, How much of the space requires renovation or repair?, Is there enough space to meet the Nation's scientific research needs?, How do colleges and universities fund their research projects?, etc.). In October 2000, the NSF released a topical report on the needs and requirements of academic research facilities.[46] This particular survey and analysis included 660 research-performing institutions, of which 57 were HBCUs.[47]

In a 1998 survey of 57 research-performing HBCUs, the institutions reported having approximately 2.3 million net assignable square feet (NASF) of science and engineering research space.[48] The majority of the space was in the biological sciences, agricultural sciences, and engineering. However, 88% of the institutions reported that the amount of existing science and engineering research space was insufficient for meeting current research efforts. When asked to evaluate the condition of the existing space, 48% of the HBCUs indicated that their existing research space was effective for most levels of research, but required limited repair/renovation. An additional 15% determined that their institutions' existing space required major renovation in order to be used effectively for research in the science and engineering disciplines.

Table 1. Federal R&D Support and Total Academic S&E Funding to the Top 20 HBCUs in FY2005, Ranked by R&D Support (Dollars in millions)

Institutions	R&D	Total S&E
All HBCUs	$294.2	$479.2
Top 20 HBCUs		
1. Hampton University	40.1	44.1
2. Howard University	24.1	32.2
3. Morehouse School of Medicine	20.9	28.7
4. Florida A&M University	18.2	23.2
5. Meharry Medical College	18.1	30.7
6. Jackson State University	16.5	22.1
7. Morgan State University	10.8	12.8
8. North Carolina A&T State University	10.8	21.4
9. Tennessee State University	9.3	16.9
10. Tuskegee University	8.1	20.5
11. Alabama A&M University	7.5	11.7
12. Lincoln University (Jefferson City, MO)	6	9.4
13. North Carolina Central University	5.9	8
14. Prairie View A&M University	5.5	10.1
15. Southern University A&M College (all campuses)	5.4	11.6
16. Fort Valley State University	4.4	8.4
17. South Carolina State University	3.8	8.5
18. Fisk University	3.7	4.9
19. Clark Atlanta University	3.7	5.4
20. Virginia State University	3.7	8.3

Source: National Science Foundation, *Federal Science and Engineering Support to Universities, Colleges, and Selected Nonprofit Institutions, Fiscal Year 2005,* Detailed Statistical Tables, NSF07- 333, Arlington, VA, October 2007, Table 24. Total academic S&E includes R&D; R&D plant; facilities for instruction in S&E; fellowships, traineeships, and training grants; general support for S&E; and other S&E activities. See footnote 42.

The NSF survey revealed that for FY1996 and FY1997, approximately 15% of HBCUs initiated repair/renovation projects, and 14% began major construction projects. In the 1998 survey, HBCUs reported $331.0 million in construction and repair/renovation projects and campus infrastructure projects that had to be deferred due to lack of funding.[49] This constitutes 2.4% of all deferred projects reported by research-performing institutions.

Aggregate data were collected from a reduced sample of 29 institutions in order to compare research facility construction with similar surveys beginning in 1988.[50] This separate analysis of 29 HBCUs revealed that the amount of science and engineering research space increased from 1.1 million NASF in 1988 to 1.9 million in 1998 (72.7%). Between the 1996 survey and the 1998 survey, research space at the original 29 HBCUs increased by 88 thousand NASF (4.9%). The amount of research space increased the most in engineering and the agricultural sciences. During the period 1988 to 1998, research space increased in every field except the medical sciences in medical schools and computer science.

An additional analysis of the 29 HBCUs revealed that in 1996 and 1997, 11 of the 29 HBCUs initiated research facility construction projects, the same number of institutions that began construction startups in the 1988 survey. During the intervening years, specifically 1992-1995, only 4 of the 29 HBCUs initiated science and engineering research construction projects on their campuses. In the 1998 survey, FY1996 to FY1997, the 29 HBCUs provided $64.3 million in support of new construction projects. (The projects cost in excess of $100,000.) It was anticipated that the new projects would translate into 335 thousand NASF of new research space, 18% above the current available space.[51]

For the periods 1986-87 and 1992-93, the federal government was the largest source of funding for science and engineering research construction projects at the 29 HBCUs. The primary source of funding changed, and during 1994-95 and 1996-97, state and local governments provided the bulk of funding to these institutions for construction projects. Federal support to the 29 institutions did increase from 1994 to 1997, but the increase had slowed relative to other funding sources. Table 2 below details the source for research facility funding (in constant dollars) for the sample of 29 HBCUs.

Table 2. Source of Funds for Science/Engineering Research Facilities at the Original 29 HBCUs: 1986-97 (in millions of constant 1997 dollars)

Funding Source	Construction			Repair/Renovation		
	1986-87	1990-91	1996-97	1986-87	1990-91	1996-97
Federal Government	43.5	14.5	4.6	11.6	4.2	2.2
State/Local Government	34.3	7.6	50.5	6.5	9.6	1.8
Private Donations	14.8	0.0	3.0	0.7	0.1	0.0
Institutional Funds/Other	3.1	5.0	6.1	0.0	0.1	3.6
Total	95.5	27.0	64.3	18.8	14.0	7.6

Source: *Scientific and Engineering Research Facilities at Universities and Colleges: 1998*, op. cit., pp. 83-84. Components may not add to totals due to rounding.

VARIOUS AGENCY PROGRAMS TO ENHANCE SUPPORT OF RESEARCH AT HBCUs[52]

The NSF has several programs supporting HBCUs and other minority institutions. The Historically Black Colleges and Universities-Undergraduate Program (HBCU-UP) funds projects to improve the quality of undergraduate scientific and technical programs through curricular reform and enhancement, faculty development, upgrading of scientific instrumentation, and improvement of research infrastructure.[53] The FY2008 estimate is $16.1 million. Centers of Research Excellence in Science and Technology (CREST) seeks to upgrade the research capabilities of the most productive minority institutions. HBCUs and other minority- serving institutions develop alliances with other universities, laboratories, and centers in order to provide their students with direct experience in science, technology, engineering, and mathematics. The FY2008 enacted level for CREST is $14.9 million.[54]

In January 2008, NSF announced a collaborative project involving eight HBCUs and seven major research institutions to encourage black students to pursue degrees in robotics and computer science.[55] The Advancing Robotics Technology for Societal Impact (ARTSI) initiative would offer outreach programs at the K-12 and college levels and support research activities at HBCUs, internships for minority students in university laboratories, and provide mentoring programs for undergraduates. ARTSI would be funded at $2.0 million for a period of three years.

The Department of Agriculture, Cooperative State Research, Education and Extension Service (CSREES), administers a Capacity Building Grants Program to assist the 1890 land-grant institutions and Tuskegee University strengthen their research and teaching capabilities in high priority areas of the food and agricultural sciences. These activities include obtaining state-of-the-art scientific instrumentation for laboratories. For FY2008, $13.7 million will be made available for this program.[56] In addition to the Capacity Building Grants Program, the CSREES provides funding for research at the 1890 institutions through the Evans-Allen formula. The FY2008 enacted level for this program is $41.3 million.

The National Aeronautics and Space Administration (NASA) has established a University Research Centers (URC) program to fund research projects in space science and applications, advanced space technology, and advanced astronautics technology. Currently, the URC provides $1.0 million a year for five years to seven HBCUs. The Curriculum Improvement Partnership Award (CIPA) is designed to improve and strengthen the scientific and technical undergraduate curricula at minority institutions. CIPA provides $125,000 per year for three years. CIPA currently supports nine minority-serving institutions, of which three are HBCUs. FY2008 is the final year of funding for this program. CIPA was restructured and combined with the Partnership Award for the Integration of Research into the Undergraduate STEM Curriculum (PAIR) to form the Curriculum Improvements Partnership Award for the Integration of Research (CIPAIR). CIPAIR will strategically enhance teaching and education strategies across academic programs. CIPAIR is effective beginning in FY2008, and will provide $100,000 to $200,000 per year for three years.[57] NASA Science and Technology Institute for Minority Institutions (NSTI-MI) has two main components — student internships and research clusters. Underrepresented and underserved students from minority institutions compete to conduct research with NASA scientists and engineers. Clusters of minority institutions also engage in specific NASA-related research at one of the 10 NASA Centers. Funding for NSTI-MI in FY2008 is $2.0 million.[58]

P.L. 109-364, The National Defense Authorization Act, FY2006 provides approximately $11,662.5 million for science and technology programs. Contained in that funding is support for, among other things, the University Research Initiative (URI) and HBCUs. It is anticipated that participating HBCUs will increase their involvement in the performance of defense research and in the scientific disciplines critical to the national security functions of the Department of Defense (DOD). P.L. 110-116, the Department of Defense Appropriations Act, FY2008 provides $20.0 million for HBCUs and other minority institutions to enhance their R&D activity, develop approaches to inter-university research in the DOD critical technology and homeland security areas, and to increase their personnel in these areas.

POLICY OPTIONS

In testimony before the House Science Committee, Sebetha Jenkins, President, Jarvis Christian College, stated that: "[G]iven the demographic changes taking place in this nation, investing more in HBCUs is, in actuality, about the future prosperity of this nation."[59] Jenkins proposed the establishment of a program for minority institutions that is similar to the Experimental Program to Stimulate Competitive Research (EPSCoR). EPSCoR is designed for those states and institutions that are perceived as being the "have-nots" and are in the most need of R&D support.[60] This proposed EPSCoR-like program would build new and expanded capacity and capability for minority-serving institutions. Key elements of the EPSCoR-like program would be technical assistance and the development of partnerships between major research institutions and minority-serving institutions. This initiative would support also an HBCU centers program for the education and training of professionals in the scientific and technical disciplines. Jenkins, and others in the academic community, believe that an EPSCoR-like program would stimulate the competitive R&D capacity of HBCUs. Success of the HBCU centers would be dependent on unfettered resources, with funding being provided until the centers were self-sustaining.

The viability of any academic institution is a function of its ability to provide a quality education for its student population. Data reveal that many HBCUs have provided their black student population with a quality education, especially in the scientific and technical disciplines. In testimony before the House Committee on Education and Labor, Dorothy Cowser Yancy, President, Johnson C. Smith University, stated that:

> HBCUs today represent only 4% of all higher education institutions, but they graduate approximately 30% of all African-American students, 40% of African American students receiving a four-year degree in [science, technology, engineering, and mathematics], and 50% of African American teachers.... The successes were achieved despite the fact that in recent year's federal support for HBCUs has only increased in very modest amounts; and in spite of the fact that HBCUs continue to receive significantly less funding for research, facilities, and programs than their historically white counterparts.[61]

However, these institutions are faced with an increased challenge of attracting and preparing an increasingly larger number of blacks in the scientific and technical disciplines.

Demographic data show a student population and workforce increasingly composed of minority groups that have been historically underrepresented in science, mathematics, and engineering. Shirley Ann Jackson, President, Rensselaer Polytechnic Institute, contends that this demographic pattern may affect the development of the scientific and engineering workforce and, consequently, the conduct of R&D during the 21st century.[62] The success of research programs at HBCUs is inextricably linked to their ability to provide an environment for fostering additional scientific talent.[63] The National Academies report, *Rising Above the Gathering Storm*, states:

> Increasing participation of underrepresented minorities is critical to ensuring a high-quality supply of scientists and engineers in the United States over the long term. As minority groups increase as a percentage of the US population, increasing their participation rate in science and engineering is critical if we are just to maintain the overall participation rate in science among the US population. Perhaps even more important, if some groups are underrepresented in science and engineering in our society, we are not attracting as many of the most talented people to an important segment of our knowledge economy.[64]

The distribution of federal funding for HBCUs is one of the critical issues facing these institutions. Some say that past and current policies have not provided effective remedies for their problems of infrastructure necessary to develop strong scientific programs. Many HBCUs are attempting to expand their research capacity by developing expertise in areas such as homeland security and national defense, cyberinfrastructure, environmental observatories, food security, energy expenditures, genomics, and material science. They contend that improved funding for facilities and instrumentation is needed to strengthen the capability of these colleges and universities to contribute to the nation's long-term economic vitality. While many HBCUs have engaged in strategic planning in order to obtain a more competitive research base, Congress may continue to consider options that would bring HBCUs closer to an equal footing with other institutions and enable them to move toward full partnerships in conducting research. This issue may be examined when assessing the capacity of HBCUs and other minority-serving institutions to contribute to the health of the nation's higher education system, and in producing an increasingly larger number of trained scientific and technical personnel needed to meet the challenge of a highly competitive international economy.[65]

CONGRESSIONAL ACTION IN THE 110TH CONGRESS

On August 14, 2008, the President signed into law P.L. 110-315, the Higher Education Opportunity Act (HEOA).[66] The HEOA establishes a new program in Title III, Section A to provide federal support to Predominantly Black Institutions (PBIs). These PBIs that qualify for funding fall outside of the definition of an HBCU.[67] To be eligible as a PBI, the institution must have, among other things, an enrollment of undergraduate students that is at least 40.0% black, and must have a total enrollment of at least 1,000 undergraduates, with half of them being in degree programs. Grant proposals for PBIs can be in the areas of science, technology, engineering, and mathematics, in addition to teacher preparation, health education, and international issues. Title III, Part E of the HEOA provides funding for two new minority science and engineering improvement programs. A partnership grant program is directed at increasing the participation of underrepresented minority youth or low-income youth in science, technology, engineering, and mathematics education. Activities to be supported include outreach, hands-on, and experiential-based learning projects. Partnership grants to be awarded are for a period of five years in an amount not less than $500,000. Non-federal matching funds are required. An additional program will be directed at encouraging minorities to pursue careers in science, mathematics, engineering, and technology.

The HEOA provides authority for loans for repair and renovation of academic research facilities, among other facilities. Language in Title III, Part B, Investing in HBCUs and Other Minority Institutions, provides formula grants to eligible institutions. The percentage of funds allocated to each institution is based on several factors, and no institution can receive less than $250,000.[68] Also under Title III, Part B, the HEOA provides assistance to Historically Black Graduate Institutions to increase the number of blacks in certain professional disciplines.[69] Title III, Part D, HBCU Capital Financing, establishes a bonding authority to raise capital to be lent to HBCUs for repair and renovation of facilities. The total amount that would be available for financing is $1.1 billion.[70] The aggregate authority principal and unpaid accrued interest on these loans are to be made for two types of institutions in the amounts of $733.3 million and $366.7 million.[71]

On September 4, 2007, the House passed, as amended, H.R. 694, Minority Serving Institution Digital and Wireless Technology Opportunity Act. The bill would provide, among other things, funding to acquire equipment, instrumentation, networking capability, hardware and software, digital and wireless networking technology, and infrastructure to improve the quality and delivery of educational services of these institutions. The institutions eligible for participation include (1) HBCUs; (2) Hispanic-, Alaskan Native-, or Native Hawaiian-serving institutions; (3) tribally controlled colleges and universities; and (4) institutions with a sufficient enrollment of needy students as defined by the Higher Education Act of 1965. Support also would enable these institutions to obtain capacity-building technical assistance through remote technical support and technical assistance workshops, and to advance the use of wireless networking technology in an effort to improve research and education, including scientific, engineering, mathematics, and technology instructions. Funding would be available through grants, cooperative agreements, or contracts. Non-federal matching requirements would be required in the amount equal to one-quarter of the award, or $500,000, whichever is the lesser amount. Matching requirements could be waived for an institution with little or no endowment. The bill would authorize $250.0 million for FY2008 and such sums as may be necessary for each of FY2009 through FY2012.[72]

On January 8, 2008, similar legislation, S. 1650, Max Cleland Minority Serving Institution Digital and Wireless Technology Opportunity Act of 2007, was reported in the Senate (S.Rept. 110-257). S. 1650 would authorize, also, $250.0 million annually for each of FY2008 through FY20 12. The bill would strengthen the ability of minority institutions to provide course offerings, faculty development, and capacity-building technical assistance in digital and wireless network technologies. S. 1650 is designed to narrow the "economic opportunity divide" that currently exists between students in minority serving institutions and their counterparts in other institutions.[73] Similar to H.R. 694, funding would be awarded through a peer-review process in the form of grants, contracts, or cooperative agreements. An eligible institution could receive as much as $2.5 million annually. The Senate committee bill would also establish an office in the Department of Commerce and there would be cost sharing requirements from grant recipients similar to that contained in H.R. 694. Cost sharing would be waived for those institutions with no endowment or an endowment valued at less than $50.0 million.[74]

End Notes

[1] House Committee on Education and Labor, *America's Black Colleges and Universities: Models of Excellence and Challenges for the Future*, 110th Cong., 2nd Sess., March 13, 2008, Written testimonies of Hazel O'Leary, President, Fisk University and Earl S. Richardson, President, Morgan State University. See also Chalokwu, Christopher I., "A Rationale for Increasing Funding for HBCUs," *Black Issues in Higher Education*, v. 20, January 1, 2004, p. 98, Frazier, Matt, "Survival Is Evolving Struggle for Black Colleges," *Fort-Worth Star-Telegram*, February 2, 2003, Metro, p. 1.

[2] See for example Powell, Tracie, "Surviving Tough Times: From Administrative Reorganizations to Finding New Streams of Revenue, Some Historically Black Colleges and Universities are Determined to Stay Afloat," *Black Issues in Higher Education*, v. 20, January 1, 2004, pp. 34 -37.

[3] See for example Minor, James T., *Contemporary HBCUs: Considering Institutional Capacity and State Priorities*, Michigan State University, College of Education, January 2008, 37 pp., Southern Education Foundation, "Education After Katrina: Time for a New Federal Response," Atlanta, GA, August 2007, 35 pp., Hamilton, Kendra, "Restructuring, Restoring and Rebuilding," *Diverse Issues in Higher Education*, v. 23, March 23, 2006, pp. 24-27, and Schuman, Jamie, "Southern U. At New Orleans May Have to Rebuild From Scratch, at a Cost of $300-Million or More," *The Chronicle of Higher Education*, v. 52, September 23, 2005, p. A16.

[4] Educational Testing Service, *A Culture of Evidence III: An Evidence-Centered Approach to Accountability for Student Learning Outcomes*, Princeton, NJ, February 2008, 24 pp., Department of Education, A Test of Leadership, *Charting the Future of U.S. Higher Education, A Report of the Commission on the Future of Higher Education*, September 2006, 76 pp., Carey, Kevin, "Make Universities Accountable for What Matters," Education Sector, November 2007, Redden, Elizabeth, "Explaining State Spending on Higher Ed," *Inside Higher Ed*, October 11, 2007, [http://www.insidehighered.com/news/2007/10/11/ spending], and National Science Foundation, "Universities Report Stalled Growth in Federal R&D Funding in FY2006," *InfoBrief*, NSF07-336, Rhonda Britt, Arlington, VA, September 2007, 6 pp.

[5] Chalokwu, Christopher I., "A Rationale for Increasing Funding for HBCUs," and House Committee on Science and Technology, Subcommittee on Research, Preparing a 21st Century Workforce: Strengthening and Improving K- 12 and Undergraduate Science, Math, and Engineering Education, 107th Cong., 2nd Sess., April 22, 2002, Testimony of Sebetha Jenkins, President, Jarvis Christina College.

[6] See for example The Southern Education Foundation, *Igniting Potential, Historically Black Colleges and Universities and Science, Technology, Engineering and Mathematics*, Summer 2005, 36 pp.

[7] The Southern Education Foundation, *Igniting Potential, Historically Black Colleges and Universities and Science, Technology, Engineering and Mathematics*, pp. 22-23.

[8] The various executive orders include Executive Order 12232, August 1980; Executive Order 12320, September 1981; Executive Order 12677, April 1989; Executive Order 12876, November 1993, and Executive Order 13256, February 2002.

[9] The White House, Executive Order 13256, Advisors for Historically Black Colleges and Universities, February 2002, [http://www.whitehouse.gov/news/releases/2002/02/2002021 2- 3.html].

[10] National Science Foundation, "Role of HBCUs as Baccalaureate-Origin Institutions of Black S&E Doctorate Recipients, " *InfoBrief*, NSF08-319, Joan Burrelli and Alan Rapoport, Arlington, VA, August 2008, 8 pp.

[11] Lomax, Michael, "The HBCU Mission: A Fresh Look for a New Congress," *Diverse Issues in Higher Education*, v. 24, February 22, 2007, p. 51, Allen, Walter R., Joseph O. Jewell, Kimberly A. Griffin, and De'Sha S. Wolf, "Historically Black Colleges and Universities: Honoring the Past, Engaging the Present, Touching the Future," *Journal of Negro Education*, Summer 2007, pp. 263-281, and *Igniting Potential, Historically Black Colleges and Universities and Science, Technology, Engineering and Mathematics*, 36 pp.

[12] Department of Education, National Center for Education Statistics, *Projections of Education Statistics to 2015*, NCES2006-084, September 2006, p. 10. Note: Demographic data indicate that blacks, Hispanics, Native Americans/Alaskan Natives, and Asians/Pacific Islanders will comprise more than 52% of the undergraduate population (18-24 years old) of the United States by 2050, an increase from the recorded 34% in 1999. National Science Foundation, *Women, Minorities, and Persons with Disabilities in Science and Engineering:2007*, NSF07-315, Arlington, VA, February 2007, p.4. See also National Science Board, *America's Pressing Challenge — Building a Stronger Foundation*, NSB06- 02, Arlington, VA, January 2006, p. 3.

[13] The U.S. Census Bureau reports that 303 counties in the nation, out of a total of 3,141, have a "majority-minority" population — more than 50% racial/ethnic minority. U.S. Census Press Releases, August 9, 2007.

[14] For discussion of the participation of underrepresented groups in the sciences see for example *Women, Minorities, and Persons with Disabilities in Science and Engineering: 2007*, 304 pp., Johnson, Angela, "Graduating Underrepresented African Americans, Latino, and American Indian Students in Science," *Journal of Women and Minorities in Science and Engineering*, v. 13, 2007, pp. 1-21, White, Jeffrey L., James W. Altschuld, and Yi-Fang Lee, "Persistence of Interest in Science, Technology, Engineering, and Mathematics: A Minority Retention Study," *The Journal of Women and Minorities in Science and Engineering*, v. 12, 2006, pp. 47-64, and CRS Report 98-871, *Science, Engineering, and Mathematics Education: Status and Issues*, by Christine M. Matthews.

[15] See for example Heriot, Gail, "Civil Rights Commission to Explore Ways to Encourage More Minorities to Enter Science, Technology, Engineering & Math," *The Right Coast*, September 4, 2008, [http://rightcoast.typepad.com/rightcoast/2008/09/civil-rights-co.html], The National Academies, *Rising Above the Gathering Storm, Energizing and Employing America for a Brighter Economic Future*, Committee on Science, Engineering, and Public Policy, Washington, DC, National Academy Press, 2007, pp. 165-168, and Commission on the Advancement of Women and Minorities in Science, Engineering and Technology Development, *Land of Plenty - Diversity as America's Competitive Edge in Science, Engineering and Technology*, September 2000, 91 pp.

[16] Pluviose, David, "The Meyerhoff Model," *Diverse Issues in Higher Education*, v. 25, July 10, 2008, pp.18-19.

[17] For an expanded history of HBCUs see for example Jackson, Cynthia L. and Eleanor F. Nunn, *Historically Black Colleges and Universities, A Reference Handbook*, Santa Barbara, California, 2003, 253 pp, and Peltak, Jennifer, *History of African-American Colleges & Universities*, Philadelphia, 2003, 120 pp.

[18] Department of Education, National Center for Education Statistics, Snyder, Thomas D., Stephen Provasnik, and Linda L. Shafer, *Historically Black Colleges and Universities: 1976 to 2001*, NCES2004-062, Washington, DC, September 2004, p. 1.

[19] The Freedman's Bureau operated from 1865-1873 to provide assistance for newly freed slaves. Ibid., p. 2.

[20] The establishment of a public land-grant system is considered to be one of the most significant developments in U.S. higher education. Prior to the First Morrill Act, higher education opportunities were limited to the very elite.

[21] *Historically Black Colleges and Universities, 1976 to 2001*, op. cit., p. 1.

[22] Ibid.

[23] For a discussion of the history of land-grant institutions, see McDowell, George R., "Land-Grant Colleges of Agriculture: Renegotiating or Abandoning A Social Contract", *Choices*, Second Quarter 1988, p. 18-21, Schuh, G. Edward, "Revitalizing Land-Grant Universities," *Choices*, Second Quarter 1986, p. 6-10, National Research Council, Board on Agriculture, *Colleges of Agriculture at the Land Grant Universities: A Profile*, Washington, DC, 1995, and Bonnen, James T, "Land Grant Universities Are Changing," November 1996, [http://www.adec.edu/clemson/papers/bonnen1.html].

[24] Most HBCUs began as "normal" schools — with the fundamental mission to train teachers. Beginning in the late 1960s and early 1970s, there was a shift in that focus to other professions. HBCUs do, however, continue to graduate and award a large number of degrees in the field of education.

[25] In 1967, the federal government provided $285,000 to be divided among 16 1890 land- grant institutions (approximately $17,812.50 per institution). House Committee on Agriculture, Subcommittee on Department Operations, Research, and Foreign Agriculture, *Hearing on H.R. 1309, 1890 Land-Grant Colleges Facilities*, 97th Cong., 1st Sess., June 4, 1981, p. 13-15.

[26] Fall 2005 enrollment data reveal that three HBCUs have predominantly white student populations — Bluefield State College (88.5%), West Virginia State College (84.5%), and Lincoln University, Missouri (60.4%). In addition, St. Phillip's College, San Antonio, a two-year institution, has a large Hispanic enrollment — 47.7%. St. Phillip's College is the only institution with the dual designation of being both an HBCU *and* a Hispanic-serving institution. The black student enrollment at St. Phillip's is 16.2%, and the white student enrollment is 33.8%. See also Goldman, Russell, ABC News, "Changing Face of Historically Black Colleges," May 19, 2008, [http://abcnews.go.com/print?id=4874870].

[27] Department of Education, *Digest of Education Statistics 2007*, NCES2008-022, Washington, DC, March 2008, Table 230, pp. 348-349. Documents provided by the White House Initiative on Historically Black Colleges and Universities list, as of September 2008, a total of 105 HBCUs. The list of the 100 institutions detailed in the *Digest of Education Statistics*, excludes those HBCUs that are not participating in Title IV programs (Higher Education Act). Title IV eligible institutions are required to meet certain criteria in order to receive federal student financial aid. A Title IV eligible institutions must have, among other things, "acceptable accreditation and admission standards, eligible academic program(s), administrative capability, and financial responsibility." *Digest of Education Statistics 2007*, p. 666.

[28] *Digest of Education Statistics 2007*, Tables 218 and 231, pp. 314, 350. ED data reveal that for the academic school year 2006-2007, there were 2,629 four-year institutions, and 1,685 two-year institutions. Disaggregated

data show that HBCUs are approximately 3.3% of all four-year institutions and less than 1.0% of all two-year institutions.

[29] The underrepresented minorities include blacks, Hispanics, Native Americans, and women. Asian Americans are excluded because they are not statistically underrepresented in science, mathematics, and engineering. See for example National Science Foundation, *Women, Minorities, and Persons with Disabilities in Science and Engineering*, Figure D-2, p. 10, and Wyer, Mary, "Intending to Stay: Images of Scientists, Attitudes Toward Women, and Gender as Influences on Persistence Among Science and Engineering Majors," *Journal of Women and Minorities in Science and Engineering*, vol. 9, 2003, pp. 1-16.

[30] Borden, Victor M. H.,"Top 100 Undergraduate Degree Producers — Interpreting the Data," *Diverse Issues in Higher Education*, v. 25, June 12, 2008, p. 28.

[31] Ibid., p. 34.

[32] National Science Foundation, *Science and Engineering Degrees, by Race/Ethnicity of Recipients: 1995-2004*, NSF07-308, Arlington, VA, January 2007, Table 13. Note: An expanded discussion of HBCUs is contained in Department of Education, *Characteristics of Minority-Serving Institutions and Minority Undergraduates Enrolled in These Institutions*, NCES2008-156, November 2007, 196 pp.

[33] Other science and engineering activities are defined as "... technical conferences, teacher institutes, and programs geared to increase the scientific knowledge of precollege and undergraduate students. Such activities comprise some of the building blocks of science education and future research capability." National Science Foundation, "The Extent of Federal S&E Funding to Minority-Serving Institutions," *InfoBrief*, NSF04-325, Richard J. Bennof, Arlington, VA, June 2004, p. 2.

[34] National Science Foundation, "Universities Report Stalled Growth in Federal R&D Funding in FY2006," NSF07-336, *InfoBrief*, September 2007, 6 pp.

[35] In 1990, the first Bush Administration proposed to categorize and classify HBCUs based on their missions and programs. The premise was that it would allow federal agencies to select the appropriate group for developing linkages, rather than having them work with the various programs in all the institutions. Considerable criticism voiced by presidents and department chairs of HBCUs contributed to the withdrawal of the proposal. Opposition was based on the concern that only a small group of the institutions would receive funding — those that were already considered to be the research "elite." It was believed that the remainder would be abandoned. Mercer, Joye, " White House Scraps Classification Plan for Black Institutions," *Black Issues in Higher Education*, v. 8, May 23, 1991, p. 7.

[36] National Science Foundation, "FY2005 Federal S&E Obligations Reach Over 2,400 Academic and Nonprofit Institutions; Data Presented on Minority-Serving Institutions," NSF07-326 (Revised), *InfoBrief*, Richard J. Bennof, October 2007, p. 2. A total of 1,227 academic institutions received federal S&E support in FY2005 (with R&D being one of the six categories of S&E support).

[37] National Science Foundation, *Federal Science and Engineering Support to Universities, Colleges, and Nonprofit Institutions: FY2005*, Table 24.

[38] See for example Anderson, Lauren Bayne, "Black Colleges Continue Fighting for Federal Funds," *The Wall Street Journal*, October 29, 2003, p. B.4J, "Pork Barrel Grants: Tidbits for Black Colleges," *The Journal of Blacks in Higher Education*, Autumn 2003, pp. 68-69, and Salandy, Anthony, "Correcting the Inequities in Federal Research Funding," *Black Issues in Higher Education*, v. 19, May 23, 2002, p. 42.

[39] The data on federal support to academic R&D result from a compilation of 19 agencies. R&D includes all research activities, both basic and applied, and all development activities that are supported at colleges and universities. Obligations reported do not include funds to federally funded research and development centers (FFRDCs). The institutions compiling this population are those receiving current year obligations. Caution should be exercised in reviewing the data. Because of the relatively small number of HBCUs, data from a few institutions can skew the quantitative findings and have a marked effect on the resulting analysis. National Science Foundation, *Federal Science and Engineering Support to Universities, Colleges, and Nonprofit Institutions: Fiscal Year 2001*, Detailed Statistical Tables, NSF 02-319, Arlington, VA, August 2003, Table B-22, pp. 173-174.

[40] National Science Foundation, *Federal Science and Engineering Support to Universities, Colleges, and Nonprofit Institutions: Fiscal Year 2005*, NSF07-333, Arlington, VA, October 2007, Tables 1 and 24, and *Federal Science and Engineering Support to Universities, Colleges, and Nonprofit Institutions: Fiscal Year 2003*, NSF06-309, Arlington, VA, June 2006, Table 22.

[41] In FY2005, approximately 30% of the total federal academic R&D expenditures in science and engineering went to the leading 20 institutions. National Science Foundation, "Universities Report Stalled Growth in Federal R&D Funding in FY2006," *InfoBrief*, NSF07-336, Richard J. Bennof, Arlington, VA, September 2007, p. 4.

[42] NSF reports that federal academic science and engineering support for HBCUs, and minority institutions as a whole (includes Hispanic-serving institutions and tribal colleges), is "allocated relatively less for R&D and relatively more for S&E capacity building activities when compared to non-minority-serving institutions." National Science Foundation, "The Extent of Federal S&E Funding to Minority-Serving Institutions," p. 1.

[43] *Federal Science and Engineering Support to Universities, Colleges, and Selected Nonprofit Institutions, Fiscal Year 2005*, Table 21, and *Federal Science and Engineering Support to Universities, Colleges, and Selected*

Nonprofit Institutions, Fiscal Year 1996, Table B-22. Howard University had consistently ranked number one in R&D support to HBCUs for several decades. In FY2003, Howard University ranked number two, fell to number three in FY2004, and again regained the ranking of number two in FY2005. For expanded discussion of academic support to HBCUs see National Science Foundation, "FY2005 Federal S&E Obligations Reach Over 2,400 Academic and Nonprofit Institutions; Data Presented on Minority-Serving Institutions," 8 pp.

[44] House Committee on Science, Subcommittee on Research, *H.R. 2183, the Minority Serving Institutions Digital and Wireless Technology Opportunity Act,* 108th Cong., 1st Sess., July 9, 2003, House Committee on Education and the Workforce, Subcommittee on Select Education and the Subcommittee on 21st Century Competitiveness, *Responding to the Needs of Historically Black Colleges and Universities in the 21st Century,* 107th Cong., 1st Sess., April 23, 2001, pp. 69-98, 107th Cong., 2nd Sess., February 13, 2002, pp. 77-94, and 107th Cong., 2nd Sess., September 19, 2002, pp. 5 1-60.

[45] See for example House Committee on Science and Technology, *Improving the Research Infrastructure at U.S. Universities and Colleges,* 98th Cong., 2nd Sess., May 8, 1984.

[46] National Science Foundation, *Scientific and Engineering Research Facilities at Colleges and Universities, 1998,* Topical Report, NSF0 1-301, Arlington, VA, October 2000. For this particular survey and analysis, research-performing institutions were defined as (1) those institutions that offer a master's or a doctorate degree in science and engineering; (2) report in excess of $50,000 expenditures in 1993 academic R&D survey; and (3) all HBCUs, nonHBCU-black institutions, and Hispanic-serving institutions with any research expenditures.

[47] The other minority institutions in the survey included 13 non-HBCU-black institutions, and 9 Hispanic-serving institutions. Non-HBCU-black institutions are those colleges and universities with at least a 25% black student enrollment according to the Integrated Postsecondary Education Data System, but do not have the designation as HBCUs.

[48] National Science Foundation, *Scientific and Engineering Research Facilities at Colleges and Universities, 1998,* NSF01-301, Arlington, VA, October 2000, 232 pp. Since 1986, the NSF has collected, on a biennial basis, data on scientific and engineering research facilities in higher education. Different analyses and various reports are released. This topical report contains data from the 1998 survey that included a total of 80 research-performing, minority-serving institutions — 57, HBCUs; 13, non-HBCU-black institutions; and 10, Hispanic serving institutions. (This is the most current published data available for an analysis of this type.) Note: "Net assignable square feet (NASF) is defined as the sum of all area, in square feet, on all floors of a building assigned to, or available to be assigned to, an occupant for specific use." p. 2.

[49] Ibid., p. 79.

[50] These were the "original" HBCUs that reported separately budgeted R&D expenditures and science and engineering research space in the 1988 survey (FY1986 and FY1987).

[51] Ibid., p. 81.

[52] This is not a complete compilation of federal agency support, but illustrates the various efforts to address the support of research infrastructure at HBCUs. Many of the programs in the various agencies are an outgrowth of Executive Orders 12232 and 12320. Note: For an expanded discussion of federal support to HBCUs see Department of Education, White House Initiative on Historically Black Colleges and Universities, Office of Postsecondary Education, *Fulfilling the Covenant — The Way Forward 2004-05 Annual Report to the President on the Results of Participation of Historically Black Colleges and Universities in Federal Programs,* by the President's Board of Advisors on Historically Black Colleges and Universities, November 2007, 53 pp.

[53] Since 2001, the HBCU-UP has provided funding for science and mathematics education and research programs at 80 HBCUs. This includes support of programs at 82.0% of four- year HBCUs and to 46.0% at two-year HBCUs.

[54] See also Robinson, Natasha, "NC Historically Black College 1st to Get NSF Grant," September 8, 2008, [http://www.dailyadvance.com/news/state]. North Carolina A&T State University will receive approximately $18.0 million over a period of five years to develop and operate the Engineering Research Center for Revolutionizing Metallic Biomaterials.

[55] Currently, approximately 2 million computer and information scientists are in the United States, of which 4.8% are black.

[56] Some matching funds are required.

[57] The CIPAIR budget for FY2008 is $2.8 million. This amount is for new project solicitation and for completion of those grants awarded within the CIPA structure.

[58] See also "NASA Awards Education Research Grants to Minority Universities," September 16, 2008, [http://blackengineer.com/artman/publish/printer_871 .shtml].

[59] House Committee on Science and Technology, Subcommittee on Research, *Preparing a 21st Century Workforce: Strengthening and Improving K-12 and Undergraduate Science, Math, and Engineering Education,* 107th Cong., 2nd Sess., April 22, 2002, Written statement of Sebetha Jenkins, President, Jarvis Christian College.

[60] CRS Report RL30930, *U.S. National Science Foundation: Experimental Program to Stimulate Competitive Research,* by Christine M. Matthews.

[61] House Committee on Education and Labor, *America's Black Colleges and Universities: Models of Excellence and Challenges for the Future*, Written statement of Dorothy Cowser Yancy, President, Johnson C. Smith University, p. 3.

[62] Jackson, Shirley Ann, President, Rensselaer Polytechnic Institute, "The Quiet Crisis and the Future of American Competitiveness," Speech before the American Chemical Society, August 29, 2005.

[63] Roach, Ronald, "The Journey for Jackson State," *Diverse Issues in Higher Education*, v. 23, February 8, 2007, pp. 22-27, and Suitts, Steve, "Fueling Education Reform: Historically Black Colleges are Meeting a National Science Imperative,"*Cell Biology Education*, v. 2, July 2, 2003, pp. 205-206.

[64] The National Academies, *Rising Above the Gathering Storm, Energizing and Employing America for a Brighter Future*, pp.1 66-167.

[65] P.L. 110-84, the College Cost Reduction and Access Act, added a program entitled "Predominantly Black Institutions." Predominantly Black Institutions (PBIs) are defined as those institutions with at least 1,000 undergraduates in which blacks comprise 40% or more of the total enrollment. In addition, 50% of the enrollment must be either low-income or first-generation students. Grants of at least $250,000 would be provided for the eligible institutions. In introducing the measure, Senator Barack Obama stated that: "To restore America's competitiveness, we must invest in the success of traditionally underrepresented groups." (Press Release, May 29, 2007). For discussion of this proposal for PBIs see CRS Report RL34283, *Higher Education Act Reauthorization in the 110th Congress: A Comparison of Major Proposals*, by Blake Alan Naughton, Rebecca R. Skinner, David P. Smole, Jeffrey J. Kuenzi, and Richard N. Apling.

[66] Signed into law on August 14, 2008, P.L. 110-315 authorizes, amends, and establishes programs under the Higher Education Act of 1965. (See H.R. 4137, Conf. Report 110-803.) The Higher Education Opportunities Act, also known as the College Opportunity and Affordability Act, was last fully authorized by P.L. 105-244. During that period of time, there were 14 extensions to the Higher Education Act. For expanded discussion of the legislation see CRS Report RL34654, *The Higher Education Opportunity Act: Reauthorization of the Higher Education Act*, by David P. Smole, Blake Alan Naughton, Jeffrey J. Kuenzi, and Rebecca R. Skinner.

[67] An HBCU is defined as an institution established prior to 1964 and have as its primary mission the education of blacks. Please see footnote 24.

[68] Previous Higher Education Act amendments set the minimum award for institutions at $500,000.

[69] The Act adds six institutions to the list of eligible institutions, with restrictions. The six institutions are Alabama State University, Prairie View A&M University, Delaware State University, Langston University, Bowie State University, and the University of the District of Columbia, David A. Clarke School of Law.

[70] Previous Higher Education Act amendments set the level of funding at $375.0 million.

[71] Previous Higher Education Act amendments set the awards at $250.0 million and $125.0 million.

[72] Authorizations are to be appropriated to the Technology Administration of the Department of Commerce to carry out section 5(c) of the Stevenson-Wydler Technology Innovation Act of 1980.

[73] Senate Committee on Commerce, Science, and Transportation, *Max Cleland Minority Serving Institution Digital and Wireless Technology Opportunity Act*, S.Rept. 110-257, Report to accompany S. 1650, 110th Cong., 2nd Sess., January 8, 2008, p. 1.

[74] See also Schmidt, Peter, "New Congressional Caucus Formed to Fight for Black Colleges," *The Chronicle of Higher Education*, v. 55, September 19, 2008, p. A16.

In: Federal Role in Funding Research and Development ISBN: 978-1-60741-486-5
Editor: Piper B. Collins © 2010 Nova Science Publishers, Inc.

Chapter 4

FEDERAL RESEARCH AND DEVELOPMENT FUNDING: FY2009

*John F. Sargent [1], Christine M. Matthews[1], John D. Moteff[1],
Daniel Morgan[1], Robert Esworthy[1], Wendy H. Schacht[1],
Pamela W. Smith[2] and Wayne A. Morrissey[3]*

SUMMARY

President Bush proposed total research and development (R&D) funding of $147.0 billion in his FY2009 budget request to Congress, a $3.9 billion (2.7%) increase over the estimated FY2008 level of $143.1 billion. The President's request included $29.3 billion for basic research, up $847 million (3.0%) from FY2008; $27.1 billion for applied research, down $1.0 billion (-3.6%); $84.0 billion for development, up 1.6 billion (1.9%); and $6.5 billion for R&D facilities and equipment, up $2.5 billion (61.7%). Congress is to play a central role in defining the nation's R&D priorities, especially with respect to two overarching issues: the extent to which the Federal R&D investment can grow in the context of increased pressure on discretionary spending and how available funding will be prioritized and allocated. A low or negative growth rate in the overall R&D investment may require movement of resources across disciplines, programs, or agencies to address priorities.

The Administration requested significantly larger percentage increases in the R&D budgets of the three agencies that are part of its American Competitiveness Initiative: the Department of Energy's Office of Science, the National Science Foundation, and the National Institute of Standards and Technology. In 2007, Congress authorized substantial R&D increases for these agencies under the America COMPETES Act (P.L. 110-69). The President's budget would reduce R&D funding for the Department of Agriculture, down $357 million; Department of Veterans Affairs, down $76 million; Department of the Interior, down $59 million; and Environmental Protection Agency, down $7 million. The FY2009 request included increases for three multiagency R&D initiatives: the National Nanotechnology

Initiative, up $35 million; Networking and Information Technology R&D program, up $194 million; and Climate Change Science Program, up $177 million.

On September 30, 2008, President Bush signed into law H.R. 2638, the Consolidated Security, Disaster Assistance, and Continuing Appropriations Act, 2009 (P.L. 110-329). This act provides FY2009 appropriations for the Department of Defense, Department of Homeland Security, and Military Construction and Veterans Affairs; continued funding for all other agencies not covered under these provisions at their FY2008 funding levels through March 6, 2009; and supplemental funding for disaster relief. Under this act, FY2009 R&D funding is approximately $147.2 billion. None of the FY2008 regular appropriations bills has been passed by both the House and Senate.

For the past two years, federal R&D funding and execution has been affected by mechanisms used to complete the annual appropriations process — the year-long continuing resolution for FY2007 (P.L. 110-5) and the combining of 11 appropriations bills into the Consolidated Appropriations Act, 2008 for FY2008 (P.L. 110-161). For example, FY2008 R&D funding for some agencies and programs is below the level requested by the President and passed by the House of Representatives and the Senate. Completion of appropriations after the beginning of each fiscal year has also resulted in delays or cancellation of planned R&D and equipment acquisition.

OVERVIEW

Congress continues to take a strong interest in the health of the U.S. research and development (R&D) enterprise and in providing sustained support for federal R&D activities. The United States government supports a broad range of scientific and engineering research and development (R&D). Its purposes include addressing specific concerns such as national defense, health, safety, the environment, and energy security; advancing knowledge generally; developing the scientific and engineering workforce; and strengthening U.S. innovation and competitiveness in the global economy. Most of the research funded by the federal government is in support of specific activities of the federal government as reflected in the unique missions of the funding agencies. The federal government has played an important role in supporting R&D efforts that have led to scientific breakthroughs and new technologies, from jet aircraft and the Internet to communications satellites and defenses against disease.

President Bush requested $147.0 billion for R&D in FY2009, a 2.7% increase over FY2008 R&D funding which is estimated to be $143.1 billion.[1] FY2008 funding is provided through the Defense Appropriations Act, 2008 (P.L. 110-116), signed into law by President Bush on November 13, 2007, and the Consolidated Appropriations Act, 2008 (P.L. 110-161), signed into law on December 26, 2007. P.L. 110-161 provides funding for departments and agencies covered in the eleven appropriations acts on which action had not been completed.

The President's FY2009 proposed R&D increase over the FY2008 funding level is due primarily to funding for the American Competitiveness Initiative (ACI) and an advance appropriation to the Department of Homeland Security (DHS) for acquisition under Project BioShield of medical countermeasures, such as vaccines, against biological terror attacks.[2] The Office of Management and Budget has classified $2.175 billion of the DHS advance appropriation as R&D facilities construction in FY2009. Some have questioned the appropriateness of classifying these funds as R&D facilities and equipment since the funds appear to be intended for product acquisition rather than research, development, or facilities construction. This advance appropriation accounts for more than half of the net increase in R&D funding in the President's FY2009 budget request.

Analysis of federal R&D funding is complicated by several factors, including the Administration's omission of Congressionally directed spending from its current year budget request, inconsistency among agencies in the reporting of R&D, and the apparent mis-categorization of some funding in the President's request. As a result of these and other factors, the R&D agency figures reported by OMB (and shown in **Table 1**) may differ somewhat from those agency budget analyses that appear later in this report.

Federal R&D Funding Perspectives

Federal R&D funding can be analyzed from a variety of perspectives that provide unique insights.

Agency Perspective

The authorization and appropriations process views federal R&D funding primarily from agency and program perspectives. **Table 1** provides data on R&D by agency for FY2007 (actual), FY2008 (estimate), and FY2009 (request) as reported by OMB. Under the President's FY2009 budget request, five federal agencies would receive 92.8% of total federal R&D funding: the Department of Defense (DOD), 54.8%; the Department of Health and Human Services (HHS) (primarily the National Institutes of Health), 20.1%; the National Aeronautics and Space Administration (NASA), 7.3%; the Department of Energy (DOE), 7.2%; and the National Science Foundation (NSF), 3.5%. This report provides an analysis of the R&D budget requests for these agencies, as well as for the Departments of Agriculture (USDA), Commerce (DOC), Homeland Security, Interior (DOI), and Transportation (DOT), and the Environmental Protection Agency (EPA). In total these departments and agencies account for more than 98% of current and requested federal R&D funding.

The Administration requested significantly larger percentage increases for the three agencies that are part of its American Competitiveness Initiative (ACI): DOE's Office of Science (up 19% above the estimated FY2008 level), the National Science Foundation (up 14%), and DOC's National Institute of Standards and Technology (NIST) (up 5%). In 2007, Congress authorized substantial R&D increases for these agencies under the America COMPETES Act (P.L. 11 0-69).[3] The President's budget would reduce R&D funding for four agencies: the Department of Agriculture, down $357 million (-15.5%); the Department of Veterans Affairs, down $76 million (-7.9%); the Department of the Interior, down $59 million (-8.7%); and the Environmental Protection Agency, down $7 million (-1.3%).

Table 1. Federal Research and Development Funding by Agency, FY2008-FY2009
(Budget Authority, Dollar Amount in Millions)

Department/Agency	FY2008 Estimate[a]	FY2009 Request	Dollar Change, 2008 to 2009	Percent Change, 2008 to 2009
Agriculture	2,309	1,952	-357	-15.5
Commerce	1,113	1,157	44	4.0
Defense	80,192	80,494	302	0.4
Energy	9,739	10,558	819	8.4
Environmental Protection Agency	557	550	-7	-1.3
Health and Human Services	29,475	29,480	5	0.0
Homeland Security	1,143	3,287	2,144	187.6
Interior	676	617	-59	-8.7
NASA	10,436	10,737	301	2.9
National Science Foundation	4,500	5,201	701	15.6
Transportation	823	901	78	9.5
Veterans Affairs	960	884	-76	-7.9
Other	1,140	1,145	5	0.4
TOTAL	**143,063**	**146,963**	**3,900**	**2.7**

Source: *Analytical Perspectives, Budget of the United States Government, Fiscal Year 2009*, Office of
  Management and Budget, The White House, February 2008.
a. The FY2008 figures in this table do not include supplemental funding for R&D for FY2008 provided
  under the Supplemental Appropriations Act, 2008 (P.L. 110-252).

Character of Work, Facilities, and Equipment Perspective

Federal R&D funding can also be examined by the character of work (basic research, applied research, and development) it supports, and funding provided for facilities and acquisition of R&D major equipment (see **Table 2**). The President's FY2009 request included $29.3 billion for basic research, up $847 million (3.0%) from FY2008; $27.1 billion for applied research, down $1.0 billion (-3.6%); $84.0 billion for development, up $1.6 billion (1.9%); and $6.5 billion for facilities and equipment, up $2.5 billion (61.7%).

Combined Perspective

Combining these perspectives, federal R&D funding can be viewed in terms of each agency's contribution to basic research, applied research, development, and facilities and equipment (see **Table 3**). The federal government is the largest supporter of basic research (funding an estimated 58.8% of U.S. basic research in 2006),[4] primarily because the private sector asserts it cannot capture an adequate return on long-term fundamental research investments. The Department of Health and Human Services (primarily HHS ' s National Institutes of Health (NIH)) accounts for more than half of all federal funding for basic research.

Table 2. Federal Research and Development Funding by Character of Work, Facilities and Equipment, FY2008-FY2009 (Budget authority, dollar amount in millions)

	FY2008 Estimate	FY2009 Request	Dollar Change, 2008 to 2009	Percent Change, 2008 to 2009
Basic research	28,472	29,319	847	3.0
Applied research	28,112	27,087	-1,025	-3.6
Development	82,432	84,013	1,581	1.9
Facilities and equipment	4,047	6,544	2,497	61.7
TOTAL	**143,063**	**146,963**	**3,900**	2.7

Source: *Analytical Perspectives, Budget of the United States Government, Fiscal Year 2009*, Office of Management and Budget, The White House, February 2008.

Table 3. Top R&D Funding Agencies by Character of Work, Facilities and Equipment, FY2008-FY2009 (Budget authority, dollar amount in millions)

	FY2008 Estimate	FY2009 Request	Dollar Change, 2008 to 2009	Percent Change, 2008 to 2009
Basic Research				
• Health and Human Services	15,897	15,884	-13	0.0
• National Science Foundation	3,689	4,336	647	17.5
• Energy	3,232	3,556	324	10.0
Applied Research				
• Health and Human Services	13,414	13,424	10	0
• Defense	5,058	4,245	-813	-16.1
• Energy	3,513	3,474	-39	-1.1
Development				
• Defense	73,358	74,393	1,035	1.4
• NASA	5,436	5,731	295	5.1
• Energy	2,232	2,472	240	10.7
Facilities and equipment				
• Homeland Security	147	2,250	2,102	1420.3
• NASA	1,922	2,175	253	13.2
• Energy	762	1,056	294	38.6

Source: *Analytical Perspectives, Budget of the United States Government, Fiscal Year 2009*, Office of Management and Budget, The White House, February 2008.

Note: Top funding agencies based on FY2009 request.

In contrast to basic research, industry is the primary funder of applied research in the United States, accounting for an estimated 58.9% in 2006, while the federal government accounted for an estimated 33.3%.[5] Among federal agencies, HHS is the largest funder of applied research, accounting for nearly half of all federally funded applied research.

Industry also provides the vast majority of funding for development, accounting for an estimated 82.5% in 2006, while the federal government provided an estimated 1 6.2%.[6] DOD is the primary federal agency development funder, accounting for 88.5% of total federal development funding in the FY2009 request.

Multi-Agency Initiatives Perspective

Federal R&D funding can also be viewed in terms of multi-agency efforts, such as the National Nanotechnology Initiative (see "Multiagency R&D Initiatives" section), and other initiatives, such as the Administration's American Competitiveness Initiative (ACI).

The ACI was proposed by President Bush in February 2006 as a response to growing concerns about America's ability to compete in the global marketplace. The $136 billion ACI proposal included $50 billion for additional research, science education, and the modernization of research infrastructure from FY2007 through FY2016. These funds were intended to double physical sciences and engineering research in three agencies — NSF, DOE's Office of Science, and NIST — over ten years.[7] Congress established authorization levels for FY2008-2010 that would put funding for research at these agencies on track to double in approximately seven years. However, FY2008 research funding provided in P.L. 110-161 for these agencies falls below these doubling targets. Estimated FY2008 funding for ACI research totals $10.61 billion, an increase of approximately $350 million (3.5%) over the FY2007 ACI funding level.

In FY2009, President Bush requested $12.21 billion in funding for ACI research at NSF, DOE's Office of Science, and the National Institute of Standards and Technology (including its core research program and facilities), an increase of $1.6 billion (15.1%) above the estimated FY2008 level of $10.61 billion.[8] The NSF funding request for FY2009 is $6.85 billion, an increase of $821 million (13.6%) above the estimated FY2008 level of $6.03 billion.[9] The FY2009 request for the DOE Office of Science is $4.72 billion, $749 million (18.9%) more than the estimated FY2008 level of $3.97 billion.[10] FY2009 proposed funding for NIST's core research program and facilities totals $634 million, an increase of $33 million (4.5%) above the estimated FY2008 level of $610 million.[11]

FY2009 Federal R&D Appropriations Status

On September 30, 2008, President Bush signed into law H.R. 2638, the Consolidated Security, Disaster Assistance, and Continuing Appropriations Act, 2009 (P.L. 110-329). This act provides FY2009 appropriations for the Department of Defense, Department of Homeland Security, and Military Construction and Veterans Affairs, as well as supplemental funding for disaster relief. In addition, Division A of the act provides continuing appropriations for FY2009 at their original FY2008 levels[12] to agencies not otherwise addressed in the act through March 6, 2009, or until the enactment into law of an appropriation for any project or activity provided for in the act, or the enactment into law of the applicable appropriations act for FY2009 without any provision for such project or activity, whichever occurs first. Under the act, estimated total R&D funding for FY2009 is $147.2 billion.

Previously, only one of the FY2009 regular appropriations bills, the Military Construction and Veterans Affairs Appropriation, FY2009 (H.R. 6599) had passed the House;

none had passed the Senate. The Senate Appropriations Committee has approved nine of the regular appropriations bills, and the House Appropriations Committee has approved four draft bills and H.R. 6599. Copies of some draft bills and draft reports considered by the House Appropriations Committee are available on the website of *Congressional Quarterly*.[13] Section 522 of the Concurrent Resolution on the Budget for Fiscal Year 2009 (S.Con.Res. 70), agreed to by the House and Senate in June 2008, expresses Congress' support for the research and education efforts authorized in the America COMPETES Act and states that "the Congress should provide sufficient funding so that our Nation may continue to be the world leader in education, innovation and economic growth."

Supplemental Appropriations for FY2008

On June 30, 2008, President Bush signed into law H.R. 2642, the Supplemental Appropriations Act, 2008 (P.L. 110-252). Among its provisions, the act provides additional funding for FY2008 of $1.75 billion to the Department of Defense for research, development, test, and evaluation (RDT&E) activities; $365 million to the Department of Defense, Defense Health Program RDT&E; and $338 million to other agencies for science-related activities. Of these funds, the National Institutes of Health received $150 million; NASA received $62.5 million for its Return to Flight activity; NSF received $62.5 million; and the Department of Energy received $62.5 million for its non-defense energy programs. In addition, the act provides $62.5 million to the Department of Energy for defense environmental cleanup.

Effect of FY2007-FY2008 Appropriations Process on R&D

For the past two years, federal R&D funding levels and execution have been affected by mechanisms used to complete the annual appropriations process — the year-long continuing resolution for FY2007 (P.L. 110-5) and the combining of 11 appropriations bills into the Consolidated Appropriations Act, 2008 for FY2008 (P.L. 110-161). For example, FY2008 R&D funding for some agencies and programs is below the level requested by the President, and originally passed by House and Senate appropriations committees.[14] The Department of Energy estimates that cuts in its FY2008 R&D budget for its Office of Science will result in layoffs of 525 personnel at the Stanford Linear Accelerator, Fermi National Accelerator Laboratory, Argonne National Laboratory, and other laboratories and universities.[15] Completion of the appropriations process after the beginning of the fiscal year may also result in delay, reduction, or cancellation of planned R&D, equipment acquisition, and facilities construction, and may impede the ability of agencies to fully obligate funds ultimately appropriated (see CRS Report RS22774, *Federal Research and Development Funding: Possible Impacts of Operating Under a Continuing Resolution*, by Dana A. Shea and Daniel Morgan).

The following sections provide analyses of the President's FY2009 R&D and related funding requests for selected Federal agencies and multiagency R&D initiatives. These sections include information on appropriations actions taken by Congress and will be updated periodically.

MULTIAGENCY R&D INITIATIVES

The President's FY2009 budget requests increased funding for three multiagency R&D initiatives. Funding for the National Nanotechnology Initiative (NNI) was requested in the amount of $1.53 billion for FY2009, an increase of 2.4% over the estimated FY2008 level of $1.50 billion (see CRS Report RL34401, *The National Nanotechnology Initiative: Overview, Reauthorization, and Appropriations Issues,* by John F. Sargent).[16] Under the President's FY2009 budget, the NNI would increase its efforts in fundamental phenomena and processes by $19.2 million (3.6%); instrument research, metrology, and standards by $21.1 million (34.9%); environmental, health, and safety by $17.8 million (30.4%); and nanomanufacturing by $11.9 million (23.7%). Smaller increases would support major research facilities and instrumentation acquisition (up $6.9 million, 4.5%) and efforts in education and societal dimensions (up $1.7 million, 4.4%). Funding would fall by $27.5 million (-10.8%) for nanomaterials research and by $15.3 million (-4.5%) for nanoscale devices and systems.

The President requested $3.57 billion in FY2009 funding for the Networking and Information Technology R&D (NITRD) program, an increase of 5.8% above the estimated FY2008 level of $3.37 billion. The NITRD increase is due primarily to requested funding increases for NSF (up $159 million, 17.1%) and DOE (up $58 million, 13.3%).[17] For additional information, see CRS Report RL33586, *The Federal Networking and Information Technology Research and Development Program: Funding Issues and Activities*, by Patricia Moloney Figliola.

The administration proposed $2.01 billion for the Climate Change Science Program (CCSP), an increase of 9.6% over the estimated FY2008 level of $1.84 billion.[18] (See CRS Report RL33817, *Climate Change: Federal Funding and Tax Incentives*, by Jane A. Leggett). Four agencies account for most of the FY2009 CCSP requested funding increase: NASA (up $126 million, 11.7%), the National Oceanic and Atmospheric Administration (NOAA) (up $20 million, 8.3%), DOE (up $18 million, 14.1%), and NSF (up $16 million, 7.8%).

DEPARTMENT OF DEFENSE (DOD)

Congress supports research and development in the Department of Defense (DOD) through its Research, Development, Test, and Evaluation (RDT&E) appropriation. The appropriation primarily supports the development of the nation's future military hardware and software and the technology base upon which those products rely.

Nearly all of what DOD spends on RDT&E is appropriated in Title IV of the defense appropriation bill (see **Table 4**). However, RDT&E funds are also requested as part of the Defense Health Program and the Chemical Agents and Munitions Destruction Program. The Defense Health Program supports the delivery of health care to DOD personnel and their families. Program funds are requested through the Operations and Maintenance appropriation. The program's RDT&E funds support Congressionally directed research in such areas as breast, prostate, and ovarian cancer and other medical conditions. The Chemical Agents and Munitions Destruction Program supports activities to destroy the U.S. inventory of lethal chemical agents and munitions to avoid future risks and costs associated with storage. Funds for this program are requested through the Army Procurement appropriation. The Joint

Improvised Explosive Device Defeat Fund also contains additional RDT&E monies. However, the fund does not contain an RDT&E line item as do the two programs mentioned above. The Joint Improvised Explosive Device Defeat Office, which now administers the fund, tracks (but does not report) the amount of funding allocated to RDT&E. Typically, Congress has funded all of these programs in Title VI (Other Department of Defense Programs) of the defense appropriations bill.

More recently, RDT&E funds have also been requested and appropriated as part of DOD's separate funding to support what the Bush Administration terms the Global War on Terror (GWOT). Congress has appropriated these funds in response to emergency supplemental requests and under a separate GWOT request. GWOTrelated requests/appropriations often include funds for a number of transfer funds. These include the Iraqi Freedom Fund (IFF), the Iraqi Security Forces Fund, the Afghanistan Security Forces Fund, and, more recently, the Mine Resistant and Ambush Protected Vehicle Fund (MRAPVF). Congress typically makes a single appropriation into each of these funds, and authorizes the Secretary to make transfers to other baseline accounts, including RDT&E, at his discretion. GWOT-related RDT&E funding is given in **Table 5**. Note that while much of these GWOT-related appropriations are distributed to a baseline account, they are accounted for separately.

For FY2009, the Bush Administration requested $79.6 billion for DOD's baseline Title IV RDT&E, roughly $2.5 billion more than Congress appropriated for Title IV in FY2008. The FY2009 requests for RDT&E in the Defense Health Program and the Chemical Agents and Munitions Destruction program were $194 million and $269 million, respectively. The Administration also submitted an FY2008 Global War on Terror request (i.e., a supplemental request), which included $2.9 billion for RDT&E. Congress only partially approved the Administration's FY2008 GWOT request made last year. The Administration hopes to make up the balance of that request this year. The Administration also made a FY2009 GWOT "Bridge" request in March. This additional request included $379 million in classified RDT&E. By requesting bridge funding, the administration hopes to have ready emergency funds at the beginning of the fiscal year (in October) rather than await passage of the entire defense appropriations.

Since FY2001, funding for RDT&E in Title IV has increased from $42 billion to $77 billion in FY2008. In constant FY2008 dollars, the increase is roughly 58%. Historically, RDT&E funding has reached its highest levels in constant dollars, dating back to 1948.[19] Congress has appropriated more for RDT&E than has been requested, every year, since FY1996.

RDT&E funding can be broken out in a couple of ways. Each of the military services request and receive their own RDT&E funding. So, too, do various DOD agencies (e.g., the Missile Defense Agency and the Defense Advanced Research Projects Agency), collectively aggregated within the Defensewide account. RDT&E funding also can be characterized by budget activity (i.e., the type of RDT&E supported). Those budget activities designated as 6.1, 6.2, and 6.3 (basic research, applied research, and advanced development) constitute what is called DOD's Science and Technology Program (S&T) and represents the more research-oriented part of the RDT&E program. Budget activities 6.4 and 6.5 focus on the development of specific weapon systems or components (e.g., the Joint Strike Fighter or missile defense systems), for which an operational need has been determined and an acquisition program established. Budget activity 6.7 supports system improvements in existing operational systems. Budget activity 6.6 provides management support, including support for test and evaluation facilities.

S&T funding is of particular interest to Congress since these funds support the development of new technologies and the underlying science. Assuring adequate support for S&T activities is seen by some in the defense community as imperative to maintaining U.S. military superiority. This was of particular concern at a time when defense budgets and RDT&E funding were falling at the end of the Cold War. As part of its 2001 Quadrennial Review, DOD established a goal of stabilizing its base S&T funding (i.e., Title IV) at 3% of DOD's overall funding. Congress has embraced this goal. The FY2009 S&T funding request in Title IV is $11.5 billion, about $1.3 billion less than what Congress appropriated for S&T in Title IV in FY2008 (not counting S&T funding requested as part of the GWOT request or S&T's share of the general reduction made to Title IV). Furthermore, the S&T request for Title IV is approximately 2.2% of the overall baseline DOD budget request (not counting funds for the Global War on Terror), short of the 3% goal. The ability for the Administration to meet its 3% goal has been strained in recent years as the overall Defense budget continues to rise. In the FY2007 defense authorization bill (P.L. 109-364, Sec. 217), Congress reiterated its support for the 3% goal, extended it to FY2012, and stipulated that, if the S&T budget request does not meet this goal, DOD submit a prioritized list of S&T projects that were not funded solely due to insufficient resources.

Within the S&T program, basic research (6.1) receives special attention, particularly by the nation's universities. DOD is not a large supporter of basic research, when compared to the National Institutes of Health or the National Science Foundation. However, over half of DOD's basic research budget is spent at universities and represents the major contribution of funds in some areas of science and technology (such as electrical engineering and material science). The FY2009 request for basic research ($1.7 billion) is roughly $65 million more than what Congress appropriated for Title IV basic research in FY2008.

Congress passed the Supplemental Appropriations Act, 2008 (P.L. 110-252) on June 30, 2008. Title IX of the act provided supplemental funding for the Department of Defense and the Global War on Terror. See **Table 5**. Chapter 1 of Title IX addressed the GWOT Pending request and Chapter 2 of Title IX addressed the FY2009 GWOT Bridge request. Congress did not provide all the RDT&E funding requested in the FY2008 GWOT Pending request for the departments and defense agencies, but added RDT&E funds for the Defense Health Program. In addition, Congress directed a general reduction of the RDT&E funds provided. Congress provided the requested level of RDT&E in the Bridge request, plus a little more for the Air Force. The act also provided a $2.5 billion for the Iraqi Security Forces Fund, $2 billion for the Joint Improvised Explosive Device Defeat Fund, and $1.7 billion for the Mine Resistant and Ambush Protected Vehicle Fund, from which the Secretary may transfer funds into RDT&E.

Congress passed a FY2009 defense appropriations as part of the Consolidated Security, Disaster Assistance, and Continuing Appropriations Act, 2009 (P.L. 101- 329, Division C). The bill provided $80.5 billion for Title IV RDT&E. This included $13.5 billion for S&T, of which $1.8 billion was for basic research (i.e. approximately $100 million more than was requested). Section 8101 reduced Title IV funding by $218 million to account for revised economic assumptions. In addition, Congress provided $903 million for RDT&E within the Defense Health Program (including $150 million and $80 million for peer-reviewed breast and prostate cancer research, respectively) and $289 million for RDT&E within the Chemical Agents and Munitions Destruction Program. **(CRS Contact: John Moteff.)**

Table 4. Department of Defense RDT&E ($ in millions)

	FY2008 Enacted[d]	FY2009 Request	FY2009 Enacted (P.L. 110-329)
Title IV - By Account			
Army	12,127	10,524	12,060
Navy	17,919	19,337	19,764
Air Force	26,255	28,067	27,084
Defense Agencies	20,791	21,499	21,423
Dir. Test & Eval	180	189	189
Adjustments improved economic assumptions	(367)[e]		(218)
Total Title IV - By Account [a]	**76,905**	**79,616**	**80,303**
Title IV - By Budget Activity			
6.1 Basic Research	1,634	1,699	1,842
6.2 Applied Research	5,096	4,245	5,113
6.3 Advanced Development	6,039	5,532	6,532
6.4 Advanced Component Development and Prototypes	15,745	15,774	15,817
6.5 Systems Dev. and Demo	18,321	19,537	18,654
6.6 Management Support [b]	4,274	4,369	4,543
6.7 Op. Systems Dev [c]	26,163	28,461	28,020
Adjustments improved economic assumptions	(367)[e]		(218)
Total Title IV - by Budget Activity [a]	**76,905**	**79,617**	**80,303**
Tanker Replacement Transfer Fund	**150**		
Title VI - Other Defense Programs			
Defense Health Program	536	194	903
Chemical Agents and Munitions Destruction	313	269	289
Continuing Resolution (P.L. 110-92) and Consolidated Appropriations Act 2008 (P.L. 110-161)	926[f]		
Grand Total	**78,830**	**80,080**	**81,495**

Sources: Title IV figures for the FY2009 request were taken from RDT&E Programs (R-1) Exhibits, Department of Defense Budget FY2009. The FY2009 RDT&E request for the Defense Health Program was taken from the Operations and Maintenance Exhibit (O-1), Department of Defense Budget FY2009. The FY2009 RDT&E request for the Chemical Agents and Munitions Destruction Program was taken from the Procurement Exhibit (P-1), Department of Defense Budget FY2009. The FY2009 enacted figures were taken from P.L. 110-329 and the Congressional Record version of the DOD explanatory statement, Sept. 24, 2008.

a. Total Budget Authority for Account and Budget Activity may not agree due to rounding.

b. Includes funds for Developmental and Operational Test and Evaluation.

c. Includes funding for classified programs.

d. Does not include subsequent rescissions or transfers, unless noted.

e. Sec. 8104 of the FY2008 Defense Appropriations Act (P.L. 110-116) required a general reduction to account for improved economic assumptions. RDT&E's designated share was $367 million. Sec. 8097 of this act also required a general reduction of $507 million to be taken proportionately from Operations and Maintenance (Title II), Procurement (Title III), and RDT&E (Title IV) to account for contractor efficiencies. The RDT&E's share of this reduction is not counted in this table.

f. Congress addressed some of the Administration's FY2008 GWOT request in one of the continuing resolutions (P.L. 110-92) which supported government operations in early FY2008 and in the Consolidated Appropriations Act of 2008 (P.L. 110-161). The continuing resolution provided additional funds for the MRAPVF. The Consolidated Appropriations Act provided funds to the IFF, some of which were transferred to RDT&E.

Table 5. Department of Defense RDT&E Associated with the Global War on Terror Funding ($ in millions)

	FY2008 GWOT Pending Request	FY2009 GWOT (Bridge Request) Request	P.L. 110-252 Supplemental Appropriations Act, 2008 Title IX Enacted	
			FY2008 Supplemental	FY2009 Bridge Funding
GWOT-Related Title IV				
By Account				
Army	163		163	
Navy	611	113	366	113
Air Force	1,487	72	400	72
Defense Agencies	684	194	816	203
Dir. Test & Eval				
Total Budget Auth.[a]	**2,945**	**379**	**1,745**	**388**
By Budget Activity				
6.1 Basic Research				
6.2 Applied Research	6			
6.3 Advanced Development	25			
6.4 Advanced Component Development and Pro-totypes	228			
6.5 Systems Dev. and Demo	514			
6.6 Management Support[b]	54			
6.7 Op. Systems Dev	2,121	379		388[d]
Sec. 8003 general reduction			?[c]	
Total Budget Auth.[a]	**2,948**	**379**		**388**
GWOT-Related Other Defense Programs				
Defense Health Program			365	
Grand Total	**2,948**	**379**	**<2,110**	**388**

Sources: The figures for the Continuing Resolution (P.L. 110-92) and the Consolidated Appropriations Act 2008 (P.L. 110-161) and the FY2008 GWOT Pending Request were taken from the Office of Secretary of Defense, FY2008 Global War on Terror Pending Request, Exhibits for FY2008, Feb. 2008.

a. Account vs. Budget Activity Total Obligational Authority numbers may not agree due to rounding.

b. Includes funds for Developmental and Operational Test and Evaluation.

c. Section 8003 of the Supplemental Appropriations Act, 2008 included a general reduction of $3.6 billion to be applied proportionately to each of the following accounts: Procurement, RDT&E, and Defense Working Capital. RDT&E's share is not calculated here.

d. P.L. 110-252 does not designate which budget activity was supported. The table presumes the enacted amounts were for the same budget activity as requested.

DEPARTMENT OF HOMELAND SECURITY (DHS)

The Department of Homeland Security (DHS) requested $1.449 billion for R&D and related programs in FY2009, an 8% increase from FY2008. This total included $869 million for the Directorate of Science and Technology (S&T), $564 million for the Domestic Nuclear Detection Office (DNDO), and $16 million for Research, Development, Test, and Evaluation (RDT&E) in the U.S. Coast Guard. The House committee recommended a total of $1.447 billion.[20] The Senate committee recommended a total of $1.476 billion.[21] The final appropriation was a total of $1.465 billion.[22] For details, see **Table 6**.

The Directorate of Science and Technology (S&T) is the primary DHS R&D organization. Headed by the Under Secretary for Science and Technology, the directorate performs R&D in several laboratories of its own and funds R&D performed by the national laboratories, industry, universities, and other government agencies. The FY2009 request for the S&T Directorate was 5% above the FY2008 appropriation. A proposed increase of $18 million for the Explosives program was to fund R&D on countering improvised explosive devices (IEDs), with an emphasis on basic research to complement shorter-term R&D being conducted by other agencies. A proposed increase of $43 million for the Laboratory Facilities program included $29 million for startup costs at the National Biodefense Analysis and Countermeasures Center (NBACC) as well as $14 million for laboratory employee salaries previously budgeted in the Management and Administration account. A proposed $27 million reduction in the Infrastructure and Geophysical program was largely the result of reducing funding for local and regional initiatives previously established or funded at congressional direction.

The House committee recommended a total of $887 million for S&T. Increases relative to the request included $11 million for the Infrastructure and Geophysical program to support the National Institute for Hometown Security; $5 million for Laboratory Facilities to accelerate ongoing construction activities at the Pacific Northwest National Laboratory (PNNL); $4 million to help develop an operational test and evaluation program for first responder technologies; $2 million for a pilot program to improve the productivity and efficiency of the homeland security industrial base; and $7 million for University Programs to support university centers of excellence and maintain the fellowship program at the FY2008 level. Decreases included $5 million for new maritime technologies "more appropriately handled by the Coast Guard" and $6 million for the Innovation program "due to a lack of budgetary details." The committee directed DHS to provide a report on issues related to the S&T Directorate's unobligated balances.

The Senate committee recommended a total of $919 million for S&T. Increases relative to the request included $25 million for cyber security research in the Command, Control, and Interoperability program; $27 million for the Infrastructure and Geophysical program to continue the Southeast Region Research Initiative; and $15 million for the ongoing construction at PNNL. Decreases included $12 million for Innovation (because of the need for "sound business plans" based on "operational requirements") and $4 million for Human Factors. The committee recommended that $5 million for the Homeland Security Institute be provided as a separate item, as it was in FY2008, rather than as part of the Transition program as the Administration requested.

The final appropriation for S&T was $933 million. Relative to the request, this total included increases of $ 10 million for cyber security research, $11 million for the National Institute for Hometown Security, $27 million for the Southeast Region Research Initiative, $15 million for the ongoing construction at PNNL, and $6 million for University Programs. Decreases included $12 million from Innovation, because the DHS Inspector General "raised concerns about how projects were selected and managed" and because S&T took nine months to inform the committee how FY2008 funding would be spent. Funding for the Homeland Security Institute was provided as a separate line item.

Among the issues facing Congress are the S&T Directorate's priorities and how they are set, its relationships with other federal R&D organizations, its budgeting and financial management, and the allocation of its R&D resources to national laboratories, industry, and universities. The directorate announced five new university centers of excellence in February 2008. Some existing centers are expected to be terminated or merged over the next few years to align with the directorate's division structure. For more information, see CRS Report RL34356, *The DHS Directorate of Science and Technology: Key Issues for Congress.*

The Domestic Nuclear Detection Office (DNDO) is the primary DHS organization for combating the threat of nuclear attack. It is responsible for all DHS nuclear detection research, development, testing, evaluation, acquisition, and operational support. The FY2009 request for DNDO was a 16% increase from FY2008. Most of the growth was in the Systems Acquisition account, where an increase of $68 million for procurement of Advanced Spectroscopic Portals (ASPs) was partly offset by a decrease of $10 million for the Securing the Cities initiative in the New York City area.

The House committee recommended a total of $544 million for DNDO. Changes relative to the request included reductions of $3 million for new headquarters employees, $1 million for a proposed fellowship program at the National Technical Nuclear Forensics Center, and $15 million for the Radiation Portal Monitoring Program. The House bill would continue the prohibition on full-scale procurement of ASPs until the Secretary certifies their performance and would prohibit DNDO from engaging in high-risk concurrent development and production of mutually dependent software and hardware. The draft House report directed DNDO to conduct a risk assessment for radiological dispersal devices.

The Senate committee recommended a total of $541 million for DNDO. The only change relative to the Administration request was a reduction of $23 million in the Radiation Portal Monitoring Program because of delays in the required certification of ASP performance. Like the House bill, the Senate bill would continue the prohibition on full-scale procurement of ASPs and prohibit high-risk concurrent development and production. The Senate committee report urged DNDO to prioritize its programs based on risk and directed it to contract with the National Academy of Sciences (or another independent organization) to develop a conceptual framework for prioritizing defensive efforts relative to mitigation measures.

The final appropriation for DNDO was $514 million. Reductions relative to the request included $10 million from new initiatives in Transformational R&D and $38 million from the Radiation Portal Monitoring Program due to development delays. Like the House and Senate bills, the final bill continued the prohibition on full-scale procurement of ASPs and prohibited high-risk concurrent development and production.

Table 6. Department of Homeland Security R&D and Related Programs ($ in millions)

	FY2008 Enacted	FY2009 Request	FY2009 H. Cte.	FY2009 S. Cte.	FY2009 Final
Directorate of Science & Technology	**830**	**869**	**887**	**919**	**933**
Management and Administration[a]	139	132	132	132	132
R&D, Acquisition, and Operations	692	737	755	787	800
Border and Maritime	*25*	*35*	*30*	*35*	*33*
Chemical and Biological	*208*	*200*	*200*	*200*	*200*
Command, Control, & Interoperability	*57*	*62*	*62*	*87*	*75*
Explosives	*78*	*96*	*96*	*96*	*96*
Human Factors	*14*	*12*	*12*	*8*	*12*
Infrastructure and Geophysical	*64*	*38*	*49*	*65*	*76*
Innovation	*33*	*45*	*39*	*33*	*33*
Laboratory Facilities[a]	*104*	*147*	*152*	*162*	*162*
Test and Evaluation, Standards	*29*	*25*	*29*	*25*	*29*
Transition[b]	*25*	*32*	*34*	*27*	*29*
University Programs	*49*	*44*	*51*	*44*	*50*
Homeland Security Institute[b]	*5*	*—*	*—*	*5*	*5*
Domestic Nuclear Detection Office	**485**	**564**	**544**	**541**	**514**
Management and Administration	32	39	35	39	38
Research, Development, and Operations	324	334	333	334	323
Systems Engineering and Architecture	*22*	*25*	*25*	*25*	*25*
Systems Development	*118*	*108*	*108*	*108*	*108*
Transformational R&D	*96*	*113*	*113*	*113*	*103*
Assessments	*38*	*32*	*32*	*32*	*32*
Operations Support	*34*	*38*	*38*	*38*	*38*
Natl. Technical Nuclear Forensics Ctr.	*15*	*18*	*17*	*18*	*17*
Systems Acquisition	130	191	176	168	153
Radiation Portal Monitoring Program	*90*	*158*	*143*	*135*	*120*
Securing the Cities	*30*	*20*	*20*	*20*	*20*
Human Portable Radiation Detn. Sys.	*10*	*13*	*13*	*13*	*13*
U.S. Coast Guard RDT&E	**25**	**16**	**16**	**16**	**18**
TOTAL	**1,340**	**1,449**	**1,447**	**1,476**	**1,465**

Source: DHS FY2009 congressional budget justification; H.R. 6947 as reported and H.Rept. 110-862; S. 3181 as reported and S.Rept. 110-396; and P.L. 110-329, Division D, and explanatory statement, *Congressional Record*, September 24, 2008, pp. H9806-H9807.

Notes: Totals may not add because of rounding.

a. Funding for the salaries of DHS laboratory employees ($14 million in FY2008) was transferred from Management and Administration to Laboratory Facilities in the FY2009 request.

b. For FY2008, Congress appropriated $5 million for the Homeland Security Institute as a separate line item. The FY2009 budget justification incorporated this amount into Transition. The FY2009 request for Transition included $5 million for the Homeland Security Institute.

Congressional attention has focused on the testing and analysis DNDO conducted to support its decision to purchase and deploy ASPs, a type of next- generation radiation portal monitor.[23] The requirement for secretarial certification before full-scale ASP procurement has been included in each appropriations act since FY2007. The expected date for certification has been postponed several times; the current target is reportedly November 2008.[24] The global nuclear detection architecture overseen by DNDO and the relative roles of DNDO and the S&T Directorate in research, development, testing, and evaluation also remain issues of congressional interest. For more information on the global nuclear detection architecture, see CRS Report RL34574, *The Global Nuclear Detection Architecture: Issues for Congress.* **(CRS Contact: Daniel Morgan.)**

NATIONAL INSTITUTES OF HEALTH (NIH)

The NIH budget request for FY2009 continued the trend of the previous five years, during which increases, if any, have been below the rate of inflation. Congressional action on FY2009 appropriations bills, not yet finalized, has recommended funding growth approximately equal to the estimated 3.5% inflation rate. Currently, NIH is operating under the FY2009 continuing resolution at a rate based on its original FY2008 appropriations.

The President's FY2009 request for $29.1 65 billion for NIH was about level with the original FY2008 amount (see **Table 7**). The Consolidated Appropriations Act, 2008 (P.L. 110-161) provided a total of $29.171 billion. Later, the Supplemental Appropriations Act, 2008 (P.L. 110-252, enacted June 30, 2008) gave NIH an additional $150 million, bringing the FY2008 program level total to $29.32 1 billion, 1.0% above FY2007. The FY2009 request was $155 million below the FY2008 enacted program level (-0.5%). In **Table 7**, FY2008 amounts are shown both before and after the supplemental appropriations.

The FY2009 Continuing Appropriations Resolution (Division A of P.L. 110- 329, the Consolidated Security, Disaster Assistance, and Continuing Appropriations Act, 2009, enacted September 30, 2008) provides funds for government operations from October 1, 2008, through March 6, 2009. For most covered agencies and programs, including NIH, funds are available at a rate for operations provided in the FY2008 appropriations acts, not counting amounts designated as emergency funding (such as the June 2008 supplemental funding NIH received). In the discussion below, most references are to FY2008 funding levels prior to the supplemental appropriations, since the FY2009 request and congressional actions were based on the original FY2008 amounts.

NIH's funding comes primarily from the appropriations bill for the Departments of Labor, Health and Human Services, and Education, and Related Agencies (Labor/HHS), with an additional amount for Superfund-related activities from the appropriations bill for the Department of the Interior, Environment, and Related Agencies (Interior/Environment). Those two bills provide NIH's discretionary budget authority. In addition, NIH receives $150 million annually from separate legislation funding diabetes research, and $8.2 million from a transfer within the Public Health Service (PHS). NIH loses part of its appropriation to a transfer to the Global Fund to Fight HIV/AIDS, Tuberculosis, and Malaria. For several years, about $100 million of the annual NIH appropriation was transferred to the Global Fund. In the FY2008 request, the President increased the amount to $300 million, and the final amount of the transfer from the NIH appropriation was $295 million. The FY2009 budget again proposed to transfer $300 million to the Global Fund. In **Table 7**, the total funding available for NIH activities, taking account of add-ons and transfers, is called the program level.[25]

In congressional action on the FY2009 request, the Senate Appropriations Committee reported S. 3230 (S.Rept. 110-410) on July 8, 2008, recommending a program level total of $30.11 3 billion for NIH within the Labor/HHS appropriations bill. Although the committee did not take action on the Interior/Environment bill, funding of approximately $78 million for the NIH Superfund account might have been projected based on past years. The NIH program level total recommended by the Senate committee would then have been about $30.19 1 billion, some $1.02 billion (3.5%) over the original FY2008 amount and $870 million (3.0%) over the revised FY2008 level.

The full House Appropriations Committee did not take final action on either its Labor/HHS bill or its Interior/Environment bill. On June 19, 2008, the House Labor/HHS subcommittee reported a draft bill to the full committee that recommended program level funding of $30.23 8 billion for NIH, $125 million more than the Senate committee amount. The total NIH program level, again assuming $78 million for the Superfund account, might have been projected at approximately $30.3 16 billion, some $1.145 billion (3.9%) over the original FY2008 total amount and $995 million (3.4%) over the revised FY2008 level.

In this decade, the peak of NIH's purchasing power was in FY2003, when Congress completed a five-year doubling of the NIH budget. Congress provided NIH with annual increases in the range of 14%-15% each year from FY1999 through FY2003. Since then, increases have been between 1%-3% each year, except that FY2006 was a 0.3% decrease. The President requested no increase for NIH for FY2009, while the advocates in the research community recommended a 6.5% increase. The projected inflation rate for medical research prices is 3.5% for both FY2008 and FY2009. In inflation-adjusted terms, the FY2008 funding level represented an estimated 10.7% decrease in purchasing power from the FY2003 peak, and the FY2009 request level was 14% below FY2003.

The agency's organization consists of the Office of the NIH Director and 27 institutes and centers. The Office of the Director (OD) sets overall policy for NIH and coordinates the programs and activities of all NIH components, particularly in areas of research that involve multiple institutes. The institutes and centers (collectively called ICs) focus on particular diseases, areas of human health and development, or aspects of research support. Each IC plans and manages its own research programs in coordination with the Office of the Director. As shown in **Table 7**, Congress provides a separate appropriation to 24 of the 27 ICs, to OD, and to a buildings and facilities account. (The other three centers, not included in the table, are funded through the NIH Management Fund, financed by taps on other NIH appropriations.)

The President's FY2009 budget gave most of the institutes and centers approximately level funding from their original FY2008 amounts, requesting increases of 0.1% or 0.2%. The President requested increases greater than 0.5% only for the National Center for Research Resources (1.0%) and the National Library of Medicine (0.8%). The Senate committee and the House subcommittee recommended increases of about 3% and 3.5%, respectively, for most of the ICs compared to the original FY2008 levels.

The two biggest changes proposed in the request were a 5.6% increase in the Buildings and Facilities account, and a 4.7% drop in funding for the Office of the Director. Many of the laboratories, animal facilities, and office buildings on the NIH campus are aging, and are in need of upgrading to stay compliant with health and safety guidelines and to provide the proper infrastructure for the Intramural Research program. The budget requested $126 million for Buildings and Facilities, an increase of $7 million. The House subcommittee agreed with that amount, while the Senate committee recommended $147 million, an increase of $28 million (23%).

In the request, the net $52 million drop in the OD account, from $1,109 million in FY2008 to $1,057 million, represented the proposed cancellation of a study combined with increases for several other OD activities. The National Children's Study was funded at $111 million in FY2008. It is a long-term (25+ year), multi- agency environmental health study that was mandated by the Children's Health Act of 2000 (P.L. 106-310). The overall projected cost for the whole study is about $2.7 billion. Starting with the FY2007 request, when the study moved from the planning phase to the more costly implementation phase, the Administration has proposed each year to end its funding. Congress has continued to support the study. Both the Senate committee and the House subcommittee included $192 million for the study, an increase of $81 million (73%).

The President proposed increases within the OD account totaling $59 million, including a $38 million increase (7.7%) for the NIH Roadmap initiatives funded through the Common Fund. The NIH Roadmap for Medical Research is a set of trans-NIH research activities designed to support high-risk/high-impact research in emerging areas of science or public health priorities. For FY2009, the President requested $534 million for the Roadmap/Common Fund, up from $496 million in FY2008. The Senate committee recommended $568 million for the Common Fund (a $73 million increase), and boosted overall funding for the OD account to $1,275 million, an increase of $ 166 million (15%). The House subcommittee recommended $544 million for the Common Fund (a $49 million increase) within overall funding of $1,255 million for the OD account, an increase of $146 million (13%). The other major increase in the President's request for OD was an additional $19 million (19.9%) for research on medical countermeasures against nuclear, radiological, and chemical threats, increasing that program to $113 million from $94 million in FY2008. That was the only significant increase for NIH's biodefense portfolio, which totaled $1,748 million in the President's FY2009 request (up 1.2%). The House subcommittee included $100 million for countermeasures research; the Senate committee did not discuss biodefense research.

NIH has two major concerns in the face of tight budgets: maintaining support of investigator-initiated research through research project grants, and expanding the supply of new investigators. Total funding for research project grants (RPGs), at $15.5 billion, represents about 53% of NIH's budget. The FY2009 request proposed to support an estimated 38,257 awards, about the same number as projected in FY2008 before the supplemental. Within that total, 9,757 awards would have been competing RPGs, 14 fewer than in FY2008. ("Competing" awards means new grants plus competing renewals of existing grants.) The Senate committee estimated that its funding level would support 10,471 competing RPGs, while the House subcommittee level would support 10,812. The request proposed that no inflationary increases be paid for noncompeting (continuation) RPGs, and that the average annual cost of competing RPGs remain at the FY2008 level, about $361,000. The House subcommittee included an average 2% increase for both new and continuing grants; the Senate report did not specify average costs. Under the request, the expected "success rate" of applications receiving funding would have declined to about 18% from the estimated rate of

19% for FY2008 (pre-supplemental). Estimated success rates for the various ICs would have ranged from 8% to 26%.

Several NIH efforts are focused on supporting new investigators to encourage young scientists to undertake careers in research and to help them speed their transition from training to independent research. The request proposed that the Pathway to Independence program support approximately 500 awardees, including 170 new awards, for a total of $71 million. The request proposed an increase of $5 million (0.6%) to $786 million for regular training mechanisms such as the National Research Service Awards, including stipend increases of 1% for both pre- and postdoctoral fellows. Clinical research training, including the Clinical and Translational Science Awards, would have been funded at a total of $475 million. The request proposed to support about 25 New Innovator Awards for a total of $56 million in the Common Fund. The NIH Director's Bridge Award is a program that can give short- term funding to established, meritorious investigators who have just missed the funding cutoff for a renewal application and who have little other support, giving them time to resubmit without disrupting the operation of their laboratory. The request included $91 million for 244 awards, an increase of $1.6 million. Both the Senate committee and the House subcommittee specifically mentioned support for most of these initiatives, as well as others; both included funding increases beyond the request for the New Innovator Awards.

Changes proposed in the request for other funding mechanisms within the NIH budget included increased support for research centers, up $20 million to $2,963 million; a $33 million increase to $3,275 million for R&D contracts, including $5 million additional for the Global HIV/AIDS Fund; $50 million more for the NIH intramural research program, for a total of $3,119 million; an increase of $20 million to a total of $1,361 million for research management and support; and a decrease of $23 million for other research grants totaling $1,786 million.

NIH and three of the other Public Health Service agencies within HHS are subject to a budget "tap" called the PHS Program Evaluation Set-Aside. Section 241 of the PHS Act (42 U.S.C. § 238j) authorizes the Secretary to use a portion of eligible appropriations to assess the effectiveness of federal health programs and to identify ways to improve them. The tap has the effect of redistributing appropriated funds among PHS and other HHS agencies. The FY2008 appropriation kept the tap at 2.4%, the same as in FY2007; the FY2009 Senate bill and the draft House bill maintain that level. NIH, with the largest budget among the PHS agencies, becomes the largest "donor" of program evaluation funds, and is a relatively minor recipient. By convention, budget tables such as **Table 7** do not subtract the amount of the evaluation tap, or of other taps within HHS, from the agencies' appropriations. For further information on the Evaluation Set-Aside, see CRS Report RL34098, *Public Health Service (PHS) Agencies: Background and Funding*, coordinated by Pamela W. Smith.

At the end of the 109th Congress, the House and Senate agreed on the first NIH reauthorization statute enacted since 1993, the NIH Reform Act of 2006 (P.L. 109- 482). The law made managerial and organizational changes in NIH, focusing on enhancing the authority and tools for the NIH Director to do strategic planning, especially to facilitate and fund cross-institute research initiatives. The measure authorized, for the first time, overall funding levels for NIH, although not for the individual ICs, and established a "common fund" for trans-NIH research. For further information on NIH, see CRS Report RL33695, *The National Institutes of Health: Organization, Funding, and Congressional Issues,* by Pamela W. Smith. **(CRS Contact: Pamela Smith.)**

Table 7. National Institutes of Health ($ in Millions)

Institutes and Centers (ICs)	FY2008 original approp.[a]	FY2008 enacted[b]	FY2009 request	FY2009 House Subcom.	FY2009 Senate Comm.
Cancer (NCI)	4,805	4,831	4,810	4,975	4,959
Heart/Lung/Blood (NHLBI)	2,922	2,938	2,925	3,026	3,006
Dental/Craniofacial Research (NIDCR)	390	392	391	404	401
Diabetes/Digestive/Kidney (NIDDK)	1,707	1,716	1,708	1,767	1,756
Neurological Disorders/Stroke (NINDS)	1,544	1,552	1,545	1,599	1,588
Allergy/Infectious Diseases (NIAID)[c]	4,561	4,583	4,569	4,716	4,689
General Medical Sciences (NIGMS)	1,936	1,946	1,938	2,004	1,992
Child Health/Human Development (NICHD)	1,255	1,261	1,256	1,299	1,291
Eye (NEI)	667	671	668	691	687
Environmental Health Sciences (NIEHS)	642	646	643	665	661
Aging (NIA)	1,047	1,053	1,048	1,084	1,077
Arthritis/Musculoskeletal/Skin (NIAMS)	509	511	509	527	523
Deafness/Communicat'n Disorders (NIDCD)	394	396	395	409	406
Nursing Research (NINR)	137	138	138	142	141
Alcohol Abuse/Alcoholism (NIAAA)	436	439	437	452	449
Drug Abuse (NIDA)	1,001	1,006	1,002	1,036	1,030
Mental Health (NIMH)[d]	1,405	1,413	1,407	1,455	1,446
Human Genome Research (NHGRI)	487	489	488	505	501
Biomedical Imaging/Bioengineering (NIBIB)	299	300	300	311	307
Research Resources (NCRR)	1,149	1,156	1,160	1,200	1,193
Complementary/Alternative Med (NCCAM)	122	122	122	126	125
Minority Health/Hlth Disparities (NCMHD)	200	201	200	207	205
Fogarty International Center (FIC)	67	67	67	69	69
National Library of Medicine (NLM)	321	322	323	332	330
Office of Director (OD)	1,109	1,112	1,057	1,255	1,275
Common Fund (non-add)	*(496)*	*(498)*	*(534)*	*(544)*	*(568)*
Buildings & Facilities (B&F)	119	119	126	126	147
Subtotal, Labor/HHS Appropriation	**29,230**	**29,380**	**29,230**	**30,380**	**30,255**
Superfund (Interior approp to NIEHS)[e]	78	78	78	78[e]	78[e]
Total, NIH discretionary budget authority	**29,307**	**29,457**	**29,307**	**30,458[f]**	**30,333[f]**

Table 7. (Continued)

Institutes and Centers (ICs)	FY2008 original approp.[a]	FY2008 enacted[b]	FY2009 request	FY2009 House Subcom.	FY2009 Senate Comm.
Pre-appropriated Type 1 diabetes funds[g]	150	150	150	150	150
PHS Evaluation Tap funding[h]	8	8	8	8	8
Global Fund transfer (AIDS/TB/Malaria)[c]	-295	-295	-300	-300	-300
Total, NIH program level	**29,171**	**29,321**	**29,165**	**30,316[f]**	**30,191[f]**

Sources: Adapted by CRS from NIH and congressional tables. FY2008 amounts are from NIH Office
  of Budget at [http://officeofbudget.od.nih.gov/ui/fy2008elws.html]. FY2009 amounts are from
  House Appropriations Committee table reflecting subcommittee action on the draft bill, and
  S.Rept. 110-410 reflecting the committee-reported bill (S. 3230). Details may not add to totals due
  to rounding.

a. FY2008 original appropriations were provided in the Consolidated Appropriations Act, 2008 (P.L.
  110-161, Division G, enacted December 26, 2007). Also includes comparative IC transfers from
  NHLBI to NIDDK ($0.8 16 million) and from NLM to NIDCR ($0.455 million). The FY2008
  amounts are the reference point for the FY2009 Continuing Resolution (CR).

b. FY2008 enacted includes $150 million from the Supplemental Appropriations Act, 2008 (P.L. 110-
  252, June 30, 2008), distributed proportionally to the ICs. Those funds were designated as
  emergency spending and are not counted for the FY2009 CR.

c. NIAID totals include funds for transfer to the Global Fund to Fight HIV/AIDS, TB, and Malaria.

d. FY2008 NIMH has $0.983m from Office of the Secretary to administer the Interagency Autism
  Coordinating Committee.

e. Separate account in the Interior/Environment appropriations for NIEHS research activities related to
  Superfund. For FY2009, neither the Senate nor the House Appropriations·Committees took action
  on the Interior/Environment bills. The $78 million figure is an estimated amount based on past
  years.

f. These totals include the estimated $78 million for Superfund-related activities.

g. Funds available to NIDDK for diabetes research under PHS Act § 330B (authorized by P.L. 106-
  554, P.L. 107-360, and P.L. 110-173).

h. Additional funds for NLM from PHS Evaluation Set-Aside (§ 241 of PHS Act).

DEPARTMENT OF ENERGY (DOE)

The Department of Energy (DOE) has requested $ 10.535 billion for R&D in FY2009,
including activities in three major categories: science, national security, and energy. See
Table 8 for details. This request is 6% above the FY2008 appropriation. The House
committee recommended $ 10.903 billion. The Senate committee recommended $1 1.010
billion. The Continuing Appropriations Resolution, 2009 (Division A of P.L. 110-329)
provides funding for continuing DOE activities at the FY2008 rate through March 6, 2009.

Table 8. Department of Energy R&D ($ in millions)

	FY2008	FY2009 Request	FY2009 H.Cte.	FY2009 S.Cte.
Science	**$3,973**	**$4,722**	**$4,862**	**$4,640**
Basic Energy Sciences	1,270	1,568	1,600	1,415
High Energy Physics	689	805	805	805
Biological and Environmental Research	544	569	579	599
Nuclear Physics	433	510	517	510
Fusion Energy Sciences	287	493	499	493
Advanced Scientific Computing Research	351	369	379	369
Other	399	408	483	449
National Security	**3,199**	**3,132**	**3,052**	**3,252**
Weapons Activities[a]	2,016	1,996	1,916	2,051
Naval Reactors	775	828	828	828
Nonproliferation and Verification R&D	387	275	276	350
Defense Environmental Cleanup TD&D	21	32	32	22
Energy	**2,730**	**2,681**	**2,989**	**3,118**
Energy Efficiency and Renewable Energy[b]	1,440	1,197	1,567	1,542
Fossil Energy R&D	743	754	854	877
Nuclear Energy R&D[c]	438	630	464	566
Electr. Delivery & Energy Reliability R&D	110	100	105	133
Total	**9,903**	**10,535**	**10,903**	**11,010**

Source: DOE FY2009 congressional budget justification; draft House-reported bill and draft House report; and S. 3258 and S.Rept. 110-416.

a. Includes Stockpile Services R&D Support, Stockpile Services R&D Certification and Safety, Reliable Replacement Warhead, Science Campaigns, Engineering Campaigns except Enhanced Surety and Enhanced Surveillance, Inertial Confinement Fusion, Advanced Simulation and Computing, and a prorated share of Readiness in Technical Base and Facilities. Additional R&D activities may take place in the subprograms of Directed Stockpile Work that are devoted to specific weapon systems, but these funds are not included in the table because detailed funding schedules for those subprograms are classified.

b. Excludes Weatherization and Intergovernmental Activities.

c. Includes Nuclear Power 2010, Generation IV Nuclear Energy Systems Initiative, Nuclear Hydrogen Initiative, and Advanced Fuel Cycle Initiative (AFCI). Note that AFCI funding appears in the Fuel Cycle Research and Facilities line item in FY2008 and the FY2009 House report, but in the Research and Development line item in the FY2009 request, and the FY2009 Senate report.

The request for the DOE Office of Science is $4.722 billion, a 19% increase from FY2008. This unusually large increase reflects the American Competitiveness Initiative (ACI), which President Bush announced in the 2006 state of the union address. Over 10 years, the ACI would double R&D funding for the Office of Science and two other agencies.[26] Congress set even faster growth targets in the America COMPETES Act (P.L. 110-69), establishing authorization levels that would double R&D funding for these agencies in seven years. The percentage increase in the President's FY2009 request for the Office of Science is higher than what would be required on an annual basis to reach the ACI doubling target. This was also the case in FY2007 and FY2008, but although the House and Senate bills for those years would have provided increases even relative to the request, the final appropriations were lower than the ACI amount. For FY2009, the House committee recommended $140 million more than the request, while the Senate committee recommended $82 million less than the request.

Within the Office of Science, the request for basic energy sciences includes increases of $153 million for a new program of Energy Frontier Research Centers, $66 million for construction of the National Synchrotron Light Source II, and $73 million to increase operating time at existing facilities. The Senate committee recommended reducing basic energy sciences by $153 million below the request; $59 million of that amount represents solar energy R&D activities transferred to another account; the remainder of the reduction was not specified. The requested 17% increase for high energy physics would go mostly to programs cut in the final FY2008 appropriation that were funded in the House and Senate bills for that year.[27] The requested 72% increase for fusion energy sciences would fund the U.S. contribution to the International Thermonuclear Experimental Reactor (ITER), which was eliminated in the final FY2008 appropriation, again despite support in the House and Senate bills for that year. In December 2007, DOE announced new estimates of the cost and schedule for ITER: between $1.45 and $2.2 billion (previously $1.122 billion) with a completion date between FY2014 and FY2017 (previously FY2014). The House and Senate committees recommended the requested amount for ITER.

The requested funding for DOE national security R&D is $3.132 billion, a 2% decrease. Increases would include $53 million for the naval reactors program, mostly to support processing and storage of spent nuclear fuel, and $10 million for the reliable replacement warhead program, which Congress zeroed in the FY2008 appropriation. The major decrease would be $79 million for proliferation detection R&D, a program that Congress increased in FY2008. The House committee recommended a total of $3.052 billion, while the Senate committee recommended $3.252 billion. Neither committee recommended any funding for the reliable replacement warhead program, and the Senate committee recommended restoring $75 million of the requested decrease for proliferation detection R&D. In the Weapons Activities account, the House committee recommended an increase of $87 million for inertial confinement fusion and a decrease of $66 million for advanced simulation and computing.

The request for DOE energy R&D is $2.681 billion, down 2% from FY2008. Within this total, R&D on nuclear energy and coal would increase, while hydrogen R&D would decrease and gas and oil technology programs would be terminated (as also proposed, unsuccessfully, in other recent years). Most of the requested 17% decrease for energy efficiency and renewable energy results from the omission of $186 million in FY2008 congressionally directed projects. The requested 44% increase for nuclear energy R&D would be mostly for the Advanced Fuel Cycle Initiative (AFCI). The House and Senate committees both recommended substantial increases in energy R&D, particularly in energy efficiency and renewable energy, but decreases in nuclear energy. Both committees recommended funding the gas and oil technology programs at approximately the FY2008 level, and both provided less than the request for the AFCI. **(CRS Contact: Daniel Morgan.)**

NATIONAL SCIENCE FOUNDATION (NSF)

The FY2009 request for the National Science Foundation (NSF) was $6.854 billion, a 13.6% increase ($822.1 million) over the FY2008 estimate of $6.032 billion (see **Table 9**). President Bush has proposed doubling the NSF budget over 10 years, from FY2007 to FY2016, as part of his American Competitiveness Initiative (ACI). The FY2009 request represents another installment toward that doubling effort. In August 2008, Congress passed the America COMPETES Act which authorizes funding for NSF for FY2008 through FY20 10 at a pace that would more than double the agency's funding in seven years. NSF has identified several strategies in the FY2009 budget request: to maintain a portfolio with "powerful momentum" across all disciplines; to build a world-class science and engineering workforce; to perform effectively with the highest standards of accountability; and to support potentially transformative research. The NSF Director describes transformative research as "a range of endeavors, which promise extraordinary outcomes; such as, revolutionizing entire disciplines, creating entirely new fields, or disrupting accepted theories and perspective."[28] Several reports have recommended that funds be allocated specifically for this type of research. NSF contends that in the global environment of science and engineering, support for transformative, high-risk, high-reward research is critical to U.S. competitiveness. These strategies parallel some of the goals contained in the President's ACI, and are designed to promote research that will drive innovation and support the design and development of world-class facilities, instrumentation, and infrastructure.

Included in the FY2009 request is $5.594 billion for Research and Related Activities (R&RA), a 16.0% increase ($772.5 million) above the FY2008 estimate of $4. 822 billion. R&RA funds research projects, research facilities, and education and training activities. The scientific and academic communities have voiced concerns about the imbalance between support for the life sciences and the physical sciences. Research is multidisciplinary and transformational in nature, and very often, discoveries in the physical sciences lead to advances in other disciplines. The America COMPETES ACT authorizes increased federal research support in the physical sciences, mathematics, and engineering. The FY2009 request provides a 20.2% increase for the Mathematical and Physical Sciences (MPS) directorate. The MPS portfolio supports investments in fundamental research, facilities, and instruments, and provides approximately 44.0% of the federal funding for basic research in mathematics and physical sciences conducted at colleges and universities. R&RA includes Integrative Activities (IA), a cross-disciplinary research and education program, and is a source of funding for the acquisition and development of research instrumentation at institutions. The FY2009 request provides $276.0 million for IA. The IA also funds Partnerships for Innovation, disaster research teams, and the Science and Technology Policy Institute. In FY2008, support for the Experimental Program to Stimulate Competitive Research (EPSCoR) was transferred from the Education and Human Resources Directorate (EHR) to IA. NSF's FY2009 request for EPSCoR is $113.5 million, which is a part of the total IA funding request. The FY2009 request would support a portfolio of three complementary strategies — research infrastructure, co-funding, and outreach — for the 27 EPSCoR jurisdictions. Approximately 67.0% of the funding for EPSCoR would be used for a combination of new awards and research infrastructure improvement grants. The balance of funding would support co-funding (31.7%) and outreach activities (1.7%).

The NSF asserts that international research partnerships are critical to the nation in maintaining a competitive edge, addressing global issues, and capitalizing on global economic opportunities. The Administration has requested $47.4 million for the Office of International Science and Engineering (OISE). The OISE manages NSF's offices in Beijing, Paris, and Tokyo that report on and analyze in-country and regional science and technology policies and developments. The OISE serves as a liaison with research institutes and foreign agencies, and facilitates coordination and implementation of NSF research and education efforts.

The Office of Polar Programs (OPP) is funded in the R&RA. The FY2009 request for addressing the challenges in polar research is $491.0 million. NSF continues in its leadership role in planning U.S. participation in observance of the International Polar Year, 2007-2009.[29] The NSF also serves in a leadership capacity for several international research partnerships in the Arctic and Antarctic. Increases in OPP in FY2009 are directed at research programs for arctic and antarctic sciences — glacial and sea ice, terrestrial and marine ecosystems, the ocean and the atmosphere, and biology of life in the cold and dark. In FY2006, responsibility for funding the operational costs of three icebreakers that support scientific research in the polar regions was transferred from the U.S. Coast Guard to the NSF.[30] NSF is responsible for the operation, maintenance, and staffing of the vessels. Beginning in FY2009, one of the icebreakers is to be in drydock. To meet the need for back-up icebreaking services, the FY2009 request includes an additional $9.0 million for contracting of other vessels.

NSF supports several interagency R&D priorities in the FY2009 request. It is a lead agency in the U.S. nanotechnology research effort, accounting for $396.8 million of the National Nanotechnology Initiative's $1.53 billion FY2009 request. Funding would support research in emerging areas of nanoscale science and technology such as new drug delivery systems, advanced materials, more powerful computer chips. Support would be directed also at research and education in the environmental, health, and safety impacts of nanotechnology. NSF's other interagency priorities include funding for the Climate Change Science Program ($220.6 million), Homeland Security ($379.2 million), Networking and Information Technology R&D ($1,090.3 million), and Climate Change Technology Program ($23.5 million).

The NSF supports a variety of individual centers and center programs. The FY2009 request provides $76.0 million for Science and Technology Centers, $53.6 million for Materials Research Science and Engineering Centers, $53.6 million for Engineering Research Centers, $44.6 million for Nanoscale Science and Engineering Centers, $15.0 million for Science of Learning Centers, $20.0 million for Centers for Chemical Innovation, and $18.4 million for Centers for Analysis and Synthesis.

The FY2009 request for the EHR Directorate is $790.4 million, $64.8 million (8.9%) above the FY2008 estimate. The EHR portfolio is focused on, among other things, increasing the technological literacy of all citizens; preparing the next generation of science, engineering, and mathematics professionals; and closing the achievement gap of underrepresented groups in all scientific fields. Support at the various educational levels in the FY2009 request is as follows: research on learning in formal and informal settings (including precollege), $226.5 million; undergraduate, $219.8 million; and graduate, $190.7 million. Priorities at the precollege level include research and evaluation on education in science and engineering ($42.0 million), informal science education ($66.0 million), and Discovery Research K-12 ($108.5 million). Discovery Research is structured to combine the strengths of three existing programs and encourage innovative thinking in K-12 science, technology, engineering, and mathematics education.

According to NSF, programs at the undergraduate level are designed to "create leverage for institutional change." Priorities at the undergraduate level include the Robert Noyce Scholarship Program ($11.6 million); Course, Curriculum, and Laboratory Improvement ($39.2 million); STEM Talent Expansion Program ($29.7 million); Advanced Technological Education ($51.6 million); and Scholarship for Service ($15.0 million). The Math and Science Partnership Program (MSP), an interagency program, is proposed at $51.0 million in the FY2009 request. The MSP in NSF coordinates activities with the Department of Education and its state-funded MSP sites. At the graduate level, NSF 's priorities are Integrative Graduate Education and Research Traineeship ($25.0 million), Graduate Research Fellowships ($116.7 million), and the Graduate Teaching Fellows in K-12 Education ($49.0 million).

Additional priorities in the EHR would support a portfolio of programs directed at strengthening and expanding the participation of underrepresented groups and diverse institutions in the scientific and engineering enterprise. Among these targeted programs in the FY2009 request are the Historically Black Colleges and Universities Undergraduate Program ($31.0 million), Tribal Colleges and Universities Program ($13.4 million), Louis Stokes Alliances for Minority Participation ($42.5 million), and Centers of Research Excellence in Science and Technology ($30.5 million).

Improving the success rate of grant applicants has been a long-term priority for NSF. The funding rate (the number of grants awarded as a share of total grant applications) declined from 30% in FY2000 to an estimated 21% in FY2008. NSF anticipates increasing the funding rate to 23.0% in FY2009 by supporting an additional 1,370 research grants.

The Major Research Equipment and Facilities Construction (MREFC) account is funded at $147.5 million in the FY2009 request, a decrease of 33.2% from the FY2008 estimate. The MREFC supports the acquisition and construction of major research facilities and equipment that extend the boundaries of science, engineering, and technology. According to NSF, it is the primary federal agency providing support for "forefront instrumentation and facilities for the academic research and education communities." NSF's first priority for funding is for ongoing projects. Second priority is given to projects that have been approved by the National Science Board for new starts. To qualify for support, NSF required MREFC projects to have "the potential to shift the paradigm in scientific understanding and/or infrastructure technology." The FY2009 request is indicative of NSF's tighter standards and requirements for receiving funding in this account. Three projects that appeared in the FY2008 request (Alaskan Regional Research Vessel, Ocean Observatories Initiative, and the National Ecological Observatory Network) have to undergo a final design review and a risk management plan to meet NSF's policy of not allowing cost overruns on major facilities projects. These projects are still supported by NSF, and will be considered for inclusion in the budget cycle following submission of their revised baseline budgets and contingencies. The FY2009 request supports three ongoing projects: Advanced Laser Interferometer Gravitational Wave Observatory ($51.4 million), Atacama Large Millimeter Array ($82.3 million), and the IceCube Neutrino Observatory ($11.3 million). The request also provides $2.5 million to support design activities for a new start, the Advanced Technology Solar Telescope.

On June 25, 2008, the House Appropriations Committee approved a Commerce, Justice, Science and Related Agencies draft bill that would provide $6. 854 billion for the NSF in FY2009, $789.1 million above the FY2008 enacted and the same as the President's request. The R&RA would receive $5.554 billion, a $722.7 million increase above the FY2008 level and $49.9 million below the request. Additional funding in the House bill includes $840.3 million for the EHR and $147.5 million for MREFC. The Senate-reported bill of June 18, 2008 would provide $6.854 billion for the NSF, the same as the House bill and the request. R&RA would be funded at $5.594 billion, $40 million above the House bill and the same as the President's request. The Senate-reported bill would fund the EHR and the MREFC at $790.4 million and $152 million, respectively.

Table 9. National Science Foundation ($ in millions)

	FY2008 Estimate	FY2009 Request	FY2009 House	FY2009 Senate
Research & Related Activities				
Biological Sciences	$612.0	$675.1		
Computer & Inform. Sci. & Eng.	534.5	638.8		
Engineering	636.9	759.3		
Geosciences	752.7	848.7		
Math and Physical Sciences	1,167.3	1,402.7		
Social, Behav., & Econ. Sciences	215.1	233.5		
Office of Cyberinfrastructure	185.3	220.1		
Office of International Sci. & Eng.	41.3	47.4		
U.S. Polar Programs	442.5	491.0		
Integrative Activities	232.3	276.0		
U.S. Arctic Research Commission	1.5	1.5		
Subtotal Res. & Rel. Act	**4,821.5**	**5,594.0**	**5,554.0**[c]	**5,594.0**[c]
Ed. & Hum. Resr.	725.6	790.4	840.3	790.4
Major Res. Equip. & Facil. Constr.	220.7	147.5	147.5	152.0
Agency Operations & Award Management.	281.8	305.1	305.1	300.6
National Science Board	4.0	4.0	4.0	4.0
Office of Inspector General	11.4	13.1	13.1	13.1
Rescission required under P.L. 110-161	-33.0	—	—	—
Total NSF [a]	**6,032.0**[b]	**6,854.1**	**6,854.0**	**6,854.1**

a. The totals do not include carry overs or retirement accruals. Totals may not add due to rounding.

b. The Supplemental Appropriations Act, 2008 (P.L. 110-252) provides NSF with $62.5 million in additional FY2008 funding. NSF obligated all of its supplemental monies by the end of the fiscal year. Emergency supplemental funds are not included in the base for a Continuing Resolution. The FY2008 supplemental funding has not been incorporated into the above table column.

c. Specific allocations for each directorate or for individual programs and activities are not yet available.

Table 10. NIST ($ in millions)

NIST Program	FY2008 Request	FY2008	FY2009 Request (amended)	FY2009 House	S. 3182
STRS[a]	$500.5	440.5	535.0	500.7	489.5
ATP/TIP	0	65.2[b]	0	65.2	65.0
MEP	46.3	89.6	2.0	122.0	110.0
Construction	93.9	160.5	99.0	129.0	149.0
NIST Total	640.7	755.8	636.0	816.9	813.5

Note: Figures may not add up because of rounding.
a. Includes funding for the Baldrige National Quality Program.
b. Funding is for the new Technology Innovation Program (TIP) that replaces ATP.

On June 30, 2008, the President signed into law the Supplemental Appropriations Act, 2008 (P.L. 110-252, H.R. 2642). The act provides, among other things, $62.5 million in emergency supplemental funding for the NSF. Included in the total is $22.5 million for R&RA, of which $5.0 million is to be available solely for the Integrative Graduate Education and Research Trainee ship program. The supplemental provides $40.0 million for the EHR, of which $20.0 million is directed for activities of the Robert Noyce scholarship program. Please note that the FY2008 supplemental funding has not been included in the table column below.

On September 30, 2008, the President signed into law the Consolidated Security, Disaster Assistance, and Continuing Appropriations Act, 2009 (P.L.1 10-329, H.R. 2638). The continuing resolution funds the NSF at the FY2008 level until passage of the Commerce, Justice, Science and Related Agencies appropriations bill or until March 6, 2009, whichever occurs first.

(CRS Contact: Christine M. Matthews.)

DEPARTMENT OF COMMERCE (DOC)

National Institute of Standards and Technology (NIST)

The National Institute of Standards and Technology (NIST) is a laboratory of the Department of Commerce with a mandate to increase the competitiveness of U.S. companies through appropriate support for industrial development of precompetitive, generic technologies and the diffusion of government-developed technological advances to users in all segments of the American economy. NIST research also provides the measurement, calibration, and quality assurance techniques that underpin U.S. commerce, technological progress, improved product reliability, manufacturing processes, and public safety.

The Administration's original FY2009 budget proposed $638.0 million in funding for NIST. On June 6, 2008, the President submitted a series of amendments to his budget including a reduction of $2.0 million in the amount requested for NIST (from the Manufacturing Extension Partnership (MEP) program). The new request of $636.0 million is 15.9% below FY2008 due to an absence of support for the Technology Innovation Program (TIP)[31] and a significant decrease in financing for MEP. Funding for in-house research and development under the Scientific and Technology Research and Services (STRS) account (including the Baldrige National Quality Program) was to increase 21.5% to $535.0 million, while MEP would be provided $2.0 million to close out the federally financed portion of the program such that ". ..MEP centers will become independent, as intended in the program's original authorization." Construction support would decline 3 8.3% to $99.0 million. (See **Table 10**.)

The draft bill approved by the House Committee on Appropriations, would fund NIST at $816.9 million, 8.1% above FY2008. The STRS account would increase 13.7% to $500.7 million while support for TIP at $65.2 million would remain constant and MEP funding would increase 3 6.2% to $122.0 million. Construction would decrease 19.6% to $129.0 million. S. 3182, as reported by the Senate Committee on Appropriations, provided $813.5 million for NIST, an increase of 7.6% over FY2008. Included was $489.5 million for the STRS account (an 11.1% increase), $65.0 million for TIP, and $110.0 million for MEP (a 22.8% increase). The construction budget would decline 7.2% to $149.0 million.

No final FY2009 appropriations legislation was enacted by the beginning of that fiscal year. P.L. 110-329, the Consolidated Security, Disaster Assistance, and Continuing Appropriations Act, 2009, provides, in part, funding for NIST at FY2008 levels through March 6, 2009.

The FY2008 Consolidated Appropriations Act, P.L. 110-161, financed NIST at $755.8 million, an increase of 11.7% over FY2007. Support for the STRS account increased 1.4% to $440.5 million (including $7.9 million for the Baldrige Quality Program). The Technology Innovation Program (formerly the Advanced Technology Program (ATP)) was appropriated $65.2 million (with an additional $5 million from FY2007 unobligated balances under ATP), 17.6% below the previous fiscal year. Funding for MEP decreased 14.4% to $89.6 million. Support for construction almost tripled to $160.5 million.

The President's FY2008 budget proposal requested $640.7 million for NIST, 5.3% below the FY2007 appropriation. The STRS account would have increased 15.2% to $500.5 million (including the Baldrige Quality Program). There was no funding for ATP and financing for MEP would have been reduced 55.8% to $46.3 million. Construction expenses were to increase 60% to $93.9 million.

No final FY2007 appropriations legislation for NIST was enacted during the 109th Congress. A series of continuing resolutions funded the program at FY2006 levels through February 15, 2007. However, P.L. 110-5, passed in the 110th Congress, provided $676.9 million in FY2007 support for NIST. Funding for the STRS account increased 10% over the previous fiscal year to $434.4 million while the construction budget decreased 66% to $58.7 million. Financing for ATP at $79.1 million and support for MEP at $104.7 million reflected similar funding in FY2006.

As part of the American Competitiveness Initiative, the Administration stated its intention to double over 10 years funding for "innovation-enabling research" performed at NIST through its "core" programs (defined as internal research in the STRS account and the construction budget). To this end, the President's FY2007 budget requested an increase of 18.3% for intramural R&D at NIST; FY2007 appropriations for these in-house programs increased 9.6%. For FY2008, the omnibus appropriations legislation provided for a small increase in the STRS account. This was in contrast to the Administration's FY2008 budget which included a 15.2% increase in funding, as did the original appropriations bill, H.R. 3093, as passed by the House, while the Senate-passed version contained a 15.6% increase.

The President's FY2009 budget request proposed a 21.5% increase in support for the STRS account. Increases in the STRS account were included in the House and Senate bills, but at amounts less than the budget request.

Continued support for the Advanced Technology Program was a major funding issue, particularly because opponents objected to large companies receiving research grants. Although Congress maintained (often decreasing) funding for ATP, the initial appropriation bills passed by the House since FY2002 failed to include financing for the program. In FY2006, support for the program was cut 41% and in FY2007, P.L. 110-69 replaced ATP with the Technology Innovation Program which focuses on small and medium sized firms. The Consolidated Appropriations Act, FY2008, provides funding for this new initiative. The Administration's FY2009 budget request did not include financing for TIP, while the House and Senate bills provided support similar to FY2008. The budget for the Manufacturing Extension Partnership, another extramural program administered by NIST, has also been debated for several years. The President's FY2009 budget proposal recommended curtailing the federally funded portion of the MEP and provided $2.0 million to accomplish this objective. The House and Senate bills included large increases in funding for the program.

For additional information, see CRS Report 95-30, *The National Institute of Standards and Technology: An Appropriations Overview;* CRS Report RS228 15, *The Technology Innovation Program;* and CRS Report 97-104, *The Manufacturing Extension Partnership Program: An Overview*, all by Wendy H. Schacht. (**CRS Contact: Wendy H. Schacht.**)

National Oceanic and Atmospheric Administration (NOAA)

For FY2009, President Bush proposed $576 million for the Department of Commerce, National Oceanic and Atmospheric Administration (NOAA) for R&D funding (**Table 11**). According to the *NOAA FY2009 Budget Summary*, released on February 4, 2008, this is about 14% of NOAA's total discretionary budget request of $4.109 billion. Also, the R&D request would consist of 93% research funding and 7% development funding. About 70% of the R&D request would fund intramural programs and 30% would fund extramural activities.

NOAA's Budget Office reported the R&D funding request for the Office of Oceanic and Atmospheric Research (OAR) to be $293 million, or 51% of total NOAA R&D funding requested for FY2009. NOAA R&D request figures indicate that there would be an increase of 38% for the National Ocean Service (NOS) and one of 24% for the National Marine Fisheries Service (NMFS). These line offices in general sustained overall budget cuts affecting R&D in FY2008. The National Environmental Satellite Data and Information Service (NESDIS) R&D budget request of $29 million is a slight increase of $2 million as compared with the FY2008 enacted appropriation. National Weather Service (NWS) R&D is essentially flat funded at $23 million. The President's budget request for FY2009 indicated that $260 million of NOAA's budget would be for the U.S. Climate Change Science Program (CCSP). Also, it indicated that the $378 million requested for OAR represents NOAA's portion of the President's "Federal Science and Technology Budget" for FY2009, of which $128.1 million would be for OAR labs and cooperative institutes.

Table 11. NOAA R&D ($ in millions)

R&D By NOAA Line Office and Program Support	FY2008 Enacted[a]	FY2009 Request	S. 3182
National Ocean Service (NOS)	57	58	71
National Marine Fisheries Service (NMFS)	45	52	56
Oceanic and Atmospheric Research (OAR)	323	288	321
National Weather Service (NWS)	23	23	24
National Environmental Satellite Data and Information Service (NESDIS)	26	29	29
Office of Marine and Aviation Services (OMAO)[b] — Program Support	107	127	132
Total Conduct of R&D[c]	**$581**	**$577**	**$633**

Source: Department of Commerce, National Oceanic and Atmospheric Administration, NOAA, "FY2007-FY2009, Research and Development," personal communication, March 13, 2008.

a. P.L. 110-161 (Reported as Amendment to the Senate Amendment to H.R. 2764, the Consolidated. Appropriations Act of 2008, Div. B, Title I, Commerce, Justice, Science and Related Agencies

b. OMAO R&D includes marine research data acquisition and services.

c. The request figures for FY2009 reported by AAAS are based on "OMB R&D data and supplemental agency budget data."

The Senate Committee on Appropriations reported S. 3182 on June 19, 2008 (S.Rept. 110-397). According to a AAAS R&D analysis, the committee recommended a total of $633 million for R&D for FY2009 (**Table 11**).[32] This amount is reported to be 9.9% greater than the FY2009 request of $576 million, or an increase of $57 million, and is proposed for NOAA's five line offices and "all other R&D." Also, it is 8.9% more than the FY2008 appropriation of $581 million. The largest monetary increase, for R&D, compared with the President's request, would be $33 million for OAR. Of that amount, climate research and high performance computing R&D would stand to benefit the most from S. 3182. The Senate's largest increase above the R&D request in terms of percentage is for NOS (23.2%), or an additional $13 million. AAAS indicated that the NOS R&D increase is for congressionally directed programs.[33]

The FY2009 Consolidated Security, Disaster Assistance, and Continuing Appropriations Act (P.L. 110-329) would freeze most NOAA funding at FY2008 levels. AAAS noted that "R&D in NOAA would have gained 8.9 percent to $633 million in the Senate plan instead of a requested cut."[34] Even so, Division B of the act provides $17 million in supplemental appropriations for NOAA to improve its hurricane track and intensity forecasts for the protection of life and property. This may boost R&D funding for experimental modeling activities at NOAA's Hurricane Research Division (HRD) at the Atlantic Oceanographic and Meteorological Lab (AOML) and foster research to operations for NOAA Central Forecast Guidance.

(CRS Contact: Wayne Morrissey.)

NATIONAL AERONAUTICS AND SPACE ADMINISTRATION (NASA)

The Administration requested $12.857 billion for NASA R&D in FY2009. This request is a 5% increase over FY2008, in a total NASA budget that would increase by 2%. The House committee recommended $ 12.967 billion.[35] The Senate committee recommended $ 13.044 billion.[36] In addition, the National Aeronautics and Space Administration Authorization Act of 2008 (P.L. 110-422) includes authorization levels for many programs for FY2009. For details, see **Table 12**. The Continuing Appropriations Resolution, 2009 (Division A of P.L. 110-329) provides funding for continuing NASA activities at the FY2008 rate through March 6, 2009. For more information, see CRS Report RS2281 8, *National Aeronautics and Space Administration: Overview, FY2009 Budget, and Issues for Congress*.

Table 12. NASA R&D ($ in millions)

	FY2008[a]	FY2009 Request	FY2009 H.Cte.	FY2009 S.Cte.	FY2009 Auth.
Science[b]	$4,456	$4,442	$4,518	$4,523	$4,932
Earth Science	*1,280*	*1,368*	*1,448*	*1,440*	*1,518*
Planetary Science	*1,248*	*1,334*	*1,411*	*1,411*	*1,483*
Astrophysics	*1,338*	*1,162*	*1,181*	*1,184*	*1,290*
Heliophysics[b]	*591*	*577*	*618*	*633*	*641*
Adjustment[c]	—	—	*-140*	*-145*	—
Aeronautics	512	446	515	500	853
Exploration	3,143	3,500	3,506	3,530	4,886
Constellation Systems	*2,472*	*3,048*	*3,028*	*3,078*	*4,148*
Advanced Capabilities	*671*	*452*	*478*	*452*	*738*
International Space Station	1,813	2,060	2,060	2,060	n/a
Subtotal R&D	**9,924**	**10,449**	**10,599**	**10,613**	**n/a**
Other NASA Programs[d]	4,142	3,866	3,925	3,880	n/a
Cross-Agency Support[e]	3,243	3,300	3,245	3,320	3,300
Associated with R&D	*2,288*	*2,409*	*2,368*	*2,431*	*n/a*
Associated with Other	*955*	*891*	*877*	*889*	*n/a*
Total R&D	**12,212**	**12,857**	**12,967**	**13,044**	**n/a**
Total NASA	**17,309**	**17,614**	**17,769**	**17,814**	**20,210**

Source: NASA FY2009 congressional budget justification; draft House-reported bill and draft House report; S. 3182 and S.Rept. 110-397; and Sec. 101 of P.L. 110-422. Amounts not specified in P.L. 110-422 are shown as n/a (not available).

a. Adjusted for accounting changes to be comparable with the FY2009 request.

b. Reduced by $250 million in FY2008 to adjust for the transfer of Near Earth Networks and Deep Space Mission Systems from Heliophysics to Space and Flight Support in FY2009.

c. Reflects reallocated funds carried over from FY2008.

d. Space Shuttle, Space and Flight Support (increased in FY2008 as in note b), Education, and Inspector General.

e. Allocation between R&D and non-R&D is estimated by CRS in proportion to the underlying program amounts in order to allow calculation of a total for R&D. The Cross-Agency Support account consists mostly of indirect costs for other programs assessed in proportion to their direct costs.

Budget priorities throughout NASA are being driven by the Vision for Space Exploration. Announced by President Bush in January 2004 and endorsed by Congress in the NASA Authorization Act of 2005 (P.L. 109-155), the Vision includes returning the space shuttle to regular flight status following the 2003 *Columbia* disaster, but then retiring it by 2010; completing the International Space Station, but discontinuing its use by the United States by 2017; returning humans to the Moon by 2020; and then sending humans to Mars and "worlds beyond." To replace the space shuttle and carry astronauts to the Moon, NASA is developing a new spacecraft and a new launch vehicle, known as Orion and Ares I. Their first crewed flight is expected in March 2015.

In general, the FY2009 request includes increases for programs related to the Vision and decreases for other programs. The request for Constellation Systems, the program responsible for developing Orion and Ares I, is an increase of $576 million or 23% relative to FY2008. The request for the International Space Station is an increase of $247 million or 14%. Among programs not focused on human space exploration, the request for Science is a decrease of $15 million or 0.3%,[37] and the request for Aeronautics is a decrease of $65 million or 13%. The Senate committee recommended $30 million more than the request for Constellation Systems, while the House committee recommended $20 million less (but $26 million more for Advanced Capabilities in the same account). Both committees recommended the requested amount for the International Space Station and more than the request for both Science and Aeronautics.

Within the nearly flat request for Science, increases for Earth Science and Planetary Science would be offset by a decrease for Astrophysics. The request for Earth Science would fund two new missions recommended by the National Research Council in its decadal survey,[38] while the request for Planetary Science would initiate a new program in lunar robotic science. In Astrophysics, two programs have been of particular congressional interest: the NASA/DOE Joint Dark Energy Mission (JDEM) and the Space Interferometer Mission (SIM). The request includes funds for JDEM, as directed by Congress in the FY2008 explanatory statement,[39] but not for SIM. NASA explains that a new exoplanet exploration initiative could include a smaller, medium-class version of SIM, as recommended by the FY2008 Senate report.[40] The House and Senate committees both recommended more than the request for each of the four Science programs. Among their recommended increases were additions to cover cost growth in the Glory, Mars Science Laboratory, and James Webb Space Telescope missions and to fund decadal survey missions in Earth Science. (**CRS Contact: Daniel Morgan.**)

DEPARTMENT OF AGRICULTURE (USDA)

The FY2009 request for research and education activities in the U.S. Department of Agriculture (USDA) was $2.280 billion, a 12.0% decrease ($310.7 million) from the FY2008 estimate of $2.59 1 billion (see **Table 13**). The Agricultural Research Service (ARS) is USDA's in-house basic and applied research agency, and operates approximately 100 laboratories nationwide. The ARS laboratories focus on efficient food and fiber production, development of new products and uses for agricultural commodities, development of effective biocontrols for pest management, and support of USDA regulatory and technical assistance programs. Included in the total support for USDA in FY2009 is $1.050 billion for ARS, $117.2 million below the FY2008 estimate. In the ARS, the Administration proposes the reduction of $41.0 million in funding add-ons designated by Congress for research at specific locations. Also, there is the proposed discontinuation and redirection of $105.0 million in lower priority programs. The amounts are to be redirected to critical research priorities of the Administration that include livestock production, food safety, crop protection, and human nutrition. Included in the FY2009 request for ARS is $13.2 million for buildings and facilities.

The Cooperative State Research, Education, and Extension Service (CSREES) distributes funds to State Agricultural Experiment Stations, State Cooperative Extension Systems, land-grant universities, and other institutions and organizations that conduct agricultural research, education, and outreach. Included in these partnerships is funding for research at 1862 land-grant institutions, 1890 historically black colleges and universities, and 1994 tribal land-grant colleges. Funding is distributed to the states through competitive awards, statutory formula funding, and special grants. The FY2009 request provides $994.1 million for CSREES, a decrease of $ 189.7 million from the FY2008 estimate. The CSREES FY2009 budget includes the proposed elimination of $144.0 million in Congressional add-ons and the reduction of $88.0 million in lower priority programs. Funding for formula distribution in FY2009 to the state Agricultural Experiment Stations is $273.2 million, approximately $1.5 million below the FY2008 estimate. Support for the 1890 formula programs is $38.3 million, $2.8 million below the FY2008 level. One of the primary goals of the FY2009 CSREES budget is to expand competitive, peer- reviewed allocation of research programs. The FY2009 budget request has proposed, as in previous years, to modify the Hatch formula program.[41] It would expand the multistate research programs share of Hatch funds from 25.0% to approximately 70.0%. The request would redirect 42.0% of Hatch funds to nationally, competitively awarded, multi-state/multi-institutional projects in the first year, with the balance of funds distributed over a four year period. In addition, the FY2009 request proposes allocating 67.0% of McIntire-Stennis funds for the creation of a competitively awarded multi-state research program. The extension programs are also proposed to be strengthened through competitively awarded grants. The programs are designed to be more responsive to critical national issues such as agricultural security, local and regional emergencies, zoonotic diseases, and pest risk management.

The FY2009 request proposes $256.5 million for the Agriculture and Food Research Initiative (AFRI), an increase of $65.6 million over the FY2008 estimate. In addition to supporting fundamental and applied science in agriculture, USDA maintains that the AFRI makes a significant contribution to developing the next generation of agricultural scientists by providing graduate students with opportunities to work on research projects. A focus of these efforts is providing increased opportunities for minority and under-served communities in agricultural science. AFRI funding also will support projects directed at developing alternate methods of biological and chemical conversion of biomass, and research determining the impact of a renewable fuels industry on the economic and social dynamics of rural communities. The Administration has proposed support for initiatives in agricultural genomics, emerging issues in food and agricultural security, the ecology and economics of biological invasions, and plant biotechnology. Research is proposed that moves beyond water quality issues to extend to water availability, reuse, and conservation.

Table 13. U.S. Department of Agriculture R&D ($ in millions)

	FY2008 Estimate	FY2009 Request[a]	FY2009 Senate (S. Rept.110- 426)
Agricultural Research Service (ARS)			
Product Quality/Value Added	$105.1	$97.6	
Livestock Production	84.8	70.1	
Crop Production	200.6	191.0	
Food Safety	104.5	105.8	
Livestock Protection	82.4	68.8	
Crop Protection	196.0	188.7	
Human Nutrition	85.3	79.5	
Environmental Stewardship	222.5	199.6	
National Agricultural Library	21.8	18.4	
Repair and Maintenance	17.5	17.5	
Subtotal	**1,120.6**	**1,037.0**	**1,134.1[d]**
Buildings and Facilities	46.8	13.2	31.0
Total, ARS	**1,167.4**	**1,050.2**	**1,165.1**
Cooperative State Research, Education, & Extension (CSREES) Research and Education			
Hatch Act Formula	195.8	139.2	205.6
Cooperative Forestry Research	24.8	19.5	26.0
Evans-Allen Formula (Payments to 1890	41.1	38.3	43.1
Special Research Grants	107.1	18.1	50.7
Agriculture & Food Research Initiative	190.9	256.5	200.0
Federal Administration	42.2	10.7	20.4
Higher Education[b]	47.8	41.6	52.0
Other Programs	18.6	11.4	32.1
Total, Cooperative Research. & Education[c]	**668.3**	**535.3**	**629.9**
Extension Activities			
Smith-Lever Sections 3b&c	274.7	273.2	288.4
Smith-Lever Sections 3d	97.5	91.5	97.6
Renewable Resources Extension	4.0	4.1	4.0
1890 Colleges, Tuskegee, & West Virginia State	17.3	16.6	37.6
Other Extension Prog. & Admin.	59.7	46.4	36.7
Total, Extension Activities	**453.2**	**431.8**	**464.3**
Integrated Activities	55.9	20.1	55.9
Outreach for Disadvantaged Farmers	6.4	6.9	0.0[e]
Total, CSREES[c]	**1,183.8**	**994.1**	**1,150.1**
Economic Research Service	77.3	82.1	78.2
National Agricultural Statistics Service	162.1	153.5	149.1
Total, Research, Education, and Economics	**2,590.6**	**2,279.9**	**2,542.5**

Note: Research activities carried out in support of Homeland Security are reflected under the Food Safety, Livestock Protection, and Crop Protection program areas — FY2008, $35.5 million; and FY2009, $64.3 million.

a. Funding levels are contained in U.S. Department of Agriculture FY2009 Budget Summary, documents internal to the agency, and S.Rept. 110-426.

b. Higher education includes payments to 1994 institutions and 1890 Capacity Building Grants program, the Native American Institutions Endowment Fund, the Alaska Native and Native Hawaiian-Serving Institutions Education Grants, and others.

c. Program totals may or may not include set-asides (non-add) or contingencies. The CSREES total includes support for Community Food Projects and the Organic Agriculture Research and Education Initiative.

d. Specific allocations for individual programs and activities are not yet available.

e. The Committee does not include funding for this program. The Food, Conservation, and Energy Act of 2009 provides $15.0 million for this activity and repeals the authorization for appropriations.

The FY2009 request for USDA provides $82.1 million for the Economic Research Service (ERS), $4.2 million above the FY2008 estimated level; and $153.5 million for the National Agricultural Statistics Service (NASS), approximately $9.9 million below the FY2008 level. The budget includes support to improve research efforts in analyzing the impacts of bioenergy production, and to examine those concerns pertaining to feedstock storage, transportation networks, and the vagaries in commodity production. Funding for NASS will allow for the creation of a data series on key elements of bioenergy production. Research areas to explore include production and utilization of biomass materials; stocks and prices of distillers' grains; and current and proposed ethanol plants. Funding is provided in the NASS FY2009 request to fully fund the last year of the 2007 Census of Agriculture. Funding will be available also for data collection to measure energy use and production on farms.

On July 21, 2008, the Senate Committee on Appropriations reported S. 3289, the Agriculture, Rural Development, Food and Drug Administration, and Related Agencies Appropriation Bill, FY2009 (S.Rept. 110-426). The bill would provide a total of $2.543 billion for research and education activities in USDA, $262.6 million above the Administrations's FY2009 request and $48.1 million below the FY2008 estimate. S. 3289 would fund the ARS at $1.165 billion and CSREES at $1.150 billion. In addition, funding in the Senate-reported bill for the ERS and the NASS would be $78.2 million and $149.1 million, respectively.

On September 30, 2008, the President signed into law the Consolidated Security, Disaster Assistance, and Continuing Appropriations Act, 2009 (P.L. 110- 329, H.R. 2638). The continuing resolution funds the USDA at the FY2008 level until passage of the regular appropriations bill or until March 6, 2009, whichever occurs first. **(CRS Contact: Christine M. Matthews.)**

DEPARTMENT OF THE INTERIOR (DOI)

President Bush has requested $617 million for Department of the Interior (DOI) R&D in FY2009, an estimated decrease of 8.7% from FY2008 funding of $676 million (see **Table 14**). The U.S. Geological Survey (USGS) is the primary supporter of R&D within DOI, accounting for nearly 90% of the department's total R&D appropriations. President Bush has proposed $546 million for USGS R&D in FY2009, a reduction of $40.6 million (-6.9%) from the estimated FY2008 level. FY2009 R&D funding would decline in three of the four USGS research divisions: Geographic Research, Geological Resources, and Water Resources. FY2009 funding for the Biological Research Division would remain flat. Funding for a new USGS program, Global Change, was authorized by Congress in FY2008 and funded at $7.4

million. The President's FY2009 budget proposes a 260.1% increase in funding for this program to $26.6 million.

No final FY2009 appropriations legislation was enacted by the beginning of that fiscal year. On September 30, 2008, President Bush signed into law the Consolidated Security, Disaster Assistance, and Continuing Appropriations Act, 2009 (P.L. 110- 329). Division A of this act provides continuing appropriations for FY2009 at their FY2008 levels to agencies not otherwise addressed in the act through March 6, 2009, or until the enactment into law of an appropriation for any project or activity provided for in the act, or the enactment into law of the applicable appropriations act for FY2009 without any provision for such project or activity, whichever occurs first. For the Department of the Interior, this provides $671 million for R&D, an increase of $43 million above the President's FY2009 request.

Previously, the House and Senate Appropriations Subcommittees on Interior, Environment, and Related Agencies have held hearings on agency budget requests, however scheduled full committee markups have been postponed and no bill to fund Interior, Environment, and Related Agencies for FY2009 has been introduced to date.

USGS Geographic Research efforts seek to describe and interpret America's landscape by mapping the nation's terrain, monitoring changes over time, and analyzing how and why these changes have occurred. The President's FY2009 budget for Geographic Research R&D proposes a $5.6 million cut (-11.8%) to $41.9 million from its estimated FY2008 level of $47.5 million.

Funding for Geological Resources R&D in FY2009 would decrease by $33.4 million (-15.2 percent) to $185.5 million from its estimated FY2008 level of $218.8 million. The Geological Resources Program assesses the availability and quality of the nation's energy and mineral resources. The Geological Resources Program researches, monitors, and assesses the landscape to understand geological processes to help distinguish natural change from those resulting from human activity. Within the earth sciences, the USGS plays a major role in important geological hazards research, including research on earthquakes and volcanoes. Enterprise Information conducts information science research to enhance the National Map and National Spatial Data infrastructure.

USGS Water Resources R&D is focused on water availability, water quality and flood hazards. The President's FY2009 budget for Water Resources R&D proposes a $21.4 million cut (-16.7%) to $106.7 million from its estimated FY2008 level of $128.1 million.

USGS Biological Research efforts seek to generate and distribute scientific information that can assist in the conservation and management of the nation's biological resources. The President's FY2009 budget request for Biological Research R&D proposes a small increase of $0.5 million (less than 1%) to $180.3 million. The USGS Biological Research program serves as DOI's biological research arm, using the capabilities of 17 research centers and associated field stations, one technology center, and 40 cooperative research units that support research on fish, wildlife, and natural habitats. Major research initiatives are carried out by USGS scientists who collect scientific information through research, inventory, and monitoring investigations. These activities develop new methods and techniques to identify, observe, and manage fish and wildlife, including invasive species and their habitats. **(CRS Contact: John Sargent.)**

Table 14. Department of the Interior R&D ($ in millions)

	FY2008 estimate	FY2009 request
Geographic Research	47	42
Geological Resources	219	185
Water Resources	128	107
Biological Research	180	180
Global Change	7	27
Enterprise Information	5	5
USGS total	**586**	**546**
Other agencies[a]	84	82
Total[b]	**671**	**628**

Source: R&D estimates are from the Department of the Interior's FY2009 agency budget justification.
   [http://www.doi.gov/budget]
a. Includes the Bureau of Reclamation, the Bureau of Land Management, the Minerals Management
   Service, and the National Park Service.
b. Totals may not add due to rounding.

ENVIRONMENTAL PROTECTION AGENCY (EPA)

The Environmental Protection Agency (EPA), the regulatory agency responsible for carrying out a number of environmental pollution control laws, funds a broad portfolio of R&D activities to provide the necessary scientific tools and knowledge to support decisions relating to preventing, regulating, and abating environmental pollution. Beginning in FY2006, EPA has been funded within the "Interior, Environment, and Related Agencies" appropriations bill.[42] Most of EPA's scientific research activities are funded within the agency's Science and Technology (S&T) appropriations account. This account is funded by a "base" appropriation and a transfer from the Hazardous Substance Superfund (Superfund) account. These transferred funds are dedicated to research on more effective methods to clean up contaminated sites. The House and Senate Appropriations Subcommittees on Interior, Environment, and Related Agencies held hearings on agency budget requests, however, scheduled full committee markups were postponed and no bills to fund Interior, Environment, and Related Agencies for FY2009 were introduced prior to the enactment of the Consolidated Security, Disaster Assistance, and Continuing Appropriations Act (P.L. 110-329).

P.L. 110-329 as enacted September 30, 2008, contained no specific provisions regarding EPA's programs and activities including the agency's R&D activities and programs. As per Section 101 in Division A of P.L. 110-329, until March 6, 2009, funds are appropriated "at a rate for operations as provided in the applicable appropriations Acts for fiscal year 2008 and under the authority and conditions provided in such Acts." For FY2008, Title II of Division F of the FY2008 Consolidated Appropriations Act (P.L. 110-161) appropriated $7.46 billion for EPA, including $785.8 million (including a transfer from the Superfund account) for the S&T account.

Including the transfer from the Superfund account, the President's original FY2009 budget request included $789.9 million for the S&T account. On August 1, 2008, the President submitted a series of amendments[43] to the FY2009 budget request including a $10.6

million increase within the EPA S&T account for homeland security bioterrorism activities.[44] The amended request after the transfers from the Superfund account was $800.5 million, a $14.7 million increase (nearly 2%) above the FY2008 appropriation of $785.8 million (see **Table 15**). The total amount requested for the S&T account represented 11% of the $7.18 billion requested for EPA overall for FY2009.

Without adjusting for inflation, requested FY2009 funding for certain research activities would have been an increase relative to FY2008 appropriated levels, however, funding for many of the program areas within the S&T account would have remained relatively constant or declined. For example, the request included decreased funding for the "Climate Change Protection Program" and "Global Change Research," but an increase for "Air Toxics and Quality" programs. Overall funding for "Human Health and Ecosystem Research," including funding for the Science to Achieve Results (STAR) program, would have decreased based on the FY2009 request. However, within this category, funding for human health "Computational Toxicology Research" would have increased. The largest requested increase for FY2009 within the S&T account was for two EPA homeland security activities: Water Security Initiative, and Decontamination Research.[45] As revised by the President's August 1st budget request amendment, the combined $62.0 million requested[46] for FY2009 was $29.9 million above the FY2008 appropriation of $32.1 million for these two activities; a 93% increase.[47]

Although the Office of Management and Budget (OMB) reports[48] historical and projected budget authority amounts for R&D at EPA (and other federal agencies), OMB documents do not describe how these amounts explicitly relate to the requested and appropriated funding amounts for the many specific EPA program activities.

EPA's annual appropriations are requested, considered, and enacted according to eight statutory appropriations accounts, which were established by Congress during the FY1996 appropriations process. The Science and Technology (S&T) account incorporates elements of the former EPA Research and Development (R&D) account, as well as a portion of the former Salaries and Expenses, and Program Operations accounts, which had been in place until FY1996. Because of the differences in the scope of the activities included in these accounts, apt comparisons before and after FY1996 are difficult.

Table 15. Environmental Protection Agency S&T Account ($ in millions)

Environmental Protection Agency	FY2008 Enacted	FY2009 Requested
Science and Technology Appropriations Account		
• *Base Appropriations*	*$760.1*	*$774.1*
• *Transfer in from Superfund Account*	*25.7*	*26.4*
Science and Technology Total	**785.8**	**800.5**
• *(Operations and Administration)*	*(72.7)*	*(74.9)*
Net Science and Technology	**713.1**	**725.6**

Source: Prepared by the Congressional Research Service (CRS) using information provided by the House Appropriations Committee, and the July 31, 2008 White House amendments to the FY2009 budget request. Enacted amounts for FY2008 in the above table reflect a 1.56 % across-the-board rescission required in P.L. 110-161 for any discretionary appropriations in Division F Titles I through IV of the law (Division F Title IV § 437 of P.L. 110-161). Numbers may not add due to rounding.

The activities funded within the Science and Technology (S&T) account include research conducted by universities, foundations, and other non-federal entities with grants awarded by EPA, and research conducted by the agency at its own laboratories and facilities. R&D at EPA headquarters and laboratories around the country, as well as external R&D, is managed primarily by EPA's Office of Research and Development (ORD). A large portion of the S&T account funds EPA's R&D activities managed by ORD, including the agency's research laboratories and research grants. The account also provides funding for the agency's applied science and technology activities conducted through its program offices (e.g., the Office of Water). Many of the programs implemented by other offices within EPA have a research component, but the research is not necessarily the primary focus of the program.

The operation and administration of the agency's laboratories and facilities necessitate significant expenditures for rent, utilities, and security. Prior to FY2007, a significant portion of the funding for these expenses had been requested and appropriated within EPA's Environmental Programs and Management (EPM) appropriations account. In FY2007, and FY2008, increasing portions of funding for these expenses were requested and appropriated within the S&T account. This change affects comparisons of the S&T appropriations over time. Funding for these latter expenses represents approximately 10% of the total S&T account in the FY2009 request and the FY2008 appropriations, compared to less than 5% in the FY2007 appropriations.[49]

Some Members of Congress and an array of stakeholders have continually raised concerns about the adequacy of funding for scientific research at EPA. The adequacy of funding for EPA's scientific research activities has been part of a broader question about the adequacy of overall federal funding for a broad range of scientific research activities administered by multiple federal agencies. Some Members of Congress, scientists, and environmental organizations have expressed concern about the downward trend in federal resources for scientific research over time. The debate continues to center around the question of whether the regulatory actions of federal agencies are based on "sound science," and how scientific research is applied in developing federal policy. **(CRS Contact: Robert Esworthy)**.

DEPARTMENT OF TRANSPORTATION (DOT)

President Bush requested $901 million for Department of Transportation (DOT) R&D in FY2009, an increase of approximately $78 million (9.5%) from FY2008 funding of $823 million (see **Table 16**). In addition to receiving R&D funds through the regular appropriations process, DOT also receives R&D funding from the Transportation Trust Fund through authorization legislation.[50] For example, P.L. 109-59, the Safe, Accountable, Flexible, Efficient Transportation Equity Act — A Legacy for Users (SAFETEA-LU), which became law in August 2005, set DOT surface transportation authorization levels for each fiscal year from FY2005 through FY2009, providing increased DOT R&D funding during this period.

No final FY2009 appropriations legislation was enacted by the beginning of that fiscal year. On September 30, 2008, President Bush signed into law the Consolidated Security, Disaster Assistance, and Continuing Appropriations Act, 2009 (P.L. 110-329). Division A of this act provides continuing appropriations for FY2009 at their FY2008 levels through March 6, 2009, to agencies not otherwise addressed in the act, or until the enactment of an appropriation for any project or activity provided for in the act, or the enactment of the applicable appropriations act for FY2009 without any provision for such project or activity, whichever occurs first. For the Department of Transportation, this provides $823 million for R&D, $78 million less than the President's FY2009 request.

The Senate Committee on Appropriations unanimously reported S. 3261, the Transportation, Housing and Urban Development, and Related Agencies Appropriations Act, 2009, on July 10, 2008. Neither the bill nor the accompanying report (S.Rept. 110-418) provide sufficient detail to allow a complete analysis of the level of R&D funding provided to DOT. Where the bill provides detailed R&D information, it is provided in the agency funding discussions below. The American Association for the Advancement of Science has estimated DOT agency R&D funding under S. 3261; this data is included in **Table 16.**

Previously, the House Committee on Appropriations, Subcommittee on Transportation, Housing and Urban Development, and Related Agencies marked-up an unnumbered draft on June 20, 2008. No details have been provided publicly in the form of a bill or report, though a related press release and a summary table of funding are available on the subcommittee's website.[51]

The Federal Highway Administration (FHWA) and the Federal Aviation Administration (FAA) together account for more than 80 percent of DOT's R&D funding request. FHWA, FAA and the Federal Transit Administration (FTA) account for all increases in the DOT FY2009 R&D budget request.

The President requested $392.8 million in FY2009 for FHWA R&D, an increase of $20.1 million (5.4%) above the FY2008 funding level of $372.6 million. FHWA's research programs include the investigation of ways to improve safety, reduce congestion, improve mobility, reduce lifecycle construction and maintenance costs, improve the durability and longevity of highway pavements and structures, enhance the cost-effectiveness of highway infrastructure investments, and minimize negative impacts on the natural and human environment.

Table 16. Department of Transportation R&D ($ in millions)

Department of Transportation	FY2008 estimated	FY2009 request	FY2009 Senate[b]
Federal Highway Administration	373	393	393
Federal Aviation Administration	271	335	335
Other agencies[a]	179	174	185
Total	823	901	912

Source: R&D estimates are from unpublished OMB tables and DOT budget justifications.

a. "Other agencies" includes National Highway Traffic Safety Administration, Federal Railroad Administration, Federal Transit Administration, Research and Innovative Technology Administration, Federal Motor Carrier Safety Administration, Pipeline and Hazardous Materials Safety Administration, and the Office of the Secretary.

b. Based on analysis by the American Association for the Advancement of Science (AAAS).

FHWA's FY2009 budget would provide $166.9 million for R&D under the Surface Transportation Research, Development, and Deployment Program, an increase of $23 million (16%) above the FY2008 level of $143.9 million, and $51.3 million for R&D for the Intelligent Transportation Systems program, an increase of $7.5 million (17%) above the FY2008 level of $43.8 million. These increases are partially offset by decreases in R&D funds for State Planning and Research (down $10.7 million, -6.4%) which would receive $156.2 million in FY2009. S.Rept. 110- 418 states that S. 3261 recommends FHWA transportation research at the level requested by the President.

The President requested $335.0 million for Federal Aviation Administration (FAA) R&D, up $64.2 million (23.2%) from the FY2008 level of $270.7 million. The request includes $171.0 million for Research, Engineering, and Development, $161.5 million for the Air Traffic Organization (ATO), $2.3 million for Safety and Operations, and $125,000 for Commercial Space Transportation. The request includes an increase in R&D funding for FAA's Next Generation Air Transportation System (NextGen) which is focused on addressing air traffic growth by increasing the nation's airspace capacity and efficiency and reducing emissions and noise. NextGen R&D funding under Research, Engineering, and Development increases from $24.3 million in FY2008 to $56.5 million in FY2009, up $32.2 million (132.5%). An additional $69.4 million is requested for NextGen R&D under ATO focused on systems development, demonstrations and infrastructure development. S.Rept. 110-418 reports that S. 3261 provides $171 million for FAA's Research, Engineering, and Development (RE&D) activity, approximately equal to the President's request. FAA's RE&D activity accounts for approximately one-half of the agency's total overall R&D funding. Additional FAA R&D funding details are not available.

The President's FY2009 budget proposes $16.8 million in R&D funding for the Federal Transit Administration (FTA), up $4.9 million over the FY2008 level of $11.9 million. **(CRS Contact: John Sargent.)**

End Notes

[1] Funding levels included in this document are in current dollars unless otherwise noted. Inflation diminishes the purchasing power of federal R&D funds, so an increase that does not equal or exceed the inflation rate may reduce real purchasing power. For example, if inflation in 2008 exceeds 2.7 %, then the President's R&D funding request for FY2009 may represent a decline in real purchasing power. The Consumer Price Index, a key measure of inflation, rose 2.8% in 2007 and is on a pace to exceed 4% in 2008.

[2] The Department of Homeland Security Appropriations Act, 2004 (P.L. 108-90), provided funding under Title III, Preparedness and Recovery, in the amount of $5.593 billion to remain available through FY2013. The act restricts DHS from spending more than $3 .418 billion in fiscal years 2004 through 2008. The balance, $2.175 billion, will become available for use by DHS in FY2009.

[3] For additional information, see CRS Report RL34328, *America COMPETES Act: Programs, Funding, and Selected Issues*, by Deborah D. Stine.

[4] *Science and Engineering Indicators 2008, Volume 2: Appendix Tables*, National Science Foundation, 2008.

[5] Ibid.

[6] Ibid.

[7] The ACI proposes to double "innovation-enabling physical science and engineering research" at the three agencies over ten years, and states that "individual agency allocations remain to be determined." (*The American Competitiveness Initiative: Leading the World in Innovation*, Office of Science and Technology Policy/Domestic Policy Council, The White House, February 2006.)

[8] American Competitiveness Initiative Research fact sheet, FY2009 request, Office of Science and Technology Policy, The White House, February 2008.

[9] Office of Management and Budget website. [http://www.whitehouse.gov/omb/budget/ fy2009/nsf.html]

[10] Office of Management and Budget website. [http://www.whitehouse.gov/omb/budget/ fy2009/energy.html]

[11] Office of Management and Budget website. [http://www.whitehouse.gov/omb/budget/ fy2009/commerce.html]

[12] The original FY2008 funding levels do not include R&D funding provided under the Supplemental Appropriations Act, 2008 (P.L. 110-252)

[13] See [http://www.cq.com/budgettracker.do].

[14] Letter from Secretary of Energy Samuel W. Bodman to Sen. Jeff Bingaman, Chairman, Senate Committee on Energy and Natural Resources, February 4, 2008. [http://energy

[15] Ibid.

[16] *National Nanotechnology Initiative: Research and Development Funding in the President's FY2009 Budget*, fact sheet, Office of Science and Technology Policy, The White House, February 2008; National Nanotechnology Initiative website. [http://www.nano.gov/html/about/funding

[17] *Analytical Perspectives: Budget of the United States Government, Fiscal Year 2009*, Office of Management and Budget, The White House, 2008. The NITRD data in OMB's *Analytical Perspectives* include the DOD Defense Information Systems Agency (DISA). According to the NITRD National Coordination Office, DISA's contribution is not included in the FY2009 *Networking and Information Technology Research and Development: Supplement to the President's Budget* report.

[18] *Analytical Perspectives: Budget of the United States Government, Fiscal Year 2009*, Office of Management and Budget, The White House, 2008.

[19] This historical data can be found in DOD's *National Defense Budget Estimates for the FY2008 Budget* (also known as the "Green Book"). Office of the Under Secretary for Defense (Comptroller).March 2007.pp 62-67. See [http://www.defenselink.mil/ comptroller/defbudget/fy2008/fy2008_greenbook.pdf]. Last viewed May 10, 2007.

[20] CRS analysis of H.R. 6947 as reported and H.Rept. 110-862.

[21] CRS analysis of S. 3181 as reported and S.Rept. 110-396.

[22] CRS analysis of P.L. 110-329, Division D, and explanatory statement, *Congressional Record*, September 24, 2008, pp. H9806-H9807.

[23] See, for example, Government Accountability Office, *Combating Nuclear Smuggling: Additional Actions Needed to Ensure Adequate Testing of Next Generation Radiation Detection Equipment*, GAO-07-1247T, testimony before the House Committee on Energy and Commerce, Subcommittee on Oversight and Investigations, September 18, 2007.

[24] Government Accountability Office, *Combating Nuclear Smuggling: DHS Need to Consider the Full Costs and Complete All Tests Prior to Making a Decision on Whether to Purchase Advanced Portal Monitors*, GAO-08-1178T, September 25, 2008.

[25] The "NIH program level" cited in the Administration's budget documents does not reflect the Global Fund transfer.

[26] The February 2006 White House document *American Competitiveness Initiative: Leading the World in Innovation* states that "ACI doubles total research fund; individual agency allocations remain to be determined." The three ACI agencies may individually receive more or less than the amount required to double their separate FY2006 levels.

[27] In response to these cuts, the Supplemental Appropriations Act, 2008 (P.L. 110-252) provided $62.5 million in supplemental FY2008 funding for the DOE Office of Science.

[28] Bement, Jr., Arden L., Director, National Science Foundation, "Transformative Research: The Artistry and Alchemy of the 21st Century," remarks, Texas Academy of Medicine, Engineering and Science Fourth Annual Conference, Austin, Texas, January 4, 2007. [http://www.nsf.gov/news/speeches/bement/07/alb070 1 04_texas.j sp]

[29] International Polar Year runs from March 2007 through March 2009. Sponsors say that a two-year period was selected to provide equal coverage of both the Arctic and Antarctic.

[30] For expanded discussion of the icebreakers see for example CRS Report RL34391, *Coast Guard Polar Icebreaker Modernization: Background, Issues, and Options for Congress*, by Ronald O'Rourke.

[31] The Technology Innovation Program replaced the Advanced Technology Program as mandated by P.L. 110-69.

[32] American Association for the Advancement of Science (AAAS), "Funding Update on Commerce R&D in Senate Appropriations" (Based on FY2009 Appropriations Bills and Including Conduct of R&D and R&D Facilities)," July 1, 2008, at [http://bakser.aaas.org/ spp/rd/doc09s.htm].

[33] Id.

[34] AAAS, "Federal Research Funding Flat in 2009 as Federal Budget Stalls," September 30, 2008, at [http://www.aaas.org/spp/rd/upd908 .htm].

[35] CRS analysis of committee-approved drafts of the House-reported bill and House report.

[36] CRS analysis of S. 3182 as reported and S.Rept. 110-397.

[37] After adjusting for transfers. See notes to **Table 12**.

[38] National Research Council, *Earth Science and Applications from Space: National Imperatives for the Next Decade and Beyond*, 2007.

[39] *Congressional Record*, December 17, 2007, pp. H15820 and H15923.

[40] S.Rept. 110-124, p. 110.

[41] Hatch Act Formula grants are provided for agricultural research to state agricultural experiment stations (SAES) in accordance with the act approved July 2, 1862 (7 U.S.C. 301 et seq.) — as amended through P.L. 107-293. SAESs are directed to support research projects that have relevance to the special needs of the respective states. SAESs are required to provide 100% in matching funds.

[42] For information on funding for all EPA accounts and each of the other agencies funded in this bill see CRS Report RL3446 1, *Interior, Environment, and Related Agencies: FY2009 Appropriations*.

[43] White House, Office of Management and Budget, *Estimate #7 — FY 2009 Budget Amendments: Departments of Agriculture, Commerce, Education, Health and Human Services, Homeland Security, the Interior, Labor, and State, and the Environmental Protection Agency*. [http://www.whitehouse.gov/omb/budget/amendments.htm]

[44] The August 1, 2008 White House amendment also included a $24.2 million increase within EPA's Hazardous Substance Superfund appropriations account for homeland security bioterrorism activities.

[45] Under the Bioterrorism Act of 2002, and Homeland Security Presidential Directives 7, 9 and 10, EPA is the lead federal agency for coordinating security of the Nation's water systems, and plays a role in developing early warning monitoring and decontamination capabilities associated with potential attacks using biological contaminants.

[46] Includes recommended increase per the August 1, 2008 White House amendments to the FY2009 budget request.

[47] The FY2009 President's budget as amended included a total of $84.5 million for Homeland Security activities within the S&T account; $30.4 million above the FY2008 enacted appropriation of $54.1 million.

[48] The Office of Management and Budget (OMB) reports R&D budget authority amounts in its Analytical Perspectives accompanying the annual President's budget, but amounts for specific programs are not included. The R&D budget authority amounts reported by OMB are typically significantly less than amounts appropriated/requested for the S&T account, but the differences are not explicitly defined. For example, for EPA R&D OMB reported actual budget authority of $606 million for FY2007, an estimated amount of $557 million for FY2008, and $550 million proposed for FY2009. See OMB, *Fiscal Year 2009 Budget of the United States: Analytical Perspectives - Cross Cutting Programs*. [http://www.whitehouse.gov/omb/budget/fy2009/]

[49] For example, for research alone (net after operations and administration expenses), the FY2008 consolidated appropriations provided a $6.4 million increase above the FY2008 request for the S&T account, but $17.5 million less than the FY2007 appropriations (includes transfers from the Superfund account).

[50] Appropriators may add to or direct funds identified in authorization legislation.

[51] See [http://appropriations.house.gov/Subcommittees/sub_tranurb.shtml].

In: Federal Role in Funding Research and Development   ISBN: 978-1-60741-486-5
Editor: Piper B. Collins   © 2010 Nova Science Publishers, Inc.

Chapter 5

FEDERAL SUPPORT FOR RESEARCH AND DEVELOPMENT

Congressional Budget Office

SUMMARY

New knowledge and continuing innovation have been major factors in increasing economic well-being. Private businesses are the largest sponsors of research and development (R&D) in the United States, producing the discoveries that in turn lead to new products and services and the growth of productivity; however, the federal government has long provided significant support for R&D activities to both supplement and encourage private efforts. The government finances research and development through spending—fiscal year 2007 appropriations for R&D activities total $137 billion—and tax benefits that give businesses an incentive to increase their R&D spending.

Studies of federally supported research and development provide multifaceted but incomplete answers to questions about those governmental activities: whether the current level of spending is appropriate, what returns taxpayers receive for public investment in R&D, and whether funds are allocated to areas of inquiry and projects that will provide the highest return on that investment. Results of the Congressional Budget Office's (CBO's) economic analysis of federal support for R&D and its review of trends in the data over time indicate the following:

Over the 1953–2004 period as a whole, federal spending for R&D has grown, on average, as fast as the overall economy. Spending rose rapidly in the 1950s and early 1960s, reaching almost 2 percent of gross domestic product (GDP) in 1964, a peak that coincided with the acceleration of the U.S. space program. Since then, with the exception of a period in the 1980s—when an expansion of national defense activities prompted more funding for research and development—federal R&D spending has generally declined as a share of GDP.

Distinguishing between research and development is important in evaluating the effectiveness of the government's R&D spending and the benefits it may provide. Research (particularly basic research) may be conducted without a specific commercial purpose in mind, but it may nevertheless have large "spillovers" in the economy because the knowledge it produces may be useful not only to researchers in other fields but also to businesses seeking to develop new products and production processes. Development occurs closer to a product's introduction so that its benefits go more directly to innovating firms and their customers. The federal government funds about half of all research in the United States but only 17 percent of development. Since the early 1 980s, federal spending for research has grown more steadily and more quickly than federal spending for development.

Federal funding of research—particularly of basic research—is generally viewed favorably because of its large potential for spillovers and the corresponding economic benefits. Nonetheless, the economic returns to basic research are difficult to measure because the progress that results from research may be hard to identify or to value and the interval between the research and its application to a product or process is sometimes long.

Studies of federal spending for basic research in the past, particularly studies of research conducted at academic institutions, have estimated that the average returns from that spending exceed the returns that might have been gained had those resources been put to other uses. Additional federal spending could generate comparable benefits, although the returns to individual projects are likely to vary. Also, the gains from large increases in spending might be constrained if sufficient scientific and technical workers and facilities were not available.

In recent years, the share of federal research funding allocated to the life sciences has expanded, an emphasis supported by the high rates of returns to life sciences research that some studies have reported. But other studies indicate that researchers reach across disciplines for new ideas and tools, which would suggest that supporting research over a wide range of scientific fields is an important element in generating an economic return from federal research funding.

Federal spending for development has generally focused on accomplishing public missions, most prominently that of national defense. Although in the past that spending has generated some commercially viable spin-off technologies, such by-products are largely unpredictable. A consideration of how supported projects would contribute to their stated mission therefore provides the best guidance to policymakers who are responsible for deciding whether to spend public funds for those activities.

In 2004, the research and experimentation (R&E) tax credit drew claims of $5.6 billion from firms, a small amount compared with the funds that lawmakers have appropriated for R&D activities. Studies have found that the credit has the desired effect of boosting R&D spending by businesses; however, those studies do not compare the benefits derived from the increase in research and development with the potential benefits from other uses of the forgone revenues. In addition, the results of those studies may be overstated because firms have an incentive to classify as many expenses as possible as credit-eligible research, even if those expenses are not associated with new R&D activities.

(Percentage of gross domestic product)

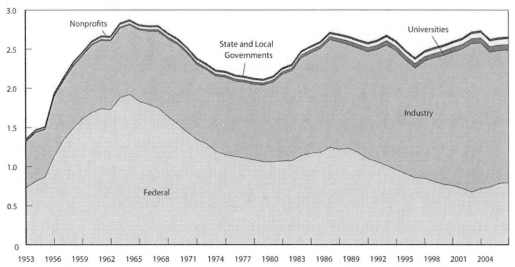

Source: Congressional Budget Office based on National Science Foundation, Division of Science
   Resources Statistics, *National Patterns of R&D Resources* (Arlington, Va., annual series).

Summary Figure 1. U.S. Spending for Research and Development, by Funding Source

(Billions of 2000 dollars)

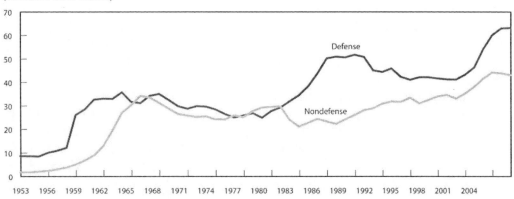

Source: Congressional Budget Office based on *Budget of the United States Government, Fiscal Year
   2008.*

Summary Figure 2. Federal Outlays for Research and Development, by Discretionary Spending
Category

Trends in Federal Support for Research and Development

From 1953 to 2004, real (inflation-adjusted) spending for R&D in the United States rose
at an average annual rate of 4.7 percent, faster than the 3.3 percent average growth of GDP.
As a result, overall R&D expenditures— including public and private spending—climbed

from less than 1.5 percent of GDP in the early 1950s to more than 2.5 percent in 2004 (see Summary Figure 1).

The federal government and industry are the primary sources of funding for research and development in the United States—in 2004 providing $93 billion and $199 billion, respectively. As those figures indicate, industry's share of total R&D funding is the larger; although the federal government's share rose rapidly during the 1 950s and early 1 960s, it has declined significantly since then. Universities and colleges, nonprofit institutions, and state and local governments account for a small share of R&D spending (about $20 billion in 2004, or roughly 6 percent of the national total).

Federal funding for defense and nondefense research and development show different trends. Real federal R&D spending for national defense purposes doubled in the 1980s and then declined in the 1 990s following the end of the Cold War (see Summary Figure 2). From 2000 to 2006, defense-related research and development grew at a real average annual rate of 7.4 percent. Nondefense R&D has increased less rapidly, growing at a real average annual rate of 4.5 percent.

In its appropriated funding of R&D activities, the federal government has expanded its support of basic research more rapidly than its support of applied research (which aims to link scientific knowledge to some practical purpose) or development (which aims to create marketable products). Between 1953 and 2004, federal funding for basic research grew at a real average annual rate of 6.3 percent, compared with rates of 3.5 percent for applied research and 2.2 percent for development. Federal spending for development has had some large swings, mainly because of increased expenditures at various times for space and defense programs (see Summary Figure 3).

Those federal funds tend to go to different entities depending on whether the work involved is research or development. In 2004, universities performed 42 percent of federally funded research but less than 2 percent of development; industry performed 13 percent of federally funded research but 49 percent of development; and the federal government itself performed 22 percent of its own research and 36 percent of its own development.

Federally supported R&D activities are spread across a number of different fields and agencies. The two agencies with the largest R&D programs—the Department of Defense and the National Institutes of Health—together accounted for 73 percent of federal R&D outlays in 2004 (see Summary Figure 4). The agencies that focus on the physical sciences and engineering—the National Science Foundation, the National Aeronautics and Space Administration (NASA), and the Department of Energy— accounted for 19 percent of outlays.

The federal research portfolio covers a broad range of scientific fields. The fields emphasized by lawmakers have changed over time, with the life sciences accounting for an increasing share of federal research spending since the 1990s (see Summary Figure 5). Federal obligations (the government's legally binding commitments that will result in spending) for life sciences research increased at a real average annual rate of 8.2 percent from 1994 to 2004, more than triple the rate of growth of the rest of the federal research portfolio. The rapid rise in federal spending for life sciences research apparently has not discouraged private-sector spending for such activities: R&D spending by pharmaceutical firms also grew rapidly during the 1994–2004 period.[1]

(Billions of 2000 dollars)

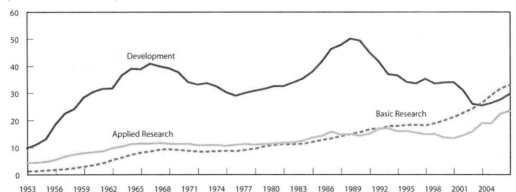

Source: Congressional Budget Office based on National Science Foundation, Division of Science
    Resources Statistics, *National Patterns of R&D Resources* (Arlington, Va., annual series).
Note: Basic research is meant to expand scientific knowledge without regard to commercial
    applications. Applied research seeks to connect scientific knowledge to some practical end.
    Development applies scientific knowledge to the creation of specific marketable products.

Summary Figure 3. Federal Spending for Research and Development, by Type of R&D
(Billions of 2000 dollars)

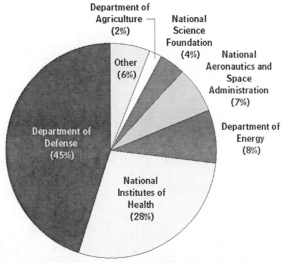

Source: Congressional Budget Office based on National Science Foundation, Division of Science
    Resources Statistics, *Federal Funds for Research and Development: Fiscal Years 2003, 2004, and
    2005* (Arlington, Va.).

Summary Figure 4. Federal R&D Outlays, by Agency, 2004

In addition to supporting research and development directly through appropriated
spending, the federal government provides a tax credit for R&D activities that firms
undertake. First introduced in the United States in 1981, the R&E tax credit lowers the tax bill
of firms that increase their spending for research and development. In general, the credit is
designed to apply to incremental spending—that is, only the R&D funds spent above a base

amount are eligible for the credit, which has three variants, each with a different base. The base amounts are meant to approximate what firms would have spent on research in the absence of the credit.

Since 1994, businesses have claimed credits (expressed in 2000 dollars) totaling as little as $1.5 billion (in 1995) and as much as $7.0 billion (in 2000). Manufacturing firms have claimed the largest share of those credits; however, over time, other sectors, including health care and construction, have accounted for increasing amounts.

Analysis

Empirical studies of past federal support for research, as opposed to all research and development, suggest that the economic returns to that spending have been positive, and on average, similar returns may be expected from more such spending. Even so, measuring the returns from research in general, and from any project in particular, is complicated by several factors: the difficulty of identifying and valuing all the potential uses of research results, the long periods likely between the decision to fund a project and the eventual uses of its findings to create products, and uncertainty about whether useful findings will arise in a specific field at a specific point in time or from any individual project.

Federal Funding of Research and Development

Federally funded R&D may be separated into two broad categories—mission-oriented activities and work that aims to advance the state of scientific and technical knowledge. That distinction may prove useful to policy- makers charged with setting funding levels for R&D programs.

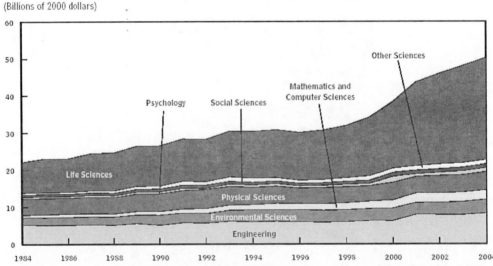

(Billions of 2000 dollars)

Source: Congressional Budget Office based on National Science Foundation, Division of Science Resources Statistics, *Federal Funds for Research and Development: Fiscal Years 2003, 2004, and 2005* and *Science and Engineering Indicators, 2006* (Arlington, Va.).

Summary Figure 5. Federal Obligations for Research, by Field

A large portion of federal support for research and development is undertaken in the service of a governmental mission—such as the development of NASA's space shuttle or of weapons for the Department of Defense. Spending for those purposes for the most part is included in the federally funded development work carried out by industry. A number of studies have found no economic return associated with such spending. Thus, decisions about undertaking those projects may be best guided by considering how the projects' anticipated results might be expected to contribute to the mission at hand, rather than how big their economic returns might be.

Other federal spending for R&D, and especially for research, is often directed at creating new knowledge and finding new applications for technology. That research includes work in a variety of scientific fields and may also cut across disciplines. This second category of support has tended to be the focus of after-the-fact empirical estimates of the rate of return to research—estimates that have been positive despite the difficulties involved in putting a value on the new knowledge.

The Research and Experimentation Tax Credit

Studies of the effectiveness of the United States' R&E tax credit (and of similar policies in other countries) have focused on estimating the additional research and development that the credit stimulates.[2] Those studies have produced a variety of results, many of which have clustered around the finding that a dollar of an R&D tax credit leads firms to spend an additional dollar of their own on research and development. Some studies of the credit in the United States suggest that its effect in inducing R&D spending may be growing over time. One group of researchers found that the tax credit had a less than one-to-one effect on R&D spending in the early 1980s but that after a change in the way the base amount was calculated—a change enacted in the Omnibus Budget Reconciliation Act of 1989—firms spent an additional $2.10 on R&D for each dollar of the credit. The same researchers also found that after 1989, fewer firms were eligible for the credit, but among those that were, a larger share were high-tech firms.

A cautionary note is warranted about those findings, however, because the data may suffer from a relabeling problem that could, over time, lead the credit's effect to be overstated. Firms have an incentive to classify as many expenses as possible as R&D spending to take advantage of the favorable tax treatment, and that incentive grows with the size of the credit. Even if those expenses were related to activities that were not new R&D efforts—just work that was newly classified that way—the activities would be included in the increase in R&D that was apparently spurred by the tax credit, thus overstating the credit's impact.

FEDERAL SUPPORT FOR RESEARCH AND DEVELOPMENT

Investments in research and development (R&D) have increased productivity, boosted economic growth, generated new products and processes, and improved the quality of people's lives.[3] The possibility of profiting from a new product or process frequently leads businesses to invest substantial amounts of money in research and development. However, private investors cannot capture many of the benefits of their R&D spending, as the knowledge it produces may be used by others; consequently, the private sector may not make some investments that have positive social, or economic, returns— gains for society and for the economy as a whole. To address that problem of incentives and encourage more R&D investment, the government uses several policy tools, including appropriated spending for R&D activities, tax preferences for private-sector research and development, and protection of intellectual property through the copyright and patent systems.

Analysts generally regard the government's funding of research and development as a way to partly offset the problems created by the difference between the returns that private parties achieve from their R&D investment—in the form of profits from new products and processes—and the returns that society may derive from those R&D activities. Federal spending has been critical to the funding of basic research (scientific inquiry that has no clear-cut commercial application but is nonetheless valued for the knowledge that results and the potential for future discoveries to grow from it). The tax preferences that policymakers have provided—the treatment of R&D spending as a fully deductible expense that can be subtracted from profits immediately rather than as an investment to be amortized and deducted over time, and the research and experimentation (R&E) tax credit— lower the cost of research and development, thereby increasing firms' after-tax returns on those activities and strengthening the incentives for firms to invest even more in research and development.

In addition, the U.S. patent and copyright systems have features that encourage the private sector to fund R&D activities. Researchers who make a discovery often find it difficult to control who makes use of their work once it becomes public because the knowledge they produce may "spill over" and be used by others. Intellectual property protections, such as patents and copyrights, afford researchers—or, in some cases, the sponsors of research— legal control over the results of their work.[4] Others wishing to make use of those results must secure permission by paying a licensing fee to the patent or copyright holder.

The patent and copyright systems offer some protections against and compensation for others' use of a researcher's results, but they are an imperfect solution to the spillover effects that diminish the incentives for firms to invest in research and development. In some instances, costly delays and court battles over intellectual property protections may ensue, and licensees may not compensate patent holders for the full value of their findings. Moreover, the limitations on the life of a patent may not create strong incentives for firms to invest in research that could have a long path to development. Finally, although patents and copyrights encourage future R&D activities, they also have a cost: deferral of the social benefits that might result from the more immediate and widespread application of currently protected innovations.

This Congressional Budget Office (CBO) study focuses on government-funded research and development— activities carried out in government laboratories or by academic researchers or private firms funded through federal grants or contracts—and tax incentives that encourage firms to perform research. For fiscal year 2007, federal budget authority (the legal authority to incur financial obligations resulting in outlays by the government) for research and development totals $137 billion.[5] Tax incentives for R&D activities are estimated to have cost $9.9 billion in forgone revenues in fiscal year 2006. CBO's analysis discusses trends in those expenditures and examines the recent economics literature that has attempted to evaluate the economic effects of federal R&D programs.

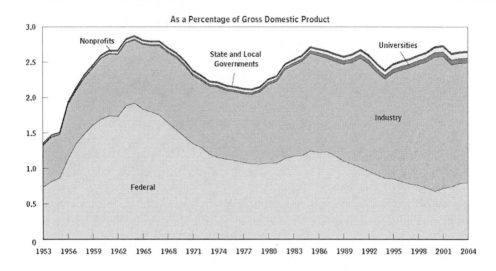

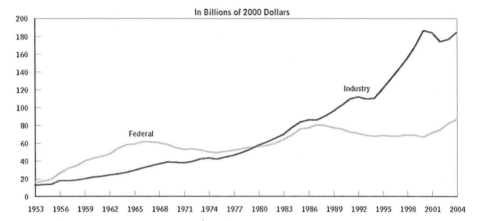

Source: Congressional Budget Office based on National Science Foundation, Division of Science Resources Statistics, *National Patterns of R&D Resources* (Arlington, Va., annual series).

Figure 1. U.S. Spending for Research and Development, by Funding Source

TRENDS IN FUNDING RESEARCH AND DEVELOPMENT

Since the late 1950s, the United States has consistently spent more than 2 percent of its gross domestic product (GDP) for research and development (see the top panel of Figure 1). From 1953 to 2004, real spending for R&D in the United States (that is, spending after an adjustment for the effects of inflation) grew at an average annual rate of 4.7 percent. The federal government and private-sector firms have been the primary sources of that funding. Spending by industry for R&D activities has grown more quickly than spending by the federal government (an average annual rate of 5.4 percent versus 3.5 percent) and has exceeded federal funding since 1980 (see the bottom panel of Figure 1). In 2004, industry's R&D spending reached $199 billion (in current dollars), and the federal government, according to the National Science Foundation (NSF), spent more than $93 billion. Other sources of R&D funding are small by comparison.[6]

The divergence between federal and industrial research and development was particularly stark in the 1990s, when real federal spending for R&D declined by an average of 1.3 percent per year while industry-sponsored R&D expanded by an average of 6.2 percent annually. Other countries have also expanded their R&D activities in recent years (see Box 1).

Historically, a large part of federal R&D spending has been devoted to agencies that have uniquely public missions, in particular national defense. Although the private sector performs much of that work under contract, the government directs such mission-oriented R&D because it, rather than private customers, is the ultimate consumer of any new technologies that might result.

Federal spending for research and development has at times accounted for a substantial portion of the government's discretionary spending (spending controlled by appropriations). Following the Soviet Union's launch of Sputnik in 1957, the United States' focus on its space program and the sciences in general led to a boost in nondefense R&D activities. As a result, by the mid-1960s, those activities accounted for 25 percent of nondefense discretionary outlays, a share that tapered off through the 1970s to remain at 10 percent to 11 percent (see Figure 2).[7] In terms of defense spending, R&D activities accounted for an increasing share in the 1980s; since then, though, their share of total defense outlays has held steady at about 14 percent.[8]

BOX 1. INTERNATIONAL RESEARCH AND DEVELOPMENT ACTIVITY

As scientific papers are published, patents are approved, and products emerge from development, the knowledge embodied in them is made available to scientific and research communities worldwide. U.S. researchers, firms, and consumers benefit from research and development (R&D) performed elsewhere in the world, and people abroad benefit from R&D activities in this country. That global diffusion of new knowledge increases the potential, both here and abroad, for substantial social returns—greater economic growth, new products and processes, improvements in the quality of people's lives—from investments in research and development.

The global context in which the U.S. government and industry provide support for R&D projects may have implications for how much the government should be spending on R&D, for how that spending is allocated between research and development, and for the mix of scientific disciplines that it is appropriate to fund.

In 2004, R&D spending worldwide totaled roughly $900 billion. More than one-third of the activities supported by those funds took place in the United States, more than one-eighth were performed in Japan, and more than one-tenth occurred in China.[1] R&D activity is expanding rapidly in Asia: From 1998 to 2004, spending for research and development in China grew at a real (inflation-adjusted) annual rate of 21 percent while R&D expenditures in South Korea rose at a real annual rate of 10 percent. An April 2006 press release by the Organisation for Economic Co-operation and Development recently predicted that in PPP terms, China in 2006 would overtake Japan in R&D expenditures. Using the official exchange rate, the Chinese government in its own press release (in January 2007) claimed a smaller amount of spending.

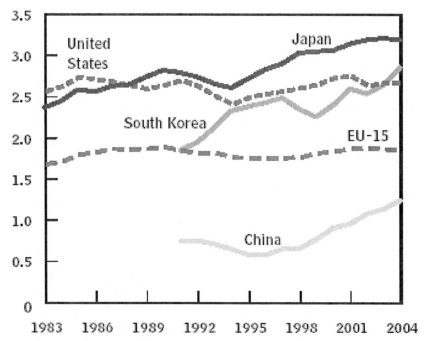

Source: Except where otherwise noted, the data presented in this figure and in the rest of the box are taken from Organisation for Economic Co-operation and Development, *Main Science and Technology Indicators*, vol. 26, release 2 (Paris, 2007), accessed through the SourceOECD database.

Note: EU-15 = the 15 European Union member countries in 1996.

R&D as a Percentage of Gross Domestic Product

Although the expansion of R&D in China and South Korea partly reflects the overall growth that the two economies are experiencing, it is also a sign of the increasing importance of science and technology in those nations: Spending for R&D during the 1998–2004 period rose at a faster rate than income in both countries (see the figure to the left). Some analysts have questioned whether the United States can maintain the size and quality of its scientific and engineering workforce in the future if recent trends in the growth of overseas R&D investment continue. A large portion of the U.S. workforce is foreign born, and as more R&D opportunities open up in their home countries, fewer such workers may choose to immigrate to the United States, and those already here may decide to return home.[2]

The source of R&D funding and the composition of such expenditures vary among countries. In the United States and Europe, governments fund a relatively larger share of research and development than they do in Asia, where industry-financed R&D is more prevalent (it accounts for 75 percent of all R&D in Japan and South Korea; see the table above). Compared with other nations, the United States directs a far larger portion of its government R&D expenditures toward defense-related projects—nearly double the amount of the second largest share (the United Kingdom's 31 percent). Basic research is emphasized more in the United States and Europe than in Asia, perhaps reflecting the government's larger role in financing R&D in those regions.

As other countries expand their R&D activities, the knowledge flowing into the United States from those projects may increase. The number of foreign scientific publications has climbed rapidly: Between 1996 and 2003, scientific articles arising from U.S.-based researchers increased by 5 percent, those from researchers in the EU-15 (the 15 European Union member countries in 1996) increased by 14 percent, and those from the rest of the world increased by 24 percent.[3] In addition, improvements in communications technologies make it easier for researchers of all nations to use findings from that research to advance their own work and may open up new possibilities for cross-border collaborations. U.S.-based researchers, for example, have increased their international collaborations: In 2003, 25 percent of articles with at least one U.S.-based author had an international coauthor, compared with only 18 percent in 1996.[4]

Composition of Research and Development

Country	Government-Financed Share of R&D, 2004	Defense Share of Government-Financed R&D, 2005	Basic Research Share of Total R&D, 2004[a]
United States	31.0	57.1	19
EU-15	35.1 (2003)	13.5	n.a.
Japan	18.1	4.0	12
South Korea	23.1	13.3	15
China	26.6	n.a.	6

Note: EU-15 = the 15 European Union member countries in 1996; n.a. = not available.

Data on basic research for the EU-15 as a whole were not available. However, as an example of those nations' investment, in 2004, basic research accounted for 24 percent of all R&D in France.

[1] In purchasing power parity, or PPP, terms (a PPP exchange rate is calculated by comparing the purchase price of a given basket of goods in e–ach country's currency), the $900 billion consists of spending of $726 billion in countries that are members of the Organisation for Economic Co-operation and Development (OECD); $143 billion in China and seven other non-OECD countries that the OECD tracks; $24 billion in India (according to OECD's *Science, Technology, and Industry Outlook 2006*, Paris, 2006, p. 42); and roughly $30 billion in other countries, based on spending in earlier years reported by the UNESCO Institute for Statistics (see "Statistics on Research and Development," May 2006, available at http://stats.uis.unesco.org/ReportFolders/reportfolders.aspx).

[2] For a discussion of that issue, see, for example, Richard Freeman, *Does Globalization of the Scientific/Engineering Workforce Threaten U.S. Economic Leadership?* NBER Working Paper No. 11457 (Cambridge, Mass.: National Bureau of Economic Research, June 2005).

[3] National Science Foundation, Science and Engineering Indicators 2006, vol. 2 (Arlington, Va., 2006), Appendix Tables 5-44 and 5-45. Those data reflect fractional counts; for example, an article that had two authors, one in a U.S. institution and one in France, would contribute 0.5 articles to the U.S. count and 0.5 articles to the EU count.

[4] Ibid., Appendix Tables 5-48 and 5-49.

In many cases, the entity that actually carries out an R&D project differs from the entity that provides the project's funding. Federal laboratories, universities, other nonprofit organizations, and industry all perform research and development that is funded by the federal government. And the R&D activities funded by the private sector may be outsourced to many of those same entities. Of the research and development performed in the United States, industry accounts for the vast majority—about 70 percent—a share that has been maintained with some consistency over the past 50 years (see Figure 3). However, firms now fund a much more substantial share—89 percent—of that R&D themselves.[9] Nonprofit organizations and federally funded research and development centers (FFRDCs) have seen little change in the share of total R&D they perform.[10]

Over the past 50 years, there has been a gradual shift in where research and development is performed outside of industry, with activities moving from the federal government's intramural programs (work performed at government labs by government employees) to universities. In 2004, the federal government conducted 8 percent of the research and development that took place in the United States, less than half the share it performed in the early 1950s. In contrast, universities and colleges have steadily increased their share of R&D activities, boosting it from 5 percent in the 1950s to 14 percent in 2004.

The sources of funding for industrial, intramural, and academic R&D have also changed over that period. In 2004, the government funded about 10 percent of industrial R&D; by contrast, in the late 1950s and early 1960s, that share peaked at more than 50 percent (see the top panel of Figure 4). Federal funding for intramural and university R&D has continued to increase in real terms over the same period (see the middle and bottom panels of Figure 4). From 1954 to 2004, federal funding for university-performed research and development grew more rapidly than did federal funding for R&D performed by others, rising at a real annual rate of 6.8 percent (compared with 3 percent for intramural government research and development) and now accounting for about 60 percent of university R&D.

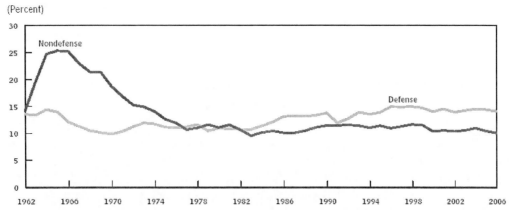

Source: Congressional Budget Office based on *Budget of the United States Government, Fiscal Year 2008: Historical Tables* (2007).

Note: Discretionary outlays constitute spending controlled by appropriations.

Figure 2. Federal Spending for Defense and Nondefense Research and Development as a Percentage of Corresponding Discretionary Outlays

(As a share of total R&D performed)

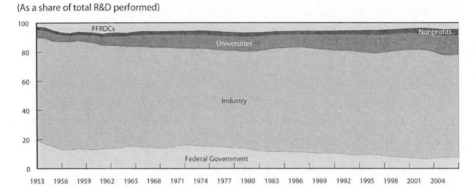

Source: Congressional Budget Office based on National Science Foundation, Division of Science
 Resources Statistics, *National Patterns of R&D Resources* (Arlington, Va., annual series).
Note: FFRDC = federally funded research and development center.

Figure 3. U.S. Research and Development, by Performer (As a share of total R&D performed)

NSF's estimates of government spending for research and development do not include
the revenues forgone as a result of the tax incentives provided to encourage the private sector
to perform more research. In 2004, firms claimed a total of nearly $5.6 billion under the R&E
tax credit.[11] Unlike appropriated federal spending for R&D, which has generally trended
upward, claims for the R&E tax credit have varied, probably in response to revisions in tax
law governing the credit and changes in economic conditions.

ASSESSING THE FEDERAL GOVERNMENT'S ROLE IN RESEARCH AND DEVELOPMENT

The difference between private financial returns to R&D activities and the social benefits
that arise from such work is often used to justify federal support for research and
development. Firms undertake R&D that promises the largest likely profit, which is not
necessarily the work that produces the greatest benefit to society. As a result, neither the
scope nor the amount of R&D initiated by the private sector—even the projects of consortia
formed by private-sector firms to conduct collective research—is likely to provide the
maximum benefits to society. Governments thus fund research and development activities
directly to supplement those private-sector activities but face the challenge of making
investments that will produce the most socially beneficial outcomes.

For both types of federal support for R&D—appropriated spending and tax incentives—
determining the "right" amount is difficult. Perhaps the biggest hurdle is measuring the
returns to R&D because it can be difficult to trace the path that an R&D discovery takes over
time, to gauge the value added at each step along the way to a final product, and to consider
what might have occurred in the absence of that discovery. In addition, policymakers must
decide not only how much to spend on R&D in total (and therefore what they will not be
spending to support other governmental priorities) but also how to allocate that funding
among fields of scientific study, agencies, constituencies, and missions.

(Billions of 2000 dollars)

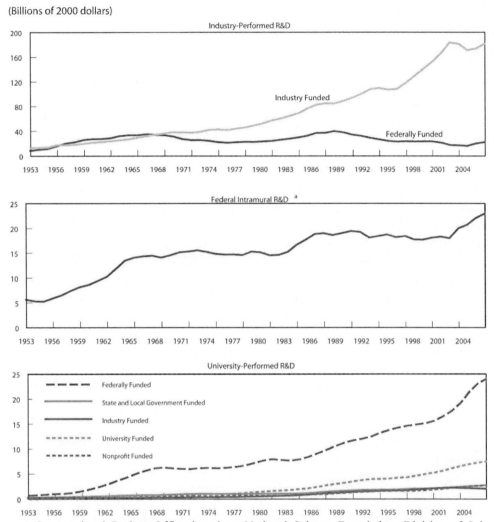

Source: Congressional Budget Office based on National Science Foundation, Division of Science
   Resources Statistics, *National Patterns of R&D Resources* (Arlington, Va., annual series).
a. Funded entirely by the federal government and performed in federal facilities by federal employees.

Figure 4. U.S. Spending for Research and Development, by Performer and Funding Source

Investment in Research and Development by the Private Sector

Private firms may invest less in R&D activities than is socially desirable because they
recognize that they will be unable to keep the full financial benefit of their research
investment for themselves.[12] Studies have documented that private firms face difficulties in
making exclusive use of their R&D and especially of their research results.[13] To reap the
rewards from its investment in R&D, a private firm might have to keep its results closely
guarded for some time until it was ready to put them to use in a product. Once a product is
marketed, the knowledge that emerged from the firm's earlier research and development work
is likely to become clear to others, often through disclosures in patents or reverse engineering,
potentially allowing others who did not invest in the research to benefit from it.

For society as a whole, however, the cost to share the knowledge generated by a firm's R&D, and in particular by its research (for example, through publication of the results), is usually less than the potential social benefits to be gained from sharing that information. Society can often benefit if new information is shared immediately because other firms with a more immediate use for the knowledge will have access to it and can then avoid costly duplicative research and development. Further, because knowledge persists even after it has been put to use, its utilization by one party does nothing to prevent another from also using it. One set of research findings could thus be used simultaneously by a variety of firms and other researchers.

In recognition of the value of R&D activities in general and the limited incentive for individual firms to conduct research in particular, industry and governments have tried to increase investment in research.[14] Private firms may initiate research joint ventures or similar collaborative research arrangements, in which they coordinate their efforts and share the results. A theoretical model has shown that if such coordinated arrangements maximize the total profits of all firms and avoid duplicating R&D activities, they can benefit the firms and produce substantial social benefits.[15] Coordination of R&D activities may improve firms' ability to secure the returns to their efforts, increase R&D spending, and reduce the risk of the investment for each participating firm, all of which would improve efficiency (that is, produce even better results from the resources that are being used).[16] However, if firms coordinate their R&D activities, they may also reduce competition by giving participants in such ventures more power in the marketplace, erecting substantial barriers to new firms that wish to enter the market, or promoting other types of anticompetitive coordination among member firms.

Research versus Development

Research—especially basic research—generally produces larger external effects, or spillovers, than development does, suggesting that the government's involvement in such research may lead to more spillovers than those generated by its support of development activities. The purpose of *basic research* (for example, physics research on the properties of elementary particles) is to make discoveries that expand scientific knowledge, even though commercial applications of that knowledge may be far in the future and not readily identifiable. *Applied research* (for example, the discovery of new materials for drug delivery) is a step closer to commercialization because it seeks to connect scientific knowledge to some practical purpose. *Development* applies scientific knowledge to the creation of specific marketable products.

The private sector has more of an incentive to invest in development activities than in basic or applied research, for several reasons: the uncertainty surrounding the results of research, the long time horizon needed to commercialize research findings, the lack of connection of research in many instances to the current demand for products, or some combination of those factors.[17] And even if all of those problems could be addressed, under-investment in research by the private sector might still occur, because the returns to research for private firms, unlike the social returns, do not encompass the benefits that research might bring to others who could also put that knowledge to use.

(Billions of 2000 dollars)

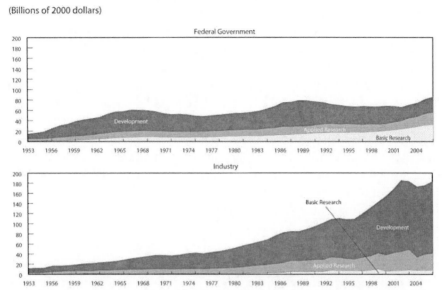

Source: Congressional Budget Office based on National Science Foundation, Division of Science
Resources Statistics, *National Patterns of R&D Resources* (Arlington, Va., annual series).

Note: Basic research is meant to expand scientific knowledge without regard to commercial
applications. Applied research seeks to connect scientific knowledge to some practical end.
Development applies scientific knowledge to the creation of specific marketable products.

Figure 5. U.S. Spending for Research and Development, by Funding Source and Type of R&D

(Billions of 2000 dollars)

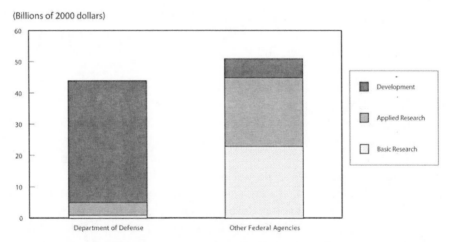

Source: Congressional Budget Office based on National Science Foundation, Division of Science
Resources Statistics, *Survey of Federal Funds for Research and Development: FY2003, 2004, and
2005.*

Notes: Obligations are legally binding commitments by the federal government that result in outlays.
Basic research is meant to expand scientific knowledge without regard to commercial applications.
Applied research seeks to connect scientific knowledge to some practical end. Development
applies scientific knowledge to the creation of specific marketable products.

Figure 6. Federal Obligations for Research and Development in the Department of Defense and Other
Federal Agencies, by Type of R&D, 2004

Whether financed by the public or private sector, research and development are characterized by the same set of external effects. But in contrast to private-sector firms, which are motivated primarily by profits, the government may take into account a number of factors, including the potential for spillovers, in choosing which research projects to support. The different objectives of the public and private sectors are evident in their patterns of spending for R&D (see Figure 5). Development activities accounted for 77 percent of industry's total R&D budget in 2004, more than twice the share of development in the federal government's R&D budget. If the Department of Defense's (DoD's) R&D spending was excluded, federal obligations—the government's legally binding commitments to spend money—for development in 2004 would account for only 11 percent of total nondefense R&D obligations, whereas the share of basic research would rise to 46 percent and that of applied research to 43 percent (see Figure 6). In contrast, the vast majority of DoD's R&D spending occurs in the development phase of projects.[18]

Questions about the relative emphasis on research and development in the federal government's spending prompted a committee of the National Academy of Sciences, in a 1995 report, to suggest the concept of a federal science and technology (FS&T) budget that would reflect the extent of the federal government's funding for investments that increased the stock of knowledge and led to new technologies and applications. The committee's report described the FS&T budget as total federal R&D spending minus funding for advanced systems development in the Department of Defense, the Department of Energy, and the National Aeronautics and Space Administration (NASA).[19] The Office of Management and Budget (OMB) reported the first FS&T budget in fiscal year 2000 ($42 billion); in 2006, the FS&T budget totaled $60 billion. According to OMB, it includes "nearly all of Federal basic research, over 80 percent of Federal applied research, and about half of Federal non-defense development."[20] Given that development accounts for only a small portion of R&D funds outside of defense-related agencies, the FS&T budget closely tracks the sum of federally funded basic and applied research (see Figure 7).

The distribution of patents among the private sector, academia, and the government further reveals their differing roles in the United States' R&D arena.[21] Universities are granted a small portion of the patents issued by the U.S. Patent and Trademark Office (PTO) to people and organizations in this country, which reflects those institutions' focus on basic research (see Figure 8). (The BayhDole Act of 1980 granted universities intellectual property control over innovations that developed out of federally funded research.) The number of such domestically owned patents that are granted annually to universities has been increasing, however, rising from fewer than 2,000 in the early 1990s to more than 3,000 since 1998.[22]

The growth of patenting and licensing by universities has raised concerns that academic research is moving away from pure science and toward work that has potential commercial applications, yet few empirical studies have investigated that issue. One study found that researchers who published reports of their work in basic-science journals were more likely to disclose their inventions than were those who published in journals that did not emphasize basic research.[23] Another study found that the growing importance of biomedical research has been a driving force in the growth of the number of patents and licenses granted to universities.[24]

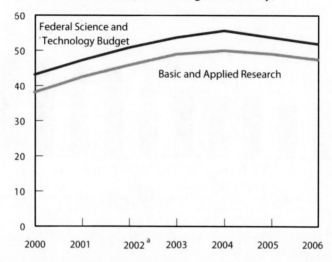

(Billions of 2000 dollars of budget authority)

Source: Congressional Budget Office based on *Budget of the United States Government, Fiscal Years 2003, 2004, 2005, 2006, 2007, and 2008: Analytical Perspectives.*

Notes: According to the Office of Management and Budget, the federal science and technology budget covers budget authority for nearly all federally suported basic research, more than 80 percent of applied research, and about half of nondefense development.

Because this figure reflects budget authority (the authority provided in law to incur financial obligations that will result in government outlays), data points may differ from the expenditures reported elsewhere in the study.

Basic research is meant to expand scientific knowledge without regard to commercial applications. Applied research seeks to connect scientific knowledge to some practical end.

a. The amounts reported for 2002 appear as estimates in the President's budget request for 2004. For all other years, amounts are the budget authority reported in the corresponding budget requests.

Figure 7. The Federal Science and Technology Budget

The bulk of the domestically owned U.S. patents granted each year go to "non-federal, non-university" organizations, according to the Patent and Trademark Office.

Those organizations, which include industrial firms, non-profit institutions, and state and local governments, accounted for approximately 63,000 to 72,000 patents annually between 1998 and 2003, or more than 75 percent of the domestically owned U.S. patents granted each year since 1998.[25] Patenting activity related to the federal government's R&D efforts occurs largely through DoD, which conducts most federally funded development (see Figure 9).[26]

Government Action

In its selection of public research and development projects, the federal government faces at least two types of potential shortcomings when it tries to efficiently address differences between the private and social returns to research and development. One problem arises from the possibility that federal agencies may not design their R&D programs in the same way that private firms would have designed theirs if private returns matched social returns. The other set of potential problems centers on the criteria that are used to choose which R&D projects the government will fund.

(Thousands)

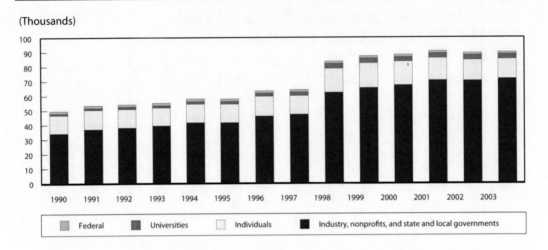

Source: Congressional Budget Office based on data from the U.S. Patent and Trademark Office, Patent
    Technology Monitoring Division.
Note: Utility patents are those granted for new or improved products or processes

Figure 8. Domestically Owned U.S. Utility Patent Grants

Much of the justification for the federal government's R&D spending rests on the notion
that the government, in its decisionmaking, can take into account the total social return that
might be generated by a specific research project but a private firm will invest only in
research that adds to its profitability. In the pursuit of profits, firms will tend to design even
their most basic research projects with a future product in mind. In contrast, federally funded
government and academic scientists might be motivated by factors other than profit, such as
opportunities for academic publications based on their research findings. Correspondingly,
those scientists might not design their research so that their findings can be easily adopted by
the private sector for its purposes, which in some cases might require firms to carry out
duplicative work to develop commercial products.

A peer-review selection process for public research, although not perfect, is often held up
as the best way to ensure that scientific merit is the basis for deciding whether to fund a
research proposal.[27] Such a system is used to select a substantial amount of public research
for funding (including much of the research funded by NSF and the National Institutes of
Health, or NIH); it seems to offer the best chance for choosing an efficient set of projects that
are most likely to advance scientific knowledge.[28] However, some observers argue that
relying on peer review may favor conservative projects (providing only incremental progress
in expanding existing knowledge) over pioneering or interdisciplinary work.[29] Others have
noted that slow-growing funding for some scientific fields, the constraints some agencies
place on the length of time research may take, and the high risk of failure are all factors in the
federal government's funding of fewer highly uncertain but potentially groundbreaking
research projects.[30]

Equity or distributional concerns may also influence decisions about funding. Concerns
about geographic fairness in allocating federal funds may motivate some awards for R&D
projects, either through programs like the Experimental Program to Stimulate Competitive
Research (EPSCoR) at NSF or as directed by legislation.[31] In addition, projects that attract
national attention may receive funding regardless of their scientific merit.[32] In other instances,

spending for R&D projects may become self- perpetuating, creating constituencies that expect continued financial support and that are willing to devote resources to secure that support outside of a peer-review process.

EVALUATING THE RESULTS OF FEDERAL FUNDING FOR RESEARCH AND DEVELOPMENT

Two rationales are typically offered in support of the federal government's involvement in the nation's R&D activity. One is that some federal spending for research and development is essential to support a uniquely governmental undertaking (such as national defense). The other arises from the consideration that firms in the private sector have insufficient incentives to finance all of the R&D that is socially beneficial.

Yet in the end, what result is the $137 billion in federal R&D spending for fiscal year 2007 likely to produce? No single answer stands out, but the following generalizations can be made from the economics literature that has considered public support for research and development:

(Percent)

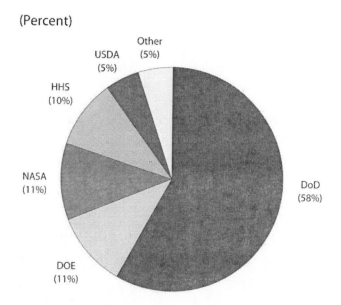

Source: Congressional Budget Office based on information from the U.S. Patent and Trademark Office, Patent Technology Monitoring Division.

Notes: During the 1990–2003 period, a total of 14,388 patents were issued to the federal government.
     DoD = Department of Defense; DOE = Department of Energy; NASA = National Aeronautics and Space Administration; HHS = Department of Health and Human Services; USDA = Department of Agriculture.
     Utility patents are those granted for new or improved products or processes.

Figure 9. Federally Owned U.S. Utility Patent Grants, 1990 to 2003

In the case of unambiguously public missions, such as national defense or space exploration, the returns to public R&D spending come as contributions to the fulfillment of that mission. Although mission-oriented projects may also produce spin-off technologies that are not linked to a project's original goals, such byproducts are inherently difficult to anticipate for any given R&D activity.

Federal spending in support of basic research over the years has, on average, had a significantly positive return, according to the best available research. That outcome is indicated in studies of the social rate of return to academic research, studies of the increasingly important role of academic research in businesses' patenting and research activity, and studies of patent and scientific journal citations, all of which suggest that academic research in primary scientific disciplines (for example, chemistry or physics) has broad and sometimes unpredictable effects across a wide variety of commercial applications.

Returns to the federal government's support of life sciences research are generally estimated to be substantial. However, those calculations are based on a somewhat different metric than that used to estimate the return to all federally supported applied and basic research, making comparisons with other disciplines difficult.[33] Spending for life sciences research is currently the largest and, since the mid-1990s, the fastest-growing area of federally supported research. That emphasis has altered the balance of scientific fields in the federal research portfolio.

Those gross generalizations are difficult to apply as guidance for spending and policy decisions across budget functions, agencies' budgets, and appropriations subcommittee jurisdictions. Any individual research undertaking or particular set of projects may produce a wide range of outcomes and returns, even though, on average, the economic returns to federal research are expected to exceed their costs. Measurement problems present another obstacle: It can be difficult to trace the path of a research finding over time and to consider what might have occurred in the absence of that finding. In addition, much of federal spending for R&D is mission oriented, and those resources are included in measures of the share of GDP that federally funded R&D accounts for and the aggregate dollar value of those activities. Thus, those measures are not indicative of the federal resource commitment to projects with the potential to produce returns that are substantial for society as a whole but that a private firm would not undertake because it could not capture enough of the returns generated by the project.

Mission-Oriented R&D

Whether a particular public-sector R&D program should be considered mission oriented and thereby justified because of its support of a uniquely governmental undertaking is not always easy to determine. R&D activities are clearly mission oriented in cases in which federal agencies are the sole customer for particular goods and services and in which those agencies tend to support R&D activities to develop and improve those goods and services. For defense R&D, as an example, the funding of development falls primarily to the government, because it is the government that produces and "consumes" the final good—national defense. Beyond national defense, however, less agreement exists about where to draw the line between R&D that is mission oriented and R&D that addresses the difference between social and private returns and the weak incentives that firms have to finance R&D.

Some research and development related to space exploration and health care might be included in a more expansive definition of mission-oriented R&D. NASA, for example, might pursue R&D activities to accomplish scientific and exploration objectives for its space missions. Disease-specific research and development supported by NIH is another such example.

With the government as the primary consumer, spending for mission-oriented R&D (such as national defense) has a different pattern from other federal R&D spending. Defense R&D spending is heavily concentrated on the development end, accounting for more than 87 percent of DoD's total R&D obligations in 2004.[34] That emphasis stands in contrast to the research and development funded by nondefense government agencies: They direct only a small portion of their spending for R&D to development and instead concentrate on basic and applied research, leaving development work to the private sector, which will ultimately produce and sell the final goods.

Despite the questions that may arise about whether certain federal R&D activities are mission oriented, methods are available to inform decisions about those undertakings. Such choices are best rooted in a consideration of how the R&D project and its expected results contribute to the overall objective that an agency is pursuing. Although mission-oriented R&D can and does produce development-worthy spin-off technologies, those byproducts are unknown at the start of an endeavor and, for the purposes of decisionmaking, difficult to anticipate.[35] Studies of all federally funded R&D—including its large mission-oriented component—have not found evidence of economic returns associated with that spending.[36]

Basic and Applied Research

Federal spending for nondefense R&D does not generally have the same unambiguously governmental mission behind it that defense R&D does (despite the fact that the "mission" of some agencies—for example, the National Science Foundation—is research itself). Instead, the non-mission-oriented R&D activities that the government supports address the lack—or insufficiency—of private-sector investment. Basic and applied research are more likely than development to fall into that category.

Accordingly, the federal science and technology budget may be a good indicator of the extent of non-missionoriented research and development, given that basic and applied research account for the bulk of the spending that the budget reports. However, the information offers little help in assessing the returns from R&D, which may vary widely from project to project.

In addition to distinguishing between research and development, it may be important for policymakers setting funding priorities and analysts studying the impact of that funding to be able to differentiate between basic and applied research. Although NSF and the Organisation for Economic Co-operation and Development (OECD) have published consistent definitions of the two kinds of research, a study has shown that neither scientists nor policymakers have a uniform understanding of the concept of basic research.[37] Yet despite their lack of agreement on definitions, many of those scientists note that funders of R&D are paying increasing attention to the applicability of research.[38] An earlier study warns that such an emphasis on applied work at the expense of research in pursuit of new knowledge and concepts could slow the pace of both scientific advancement and its application.[39] That blurring of the line between basic and applied research might present another obstacle to obtaining estimates of the returns to federal spending for research.

Academic Research as a Proxy for the Use of Federally Funded Research

Universities perform a substantial share of federally funded research—in 2004, 57 percent of basic and 20 percent of applied research (see Figure 10).[40] Analysts who focus on federally funded research often rely on the returns to academic research as a proxy for federally funded research returns. Reports of research findings in scientific publications are typically attributed to the author or investigator and his or her institution rather than to a study's funding source. Tracking citations to those publications can provide insight into how those research findings are put to use.

Nevertheless, measuring the rate of return to public research is a difficult endeavor. Although such returns are held to be positive by a broad consensus of analysts, their effects cannot be clearly traced through the economy. Thus, economists have devised other ways to assess the value of public research.

Survey-Based Studies. One segment of the economics literature that studies public research has relied on surveys of the private sector that inquire about how industry uses academic research. A 1985 survey of 76 firms served as the basis for one study that estimated an average rate of return to academic research of 28 percent.[41] That finding was based on firms' reports that without the previous 15 years of academic research, they would have faced delays of at least a year in their introduction of 11 percent of new products or their implementation of 9 percent of new production processes. To arrive at the estimated 28 percent average rate of return, researchers compared the value of the sales of new products and the process cost savings that would have been lost without the earlier spending on academic research.[42] The study emphasized that the 28 percent figure is an average rate of return on the total amount spent on academic research in the past and avoided predicting the return that would result from any increase in funding for academic research.[43]

A later study is based on a broader 1994 survey of U.S.- owned firms.[44] It offers no estimate of returns to public research but instead recounts how industry R&D makes use of public research, which in the study includes that performed at both universities and government laboratories. The sample of more than 1,200 manufacturing firms revealed that firms did not find public research to be an important source of new ideas for their R&D projects. However, more than a third of the firms reported using public research results— research findings, prototypes, and new instruments—in their own R&D activities. In addition, the study found that firms in different industries vary in their reliance on public research. The pharmaceutical industry, for example, reported much more intensive use of public research than is the average among other industries.

Citations to Academic Research. Other studies have used patents and the scientific literature to track how industry uses the results of academic science. A recent paper compares the effects of publications by academic and industrial researchers on the scientific output of industrial firms—that is, the published papers of industry scientists.[45] When weighted by each sector's accumulated spending for research, academic research was found to have a larger influence than industrial research on the scientific output of researchers in industry. In addition, the study, which was limited to the impact of basic research, found that academic research had larger spillover effects than industrial research had—which suggests that firms may perform more narrowly focused basic research than university researchers conduct, leading to fewer spillovers.

The study does not discuss the relationship between published industrial research and firms' product development. In the case of R&D that relates more directly to the products and processes being generated, firms may require researchers to keep the results of such activities confidential. If that is so, the published work of industrial researchers may be a poor proxy for estimating the value of academic research to industry.

Patent citations to the academic literature are another way of assessing the use of academic research by industry. Studies have noted a sharp increase from the mid-1980s to the 1990s in the rate at which patents cite the academic science literature, an increase that outstrips growth in the number of patents granted, in real expenditures on R&D, and in the output of scientific papers. One study considers a number of possible explanations for the increase in the citation rate;[46] one important impetus appears to be the relatively strong growth of patenting in the biomedical fields, with their traditionally strong links between academic research and industrial activity. The study also finds evidence of a change in the way firms invent new products and processes, suggesting that knowledge spillovers from academic research grew stronger in the 1990s.

Does Public R&D Crowd Out Private R&D?

One concern about governmental support for research and development is that public R&D may crowd out R&D by the private sector. However, statistical data suggest that over-all, firms' spending for private R&D increases in response to federal R&D spending.[47] In specific cases, the government may have funded some R&D activities that the private sector would otherwise have financed, but identifying the instances in which such crowding out has occurred is difficult. It is probably more likely to happen in areas in which potentially valuable commercial applications of government-funded research and development can be identified.

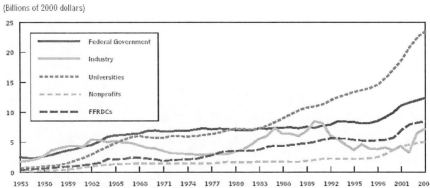

Source: Congressional Budget Office based on National Science Foundation, Division of Science
   Resources Statistics, *National Patterns of R&D Resources* (Arlington, Va., annual series).
Note: FFRDC = federally funded research and development center.

Figure 10. Federal Spending for Research, by Performer

An indirect form of crowding out may occur if increases in federal R&D spending cause the demand for workers in a particular field of scientific inquiry to rise. Greater demand for research scientists could lead to an increase in salaries—and thus in firms' labor costs.[48]

Salaries may be more likely to rise when federal funding is growing at a fast pace. Between 1997 and 2003, when NIH's funding climbed rapidly, the rate of employment for holders of doctorates in the biological, health, and life sciences declined slightly, just as it did for doctoral-level scientists overall. Meanwhile, the median salary for such workers in the life sciences grew at a real average annual rate of 2.2 percent, faster than the 1.9 percent rate for similar workers in the physical sciences but slower than the growth of salaries for those with doctorates in engineering, computer science, and math.[49]

One recent study examines the effects of different types of government funding of R&D on the amount that firms themselves spend on such activities.[50] In a sample of 17 OECD countries between 1981 and 1996, the study found that when firms received federal R&D funds, they were induced to spend, on average, 70 cents of their own money on R&D for each dollar of government funding. The study also found that if the government-funded R&D was more oriented toward defense, that complementary effect diminished, probably because defense-related R&D may lead to fewer spillover effects or because security concerns may make it difficult to use the work in civilian applications.

Other findings from the same study include the following:

Government-funded university R&D had a positive effect on industrial R&D spending after analysts controlled for defense R&D activities.

Intramural government research was not clearly found either to stimulate or crowd out industrial R&D spending. One explanation for that result is that businesses may have needed more time than the study allowed to adapt findings from government-supported R&D activities to their own endeavors.

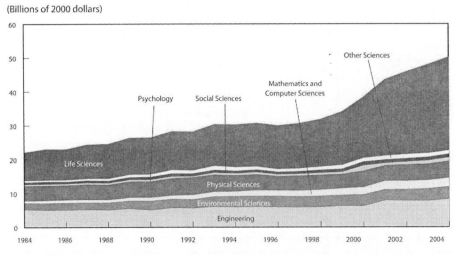

(Billions of 2000 dollars)

Source: Congressional Budget Office based on National Science Foundation, Division of Science Resources Statistics, *Federal Funds for Research and Development: Fiscal Years 2003, 2004, and 2005* and *Science and Engineering Indicators, 2006* (Arlington, Va.).

Figure 11. Federal Obligations for Research, by Field

The Shift in the Federal Research Portfolio

The mix of research supported by the federal government has changed in recent years. Starting in the late 1990s, policy-makers doubled funding to the National Institutes of Health, which left the government's research portfolio much more concentrated in the life sciences.[51] From 1984 to 2004, the life sciences saw their share of federal research obligations increase from 38 percent to 55 percent (see Figure 11). Between 1997 and 2004, real federal research obligations for the life sciences grew at an average annual rate of 11 percent, compared with 3.9 percent for all other research areas.[52] Funding for research in engineering and the physical sciences (including astronomy, chemistry, and physics) grew slowly, rising at annual rates of 5 percent and 2 percent, respectively.

That trend has prompted calls for a renewed emphasis on engineering and the physical sciences in federal research spending. Under recent proposals, increases in federal funding for research in the physical sciences and engineering would be accelerated, much like the growth that occurred in NIH's budget. Under President Bush's American Competitiveness Initiative, the research budget of the National Science Foundation and other agencies that focus on the physical sciences and engineering would double by 2016.[53] Similar action, with a particular emphasis on basic research, was recommended in a report from the National Academies of Sciences and Engineering and the Institute of Medicine.[54]

The shift to increased funding for the life sciences highlights another question that arises in decisionmaking about federal funding for R&D: not just how much to spend but on what types of research. The increasing emphasis on the life sciences in the federal research portfolio finds some support in the high returns to medical research that some economists have found.

In the literature on the effects of medical research, some recent studies have attempted to estimate the value of improvements in health and in life expectancy that result from the new treatments and knowledge that such research has produced.[55] One study suggests that the value of improvements in life expectancy is large.[56] Another agrees that the amounts spent on medical research are small in comparison with the value of the longer lives and improved quality of life that results, but it suggests that determining the returns to medical research is not simply a matter of comparing the benefits with the cost of the actual research performed.[57] If a particular piece of medical research leads to large enough increases in health care costs, the study cautions, there may in fact be a negative return to that research, especially in a health care system dominated by third-party payers.[58]

A substantial related literature examines the social benefits (including direct and indirect cost savings and improvements in people's health and life expectancy) that follow the implementation of break-through treatments for particular diseases.[59] (Such benefits would include direct savings in the cost of health care, indirect savings resulting from a healthier workforce, and any commercial developments that followed the medical research.) The focus in those studies on a specific medical condition may make the problem of estimating returns to research more tractable, but the studies' narrow scope limits the ability to generalize their results.

Box 2. Federal Support for Graduate Students in Science and Engineering

(Thousand of students)

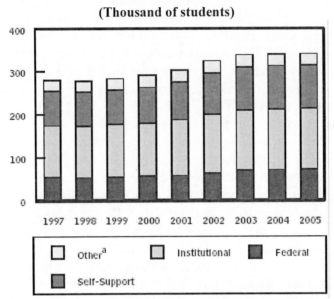

Source: National Science Foundation, Division of Science Resources Statistics, *Graduate Students and Post- doctorates in Science and Engineering: Fall 2004* (August 2006) and *Fall 2005* (May 2007).

b. Other sources of funding include industry, nonprofit organizations, and foreign governments.

Science and Engineering Graduate Students, by Primary Source of Funding (Thousands of students)

Graduate studies in science and engineering in this country are supported through a variety of means, including funding from the federal government. Institutional support, provided by students' own universities, is the largest source of funding; in 2005, 42 percent of science and engineering graduate students received such support. Just under 30 percent of students (the next largest share) provided their own funding in that year, which included loans and family and personal support. For 22 percent of U.S. graduate students in scientific and engineering fields, however, the federal government is the primary source of financial support, providing funding in 2005 to more than 74,600 students (see the figure above). Two federal agencies—the National Institutes of Health and the National Science Foundation—provided support for more than half of those students.

Research assistantships are the most common mechanism by which science and engineering graduate students receive federal support—more than 55,000 students received them in 2005 (see the figure below). Such assistantships are frequently part of the research grants awarded by government agencies to faculty researchers at a university—who in addition to graduate students often employ undergraduate students and young postdoctoral researchers in their laboratories. As a result, federal grants for research and development support science and engineering students by allowing them to gain experience in performing research during their graduate training.

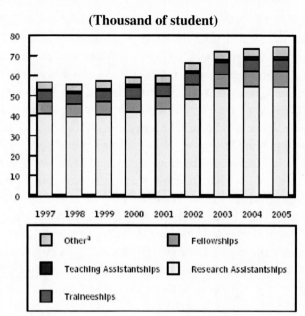

(Thousand of student)

Source: National Science Foundation, Division of Science Resources Statistics, *Graduate Students and Post- doctorates in Science and Engineering: Fall 2004* (August 2006) and *Fall 2005* (May 2007).

a. Examples of other types of support include that provided for veterans under the GI Bill and tuition paid by the Department of Defense for members of the armed forces.

Federally Supported Science and Engineering Graduate Students, by Type of Funding (Thousands of students)

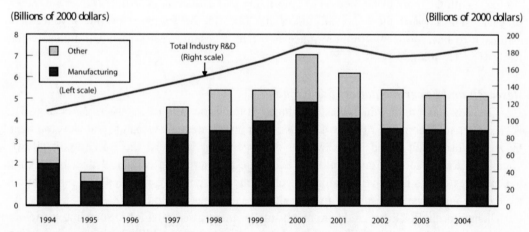

Source: Congressional Budget Office based on Internal Revenue Service, *Statistics of Income, Corporation Complete Report* (annual series), and National Science Foundation, Division of Science Resources Statistics, *National Patterns of R&D Resources* (Arlington, Va., annual series).

Note: R&E = research and experimentation; R&D = research and development.

Figure 12. R&E Tax Credit Claims and R&D Spending by Industry

A 2001 report by the National Research Council (NRC) offers a detailed picture of trends in federal research support, by scientific field, in the 1 990s, when the growing role of the life sciences first emerged.[60] The NRC recommends that the government pay close attention to the weight it gives to different fields of science in its research efforts. The most important problems for science to solve, the NRC suggests, are interdisciplinary, and the uncertainty surrounding the results of research makes it difficult to know where new advances are likely to emerge.[61] The NRC also notes that current trends in research funding may influence future scientific advances because of the close association between federal research funding and enrollment in graduate schools.[62] More than one-fifth of science and engineering graduate students rely on federal funding to support their graduate studies (see Box 2).

Some of the literature that examines how the private sector uses public research offers evidence to support the idea that scientific research has results that affect multiple disciplines—basic biology research, for example, may be able to proceed because of new instruments derived from work by engineers or physicists. The scientific papers published by industry researchers cite both academic and industry research from other fields, with computer sciences having the largest spillover effects outside its own field.[63] Surveys of R&D managers also reveal that they make use of research from outside their primary field.[64]

TAX PREFERENCES FOR RESEARCH AND DEVELOPMENT

The government also uses the tax system to encourage the private sector to invest in research and development. The research and experimentation tax credit provides an incentive to undertake new research by giving firms a credit for expenses related to those new activities against the taxes they owe. In addition, R&D expenses that are not covered by the credit can be fully deducted from income as a business expense when incurred, a treatment that contrasts with the more usual method of amortizing and deducting investments over a number of years. The cost of those tax incentives in 2006, in the form of forgone revenues, is estimated to have been $9.9 billion, much less than the same year's spending authority for R&D of $131 billion.[65]

Research and Experimentation Tax Credit

The R&E tax credit, which was introduced in the Economic Recovery Tax Act of 1981, is designed to encourage firms to increase their investment in research and development through a tax credit based on growth in that spending. In short, the R&E credit allows companies to reduce their tax liability in exchange for increasing certain of their qualifying expenditures on R&D above their past levels. Policymakers have renewed and restructured the credit a number of times; it is currently slated to expire at the end of 2007.

Claims for the R&E tax credit are much smaller than firms' total R&D spending, which is in keeping with the credit's incremental nature. In 2004, the $5.1 billion in tax credit claims (2000 dollars) amounted to only 2.8 percent of the $184 billion that industry spent on research and development that year (see Figure 12).[66] When compared only with industry-sponsored research —the sum of firms' basic and applied research spending but excluding their expenditures for development—the tax credit claims are somewhat more significant. In 2004, such claims represented just over 12 percent of basic and applied research funded by firms.

Comparisons over time of the amount of the R&E tax credit that firms have claimed are complicated by the numerous revisions to the credit and by the introduction on several occasions of associated research tax credits. The incremental research tax credit is the longest-standing part of the incentive. It offers firms three alternative calculation methods: the standard research credit; the alternative incremental credit; and, for tax years ending after December 31, 2006, the alternative simplified credit (see Box 3). Payments to universities and other tax-exempt research organizations to conduct basic research are eligible for a similar incremental tax credit. If those payments are for energy research, larger tax credits are now available following enactment of the Energy Policy Act of 2005, which introduced a flat credit for spending on energy research.

In all other cases, the credit is incremental—that is, it applies only to R&D spending above a base amount. The incremental design follows from the aim of the tax credit: to encourage firms to do more R&D than they otherwise would. The base amounts for each type of credit are intended to approximate the amount that would be spent on research and development in the credit's absence.

Effectiveness of the Credit in Stimulating R&D

The rationale behind the R&E tax credit is that if the credit makes research and development less costly, firms will realize larger expected returns to that investment, thus encouraging them to undertake projects that would not have been funded in the credit's absence. Studies suggest that the tax credit does stimulate additional R&D activity; however, no basis exists for judging whether such additional expenditures provide a high value to society relative to their value to private enterprises.

Economists who have studied the effectiveness of the R&E tax credit in the United States and similar incentives in other countries generally conclude that each additional dollar of forgone revenue attributable to the R&D- promoting tax credit causes companies to spend another dollar on R&D projects. Such studies have tended to focus on estimating the additional research and development that occurs as a result of the tax credit, usually through a two-part process: first, a calculation of how the tax credit and other tax preferences alter the cost of R&D; and second, an estimation of the price elasticity of R&D—or how much spending for R&D would change in response to a change in the cost of performing those activities. Combining those two numbers provides an estimate of how much research and development the tax credit stimulates. Studies have produced a variety of results, but many have clustered around the finding that a dollar claimed under an R&D tax credit leads firms to spend an additional dollar on R&D.[67]

Some studies suggest that the effect of the tax credit may be growing over time. The credit had a less than one-to- one effect on industrial R&D spending in the early 1 980s, when firms were still becoming accustomed to the credit and implementing systems to take advantage of it.[68] Fewer studies examine the tax credit in the 1990s and beyond; however, one that compares the credit's effects before and after the change in the base calculation enacted in 1989 found that after the change, firms spent an additional $2.10 on research and development for each dollar of the tax credit they claimed.[69] The same study also found that after 1989, fewer firms were eligible for the credit but of those that were, a larger share than before 1989 were in high-tech industries.

With few other studies of the credit in the 1990s, it cannot be determined whether the credit's effect has continued to grow. In addition, the data may suffer from a relabeling problem that could overstate the credit's effect over time. To take advantage of the favorable tax treatment of spending for research and development, firms have an incentive to classify as many expenses as possible as R&D related, an incentive that grows with the credit's generosity. Thus, activities that are not new—merely newly classified as R&D—might be counted as part of the increase in R&D activities stimulated by the tax credit, leading to an overstatement of its impact.

BOX 3. CALCULATING THE TAX CREDIT FOR RESEARCH AND EXPERIMENTATION

Since it was instituted, the research and experimentation (R&E) tax credit has been calculated in different ways. The current formulation sets the *standard credit* at 20 percent of a firm's qualified research expendi-tures (QREs) above a base amount that is the product of the firm's average annual gross receipts over the four previous tax years and a fixed-base percentage.[1] The fixed-base percentage is derived by using one of two methods, depending on when the firm first conducted research and had taxable receipts. For firms that had both receipts and QREs in tax years 1984 to 1988, the fixed-base percentage is the ratio of total research spending to total gross receipts over that period. For start-up companies (those that had neither receipts nor spending for research in tax years 1984 to 1988), the fixed-base percentage grows steadily. In the first five years that a firm is eligible for the credit, the fixed base is 3 percent; the percentage rises by the 11th year of eligibility to the ratio of total QREs to total receipts over the same five-year period. Two other restrictions apply to both kinds of firms: The fixed-base percentage may not exceed 16 percent, and the base amount must be at least 50 percent of current-year research expenditures.

Two other calculation methods are also available:

As of January 1, 2007, firms are allowed an *alternative incremental tax credit* equal to the sum of the following: 3 percent of a firm's QREs that are more than 1 percent and less than or equal to 1.5 percent of its average annual gross receipts over the four previous years; 4 percent of its QREs that are between 1.5 percent and 2 percent of those same average gross receipts; and 5 percent of QREs that exceed 2 percent of such receipts.

The *alternative simplified credit* was added in the latest extension of the tax credit at the end of 2006. Firms that elect this method may take a credit equal to 12 percent of their qualified research expenses that exceed 50 percent of their average QREs in the three preceding tax years. For firms that do not have expenses for research in all three previous tax years, the alternative simplified credit equals 6 percent of their QREs.[2]

If a firm chooses to calculate the tax credit by using an alternative method, it must continue to use that method in all future tax years.

Two other credits in addition to the main R&E tax credit offer firms an incentive to invest in R&D. Firms can claim the *basic research credit* for payments they make to qualified organizations (usually universities or other tax-exempt institutions) for performing basic research. The credit is equal to 20 percent of the amount a firm pays a qualified organization in excess of a base amount. (Calculation of that base amount is more complicated than the base-amount calculation for the standard credit, but like the latter, it is also a function of a firm's spending for research in previous years.) Any expenses that a firm applies to the basic research credit may not also be applied to the main research credit.

The *energy research credit*, created in the Energy Policy Act of 2005, extends a flat tax credit of 20 percent to firms that fund energy research through a tax- exempt energy research consortium.

---

[1] For more details on this and the other methods of calculating the tax credit, see Gary Guenther, *Research Tax Credit: Current Status and Selected Issues for Congress*, CRS Report RL31181 (Congressional Research Service, April 26, 2007).

[2] The method for calculating the alternative simplified credit is similar to the way the standard credit was calculated prior to 1990, when the base amount was the greater of a three-year moving average of research spending or 50 percent of the current year's research expenditures. That method was criticized for diminishing a firm's incentives to increase its current spending: An increase in research would generate a tax credit for the current year, but it would also set a higher base amount for ensuing years, making it more difficult for a firm to claim the credit in the future. The Omnibus Budget Reconciliation Act of 1989 put in place the current method for calculating the standard research credit.

Limitations in the available data constrain analysts' ability to draw definitive conclusions about the efficiency of the R&E credit in encouraging new private-sector R&D spending. Most studies use only publicly available data, which leaves analysts to infer the amount of firms' reported R&D that would be eligible for the credit, the amount firms claim for the credit, and the amount of the credit they actually receive. The investment in research and development that firms report in their financial statements is not the same as the "qualified research expenditures" that may be used to calculate the credit.[70] In some cases, the tax credit's effects are estimated on the basis of the amount of credits that firms claim, which may differ from the amount of credits they actually receive (given that the R&E credit is nonrefundable).

Two factors may contribute to an understatement of the cost of the R&E tax credit in these studies. First, the cost is measured only in terms of forgone revenues, with no mention of those revenues' "opportunity cost"—the benefits that their next-best use would have generated. Second, the studies ignore the cost of administering the credit—both the cost incurred by the Internal Revenue Service (IRS) to design guidelines and audit returns and by the firms to comply with the credit's requirements.[71]

Criticisms of the Credit

Economists, industry analysts, and others have offered numerous criticisms of the R&E tax credit (although few mention the potential other uses of the forgone revenues it generates). Most critiques claim that some aspects of the credit's design limit its effectiveness in stimulating research and development by firms— in particular its temporary status, nonrefundability, incremental formula, and definition of qualified research.

Temporary Status. The credit has been in place with few interruptions since it was introduced in 1981, but it has always been temporary. The credit has been extended 12 times, 9 of those times for a period of two years or less but never for more than five years. For one year—July 1995 through June 1996—the research credit lapsed, and the renewal was not extended back to its most recent expiration.

The effectiveness of the R&E tax credit may be limited by its temporariness, an attribute that does not mesh with the (generally) long time horizon of R&D projects.[72] In many cases, businesses plan their R&D projects years in advance because it takes time to build labs, acquire the right equipment, design experiments, and test products. An extension of the tax credit by one or two years may not offer enough certainty that the credit will be available over the life of a project to reduce firms' costs. As a result, the temporary credit may offer a limited incentive to firms to undertake new research and development. However, the repeated renewals of the tax credit may lead firms to expect future renewals beyond its currently stated expiration date and to invest in R&D accordingly.

Refunds and Deductions. The effectiveness of the R&E tax credit is limited, some observers say, because it is not refundable and as a result, certain companies, especially firms that are just starting up, cannot realize the value of the credit. The credit's not being refundable means that firms with tax liabilities of less than the value of the credit cannot claim it immediately. (Firms may, however, claim the credit and carry it forward or backward to reduce their tax bill in other years.) The nonrefundability of the credit may make it difficult for new firms to benefit from it: They are likely to incur expenses for research for a number of years before selling any products, and that lag is likely to reduce the credit's value for them and for other firms that must wait to claim it. Moreover, firms that do not survive long enough to apply the credit may lose its value entirely.

For firms that are more established and profitable, claiming the credit limits the deductions that firms may take, which reduces the nominal value that the credit provides. Firms may deduct their expenditures for research and development in the current year. Some of those expenses are also eligible for the R&E tax credit, but firms must reduce their deductions by the amount of the tax credit they claim to avoid applying two tax benefits to the same spending. For a firm that uses the standard R&E tax credit and is taxed at the top corporate rate of 35 percent, the credit of 20 percent for R&D spending above the base amount effectively falls to 13 percent when the firm's deductions are adjusted for the credit.[73] As a result, the value of the effective tax credit is less than the full value of the statutory credit.

Formulas for Calculating the Credit. The formulas that are currently used to calculate the credit may not be the most efficient way to encourage additional R&D activities. The R&E tax credit is intended to give firms an incentive to spend more on research and development than they would otherwise have spent. For that reason, the credit, in all its variations except for the energy research tax credit, has an incremental component: Firms may collect the credit only if they direct a larger portion of their revenues toward research and development than they did during a base period, which since 1989 has been set at the years 1984 to 1988. Over time, however, firms, technologies, and products have changed, and little connection may remain between what firms spent during the mid-1980s and what they would have spent now if there were no tax credit. Those circumstances suggest that it is difficult to know how much additional R&D activity can be attributed to the credit.

For firms that have become eligible for the credit only since 1989, its structure differs from the structure that applies to firms that became eligible before that date (see Box 3 for details). In their early years of operation, those firms may have had a relatively high ratio of research and development spending to receipts because they were still researching, designing, and introducing new products. If that period has left those firms with a large base percentage, it might set a high hurdle for them to overcome to be able to claim the credit in later years.

What Is Qualified Research? The definition of research that is eligible for the credit may limit the credit's effectiveness because the expenses that are eligible may not be applicable to new activities that would be valuable to the firm or to society. The R&E tax credit is directed toward so-called qualified research expenditures, which do not generally match the R&D figures that firms report to shareholders. Only expenses that would normally be deductible are eligible for the credit; such expenses exclude capital equipment, land, and exploration for oil, gas, and other minerals, all of which might be an important part of the R&D process. In contrast, section 41(d) (1) of the Internal Revenue Code requires that qualified research pursue something "technological in nature" to develop or improve some aspect of the firm's business. In addition, the qualified activity should involve experimentation. The firm's in-house R&D and the R&D that it contracts out to others are both eligible for the credit.

Despite new regulations that were issued in 2003 to clarify the definition, some confusion still exists over the spending that qualifies for the credit.[74] (For example, the eligibility of spending for development of software to be used only by the firm for internal purposes remains a subject of debate.) In addition, questions remain about whether R&D activity that is directed at reducing costs qualifies.[75] A further area of uncertainty is the treatment of research and development by firms in the service industries. The R&D those industries conduct is more likely to be performed on a computer than to take place in a laboratory, making it difficult for such firms to meet the experimentation requirement for the credit.

Deductibility of R&D Expenditures

In addition to the tax preference firms receive by claiming the R&E tax credit, they may also benefit from deducting R&D expenses from corporate income in determining their corporate income taxes. The Office of Management and Budget estimated that the lost revenues from firms' ability to deduct expenses for research activities in the current tax year totaled $7.8 billion in 2006.[76] R&D activities are essentially an investment because they are conducted today in anticipation of returns in future periods, once their results can be commercialized. Like other investments, spending for R&D entails risk; those activities may or may not produce a marketable result, just as a new factory or machine may or may not produce cost savings for a firm.

In most instances, the funds that a firm spends today on an investment, such as a new factory, must be amortized and deducted on the firm's tax returns over a number of years. R&D investments are treated differently: The IRS allows firms to deduct R&D expenditures in the year in which they are made; amortize them over at least 60 months, once the work begins to benefit the firm; or write them off over a 10-year period. If a firm opts to take the current-year deduction, its current tax liability will be lower, although its taxes in future years may be higher if the R&D generates a positive return.

Deducting R&D expenses as they are incurred lowers a firm's costs for performing research and development. That factor may stimulate the firm to do more such work because the lower cost may make R&D a more attractive alternative than other investment opportunities that do not have the same favorable tax treatment.

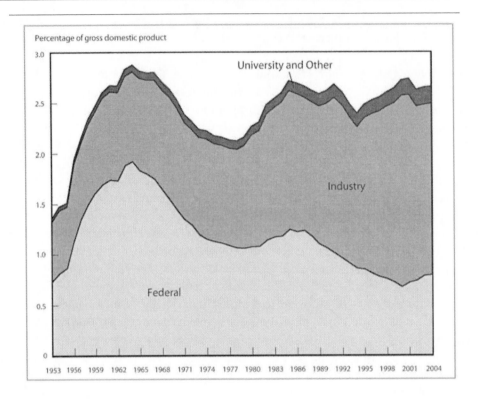

Percentage of gross domestic product

University and Other

Industry

Federal

1953 1956 1959 1962 1965 1968 1971 1974 1977 1980 1983 1986 1989 1992 1995 1998 2001 2004

End Notes

[1] See Congressional Budget Office, *Research and Development in the Pharmaceutical Industry* (October 2006).

[2] The U.S. credit is referred to as the research and experimentation tax credit because to qualify for it, activities must be experimental in nature. The credit is usually understood to apply to R&D activities, although some development work related to the design of a product may not qualify. In other countries, the experimentation distinction may not be explicit, and the class of tax credits that includes the United States' R&E credit is generally referred to as R&D tax credits.

[3] For a detailed look at the relationship between R&D and productivity as well as a discussion of estimates of the rates of return to private R&D, see Congressional Budget Office, *R&D and Productivity Growth* (June 2005).

[4] For a discussion of similar issues as they relate to copyrighted works, see Congressional Budget Office, *Copyright Issues in Digital Media* (August 2004).

[5] Intersociety Working Group, *AAAS Report XXXII: Research and Development FY2008* (American Association for the Advancement of Science, Washington, D.C., April 2007), p. 53.

[6] Together, the federal government and industry provide well over 90 percent of R&D funding, a share that has fallen from 98 percent in the 1950s and 1960s to 94 percent since 2000. Accordingly, funding from other groups has accounted for a growing share. By 2004, universities and nonprofit organizations each provided just under 3 percent of funds ($8.2 billion and $8.6 billion, respectively), and state and local governments provided approximately 1 percent ($2.9 billion). For additional information, see National Science Foundation, Division of Science Resources Statistics, *National Patterns of R&D Resources* (Arlington, Va., annual series). Although universities, nonprofits, and state and local governments have increased their R&D funding, the level of support they provide is unlikely to be large enough to offset the industrial R&D that is forgone because of the difference between private and social returns to R&D.

[7] For example, NSF, which was created in 1950, saw its budget more than double from 1956 to 1957 and again from 1958 to 1959. In other years in the 1950s and most of the 1960s, the rate of growth of NSF's budget from one year to the next was in the double digits. See National Science Foundation, Budget Division, "NSF by Account (FY Actuals—FY2006, Constant Dollars in Millions)" (Arlington, Va., 2006), available at http://dellweb.bfa.nsf.gov/NSFHist_constant.htm.

[8] For a more detailed history of federal R&D funding, see Richard Rowberg, *Federal R&D Funding: A Concise History,* CRS Report 95-1209 (Congressional Research Service, updated August 14, 1998).

[9] National Science Foundation, Division of Science Resources Statistics, *National Patterns of R&D Resources: 2004 Data Update* (Arlington, Va., September 2006).

[10] FFRDCs often host especially capital-intensive R&D projects. In May 2006, the National Science Foundation counted 37 FFRDCs under the auspices of a variety of federal agencies. Although federally funded, FFRDCs may be administered by industrial firms, universities, or other nonprofit institutions. For details of such centers, see National Science Foundation, Division of Science Resources Statistics, *Master Government List of Federally Funded R&D Centers* (Arlington, Va., May 2006).

[11] Internal Revenue Service, *Statistics of Income: Corporation Complete Report* (2004), Table 21.

[12] Some analyses examine the potential for overinvestment in R&D, which may result from duplicative efforts among firms that are racing to patent findings, deter the entry of new firms or products, or develop small innovations that destroy the market for existing products. See, for example, Kalyan Chatterjee and Robert Evans, "Rivals' Search for Buried Treasure: Competition and Duplication in R&D," *RAND Journal of Economics*, vol. 35, no. 1 (Spring 2004), pp. 160–183; Charles I. Jones and John C. Williams, "Measuring the Social Return to R&D," *Quarterly Journal of Economics*, vol. 113, no. 4 (November 1998), pp. 1119–1135; and A. Michael Spence, "Entry, Capacity, Investment, and Oligopolistic Pricing," *Bell Journal of Economics*, vol. 8, no. 2 (Autumn 1977), pp. 534–544.

[13] Two early papers frequently cited in the literature are Kenneth J. Arrow, "Economic Welfare and the Allocation of Resources for Invention," in Richard R. Nelson, ed., *The Rate and Direction of Inventive Activity* (Princeton, N.J.: Princeton University Press, 1962), pp. 609–626; and Richard R. Nelson, "The Simple Economics of Basic Scientific Research," *Journal of Political Economy*, vol. 67, no. 3 (1959), pp. 297–306. Later studies that have revisited the issues include Zvi Griliches, "The Search for R&D Spillovers," *Scandinavian Journal of Economics*, vol. 94, supplement (1992), pp. S29–S47; and Bronwyn H. Hall, "The Private and Social Returns to Research and Development," in Bruce L.R. Smith and Claude E. Barfield, eds., *Technology, R&D, and the Economy* (Washington, D.C.: Brookings Institution and American Enterprise Institute for Public Policy Research, 1996), pp. 140–162.

[14] The private sector has turned to prizes to stimulate research to solve specific problems. For a discussion of research prizes, see Congressional Budget Office, *Evaluating the Role of Prices and R&D in Reducing Carbon Dioxide Emissions* (September 2006), pp. 12–13.

[15] Morton I. Kamien, Eitan Muller, and Israel Zang, "Research Joint Ventures and R&D Cartels," *American Economic Review*, vol. 82, no. 5 (December 1992), pp. 1293–1306.

[16] Kathryn L. Combs and Albert N. Link, "Innovation Policy in Search of an Economic Foundation: The Case of Research Partnerships in the United States," *Technology Analysis and Strategic Management*, vol. 15, no. 2 (2003), pp. 177–187.

[17] "Out of the Dusty Labs: The Rise and Fall of Corporate R&D," *The Economist* (March 1, 2007).

[18] There is a difference between so-called performer-reported federal R&D (which appears in NSF's *National Patterns of R&D Resources*) and the R&D obligations reported by federal agencies (which are the foundation for NSF's *Federal Funds for Research and Development*). According to the National Science Board, which oversees NSF and offers advice to policymakers on issues involving science and engineering research and education, the problem is not unique to the United States. The discrepancy is due at least in part to differences in timing and accounting. For example, although a federal agency has obligated R&D funds, the organization or individual performing the research may not yet have spent those funds and done the work. For a discussion of the problem, see National Science Board, *Science and Engineering Indicators 2006,* vol. 1 (Arlington, Va.: National Science Foundation, 2006), pp. 4–25.

[19] National Academy of Sciences, Committee on Criteria for Federal Support of Research and Development, *Allocating Federal Funds for Science and Technology* (Washington, D.C.: National Academy Press, 1995), p. 56.

[20] *Budget of the United States Government, Fiscal Year 2002: Analytical Perspectives* (2001), p. 135.

[21] The patents referred to here and in Figures 8 and 9 are utility patents, which, according to the U.S. Patent and Trademark Office, are granted for new or improved products or processes. There are also two other types of patents—design patents, for the external design of a product, and plant patents, for new varieties. For further information, see www.uspto.gov/webgeneral/index.html.

[22] According to the PTO, the large jump from 1997 to 1998 in the number of total patents granted is largely the result of a significant expansion in the staff of patent examiners (personal communication to the Congressional Budget Office from Jim Hirabayashi, Electronic Information Products Division, U.S. Patent and Trademark Office, March 8, 2007). The PTO's 1999 annual report states that more than 800 new examiners were hired in fiscal year 1999 and more than 700 in 1998 (U.S. Patent and Trademark Office, *Century of American Innovation, A Patent and Trademark Office Review, Fiscal Year 1999*, p. 7).

[23] Jerry G. Thursby and Marie C. Thursby, "Patterns of Research and Licensing Activity of Science and Engineering Faculty" (working paper, Georgia Institute of Technology, Technological Innovation: Generating Economic Results program, April 2003), available at http://tiger.gatech.edu/files/gt_tiger_patterns.pdf.

[24] David C. Mowery and others, "The Growth of Patenting and Licensing by U.S. Universities: An Assessment of the Effects of the Bayh-Dole Act of 1980," *Research Policy*, vol. 30, no. 1 (2001), pp. 99–119.

25 Domestically owned patents represent more than half the utility patents granted each year by the PTO. The federal government and individuals account for a larger share of domestically owned patents than the share of foreign-owned U.S. patents accounted for by their foreign counterparts. However, no similar comparison may be made for universities, businesses, and other nongovernmental organizations because the data on foreign-owned patents are not broken down by those categories. See U.S. Patent and Trademark Office, "Historic Data, All Technologies (Utility Patents) Report," Table A1-1b, available at www.uspto.gov/go/taf/h_at.htm.

26 According to the Department of Commerce (*Summary Report on Federal Laboratory Technology Transfer: Activity Metrics and Outcomes FY 2003*, December 2004, p. 37), the federal government in 2003 collected $97 million in licensing income, most of which was channeled through the Department of Health and Human Services ($55 million), which is home to the National Institutes of Health, and the Department of Energy ($26 million).

27 In a peer-review selection process, research proposals are typically evaluated by other scientists in the relevant field who then recommend projects to receive funding on the basis of their scientific merit. See James D. Savage, *Funding Science in America* (New York: Cambridge University Press, 1999), pp. 9–12.

28 Of the projects rated excellent by NSF reviewers in fiscal year 2005, 74 percent were awarded funding. The percentage of projects funded decreased with the rating: very good to excellent, 43 percent funded; good to very good, 11 percent funded; and good or lower, 0.5 percent funded. See National Science Foundation, *Report to the National Science Board on the National Science Foundation's Merit Review Process, Fiscal Year 2005*, NSF Report NSB-06-21 (Arlington, Va., March 2006), p. 21.

29 S. Fölster, "The Perils of Peer Review in Economics and Other Sciences," *Journal of Evolutionary Economics*, vol. 5, no. 1 (March 1995), pp. 43–57.

30 National Academy of Sciences, National Academy of Engineering, and Institute of Medicine, *Rising Above the Gathering Storm* (Washington, D.C.: National Academies Press, 2006), pp. 6–12.

31 Under EPSCoR, states that have received less than 0.75 percent of NSF research funding in the three preceding years are eligible for additional grants and assistance in building research institutions and programs.

32 See Linda R. Cohen and Roger G. Noll, *The Technology Pork Barrel* (Washington, D.C.: Brookings Institution, 1991).

33 At times, the returns to medical research have been measured in terms of the value of the statistical lives saved as a result of an innovation. Statistical lives saved are the "reduction of some mortal hazard to some part of the population." See Thomas C. Schelling, "Value of Life," in John Eatwell, Murray Milgate, and Peter Newman, eds., *The New Palgrave Dictionary of Economics*, vol. 4 (New York: Stockton Press, 1987), p. 793.

34 National Science Foundation, Division of Science Resources Statistics, *Federal Funds for Research and Development: Fiscal Years 2003–05*, NSF 06-313 (Arlington, Va., 2006), Table 6.

35 For a review of the problems in assessing the benefits of spin-offs, see John A. Alic and others, *Beyond Spinoff: Military and Commercial Technologies in a Changing World* (Cambridge, Mass.: Harvard University Press, 1992), pp. 60–64.

36 See Office of Technology Assessment, *Research Funding as an Investment: Can We Measure the Returns? A Technical Memorandum*, OTA-TM-SET-36 (April 1986); and Paul A. David, Bronwyn H. Hall, and Andrew A. Toole, "Is Public R&D a Complement or Substitute for Private R&D? A Review of the Econometric Evidence," *Research Policy*, vol. 29, no. 4–5 (April 2000), pp. 497–529.

37 Jane Calvert and Ben R. Martin, "Changing Conceptions of Basic Research?" (SPRU [Science and Technology Policy Research], University of Sussex, prepared as a background document for the OECD/Norwegian Workshop on Policy Relevance and Measurement of Basic Research, Oslo, October 29–30, 2001).

38 A recent example is the claim in 2005 by computer scientists that the Defense Advanced Research Projects Agency had sharply cut support for basic research in favor of short-term, narrowly focused projects (see John Markoff, "Pentagon Redirects Its Research Dollars," *New York Times*, April 2, 2005). The House Science Committee held a hearing on the matter on May 12, 2005.

39 Richard R. Nelson and Paul M. Romer, "Science, Economic Growth, and Public Policy," in Smith and Barfield, eds., *Technology, R&D, and the Economy*, p. 70.

40 Together, universities account for about 42 percent of all federally funded research. However, academic research is supported by a number of other funding sources as well, such as state and local governments, nonprofit agencies, industry, and the universities themselves (see the bottom panel of Figure 4 on page 8). Of those sources, industry-funded research is likely to be the only one whose character differs substantially from government-funded research, because a private-sector research sponsor may seek to prevent or delay the publication of research findings. According to NSF, industry has consistently been the smallest source of funds for university-conducted R&D, never accounting for more than 9 percent of funding.

41 Edwin Mansfield, "Academic Research and Industrial Innovation," *Research Policy*, vol. 20, no. 1 (1991), pp. 1–12.

42 Mansfield suggests that 28 percent is a conservative estimate because the survey's methodology limited the period over which firms make use of academic research and excluded spillover effects.

43 A 1993 CBO publication (Congressional Budget Office, *A Review of Edwin Mansfield's Estimate of the Rate of Return from Academic Research and Its Relevance to the Federal Budget Process*, April 1993) also cautions

against relying on the 28 percent figure as an estimate of the returns to federal R&D. CBO's skepticism was based on the assumptions the researchers made to arrive at that result and its exclusion of several factors, including the benefits to be derived from training students to conduct academic R&D and the research performed at federally funded research and development centers.

[44] Wesley M. Cohen, Richard R. Nelson, and John P. Walsh, "Links and Impacts: The Influence of Public Research on Industrial R&D," *Management Science*, vol. 48, no. 1 (2002), pp. 1–23.

[45] James D. Adams and J. Roger Clemmons, *Science and Industry: Tracing the Flow of Basic Research Through Manufacturing and Trade,* NBER Working Paper No. 12459 (Cambridge, Mass.: National Bureau of Economic Research, August 2006).

[46] Lee Branstetter and Yoshiaki Ogura, *Is Academic Science Driving a Surge in Industrial Innovation? Evidence from Patent Citations,* NBER Working Paper No. 11561 (Cambridge, Mass.: National Bureau of Economic Research, August 2005).

[47] David, Hall, and Toole, "Is Public R&D a Complement or Substitute for Private R&D?"

[48] Austan Goolsbee, "Does Government R&D Policy Mainly Benefit Scientists and Engineers?," *American Economic Review*, vol. 88, no. 2 (May 1998), pp. 298–302.

[49] National Science Foundation, *Characteristics of Doctoral Scientists and Engineers in the United States: 2003* and *Characteristics of Doctoral Scientists and Engineers in the United States: 1997* (Arlington, Va., June 2006 and November 1999).

[50] Dominique Guellec and Bruno van Pottelsberghe de la Potterie, "The Impact of Public R&D Expenditure on Business R&D," *Economics of Innovation and New Technology*, vol. 12, no. 3 (June 2003), pp. 225–243.

[51] Since 2003, those increases have slowed sharply, which leaves NIH's budget declining in real terms when the biomedical research and development price index is used as a deflator. (For additional information, see officeofbudget.od.nih.gov/UI/GDP_FromGenBudget.htm.)

[52] Obligations for applied research in the life sciences increased at an average annual rate of 12.7 percent over the 1997–2004 period, and obligations for basic research grew at an average annual rate of 9.6 percent.

[53] President Bush announced the initiative in his 2006 State of the Union address. Details of the original proposal may be found at www.ostp.gov/html/ACIBooklet.pdf.

[54] National Academy of Sciences, National Academy of Engineering, and Institute of Medicine, *Rising Above the Gathering Storm*, p. 6-2. The report also recommended a number of other actions, including providing grants for researchers in the early stages of their career, promoting energy and high-risk research, and improving science, mathematics, and engineering education.

[55] Kevin M. Murphy and Robert H. Topel, eds., *Measuring the Gains from Medical Research* (Chicago: University of Chicago Press, 2003).

[56] William Nordhaus, "The Health of Nations: The Contribution of Improved Health to Living Standards," in Murphy and Topel, eds., *Measuring the Gains from Medical Research*, pp. 9–40.

[57] Kevin M. Murphy and Robert H. Topel, "The Economic Value of Medical Research," in Murphy and Topel, eds., *Measuring the Gains from Medical Research*, pp. 41–73.

[58] Ibid., p. 71.

[59] For a review of a number of those papers, see Martin Buxton, Steve Hanney, and Teri Jones, "Estimating the Economic Value to Societies of the Impact of Health Research: A Critical Review," *Bulletin of the World Health Organization*, vol. 82, no. 10 (October 2004), pp. 733–739.

[60] National Research Council, Board on Science, Technology, and Economic Policy, *Trends in Federal Support of Research and Graduate Education* (Washington, D.C.: National Academy Press, 2001).

[61] Ibid., pp. 87–88.

[62] Ibid., p. 50.

[63] Adams and Clemmons, *Science and Industry.*

[64] Cohen, Nelson, and Walsh, *Links and Impacts.*

[65] *Budget of the United States Government, Fiscal Year 2008: Analytical Perspectives* (2007), pp. 51 and 291.

[66] As discussed later, firms do not actually receive all of the R&E tax credit they claim in a given year.

[67] See Bronwyn H. Hall and John Van Reenen, "How Effective Are Fiscal Incentives for R&D? A Review of the Evidence," *Research Policy*, vol. 29 (2000), pp. 449–469; and Nick Bloom, Rachel Griffith, and John Van Reenen, "Do R&D Tax Credits Work? Evidence from a Panel of Countries, 1979–1997," *Journal of Public Economics*, vol. 85 (2002), pp. 1–31.

[68] Hall and Van Reenen, "How Effective Are Fiscal Incentives for R&D?," p. 462.

[69] Sanjay Gupta, Yuhchang Hwang, and Andrew Schmidt, "An Analysis of the Availability and Incentive Effects of the R&D Tax Credit After the Omnibus Budget Reconciliation Act of 1989" (draft, W.P. Carey School of Business, Arizona State University, August 2006), available at www1.gsb.columbia.edu/mygsb/faculty/research/pubfiles/2366/GHS%20082606%2Epdf.

[70] According to the General Accounting Office (now the Government Accountability Office), COMPUSTAT data, which are used in many of these studies, are a poor proxy for confidential tax data from the Internal Revenue Service. For a discussion of the issue, see General Accounting Office, *Review of Studies of the Effectiveness of the Research Tax Credit*, GAO/GGD-96-43 (May 1996).

[71] A September 1989 GAO report (*The Research Tax Credit Has Stimulated Some Additional Research Spending,* GGD-89-114) estimated that the IRS audited 74 percent of the firms that claimed the credit. It is not known whether that pattern has persisted.

[72] For example, President Bush, in his 2006 American Competitiveness Initiative (a description is available at www.ostp.gov/html/ACIBooklet.pdf), called for the R&E tax credit to be made permanent. See also Congressional Budget Office, "Revenue Option 36: Permanently Extend the Research and Experimentation Tax Credit," *Budget Options* (February 2007), p. 305.

[73] For example, consider a firm that uses the standard method to calculate its tax credit and has $1 million in R&D expenditures above the base amount. That firm's R&E tax credit would be $200,000, which would reduce the firm's deductions by $200,000 and have the effect of increasing its taxable income by the same amount. For a firm in the 35 percent tax bracket, that additional $200,000 of taxable income would increase the firm's tax liability by $70,000. In the end, the R&E tax credit would reduce the firm's tax liability by $130,000, or 13 percent of the firm's R&D expenditures above the base amount. Alternatively, the firm might simplify its accounting and take a tax credit of only 13 percent. Similar adjustments would also be required for firms that opted to use one of the alternative methods for calculating the R&E tax credit (see Box 3).

[74] Julian Y. Kim, "The Federal Research Credit—The Definition of Research," presented at the American Enterprise Institute Forum *The Research Tax Credit: Gone Today, Here Tomorrow?*, November 15, 2006.

[75] Gary Guenther, *Research Tax Credit: Current Status and Selected Issues for Congress,* CRS Report RL31181 (Congressional Research Service, April 26, 2007).

[76] *Budget of the United States Government, Fiscal Year 2008: Analytical Perspectives.*

In: Federal Role in Funding Research and Development   ISBN: 978-1-60741-486-5
Editor: Piper B. Collins   © 2010 Nova Science Publishers, Inc.

Chapter 6

FEDERAL RESEARCH: OPPORTUNITIES EXIST TO IMPROVE THE MANAGEMENT AND OVERSIGHT OF FEDERALLY FUNDED RESEARCH AND DEVELOPMENT CENTERS

United States Government Accountability Office

WHY GAO DID THIS STUDY

In 2006, the federal government spent $13 billion—14 percent of its research and development (R&D) expenditures—to enable 38 federally funded R&D centers (FFRDCs) to meet special research needs. FFRDCs—including laboratories, studies and analyses centers, and systems engineering centers—conduct research in military space · programs, nanotechnology, microelectronics, nuclear warfare, and biodefense countermeasures, among other areas. GAO was asked to identify (1) how federal agencies contract with organizations operating FFRDCs and (2) agency oversight processes used to ensure that FFRDCs are well-managed.

GAO's work is based on a review of documents and interviews with officials from eight FFRDCs sponsored by the departments of Defense (DOD), Energy (DOE), Health and Human Services (HHS), and Homeland Security (DHS).

WHAT GAO RECOMMENDS

To improve the effectiveness of FFRDCs, GAO recommends that (1) DHS and HHS revise their personal conflict-of-interest policies to specifically address FFRDC contractor employees in a position to influence research findings or agency decision making and (2) agencies create an ongoing forum to share best practices for FFRDC oversight. DHS, DOD, and DOE concurred with GAO's recommendations, while HHS concurred with the need to revise its policies and is considering a best practices forum for FFRDCs.

WHAT GAO FOUND

Federal agencies GAO reviewed use cost-reimbursement contracts with the organizations that operate FFRDCs, and three of the agencies generally use full and open competition to award the contracts. Only DOD consistently awards its FFRDC contracts on a sole-source basis, as permitted by law and regulation when properly justified. FFRDCs receive funding for individual projects from customers that require the FFRDCs' specialized research capabilities. Because FFRDCs have a special relationship with their sponsoring agencies and may be given access to sensitive or proprietary data, regulations require that FFRDCs be free from organizational conflicts of interest. DOD and DOE also have policies that prescribe specific areas that FFRDC contractors must address to ensure their employees are free from personal conflicts of interest. In a May 2008 report, GAO recognized the importance of implementing such safeguards for contractor employees. Currently, although DHS and HHS have policies that require their FFRDC contractors to implement conflicts-of-interest safeguards, these policies lack the specificity needed to ensure their FFRDC contractors will consistently address employees' personal conflicts of interest.

Sponsoring agencies use various approaches in their oversight of FFRDC contractors, including:

- Review and approval of work assigned to FFRDCs, or conducted for other agencies or entities, to determine consistency with the FFRDC's purpose, capacity, and special competency. In this process, only DOD must abide by congressionally imposed annual workload limits for its FFRDCs.
- Conduct performance reviews and audits of contractor costs, finances, and internal controls.
- Conduct a comprehensive review before a contract is renewed to assess the continuing need for the FFRDC and if the contractor can meet that need, based on annual assessments of contractor performance.

Some agencies have adopted other agencies' FFRDC oversight and management practices. For example, DHS mirrored most of DOD's FFRDC Management Plan—an internal DOD guidance document—in developing an approach to FFRDC oversight, and DHS officials told us they learned from DOE's experience in selecting and overseeing contractors for laboratory FFRDCs. In addition, HHS plans to implement certain DOE practices, including rewarding innovation and excellence in performance through various contract incentives. While agency officials have acknowledged the potential benefits from sharing best practices, there is currently no formal cross-agency forum or other established mechanism for doing so.

ABBREVIATIONS

C3I	command, control, communications, and intelligence
DCAA	Defense Contract Audit Agency
DHS	Department of Homeland Security

DOD   Departments of Defense
GAAP   generally accepted accounting principles
GAGAS   generally accepted government auditing standards
FAR   Federal Acquisition Regulation
FFRDC   federally funded research and development center
HHS   Department of Health and Human Services
HSI   Homeland Security Institute
IDA   Institute for Defense Analyses
MIT   Massachusetts Institute of Technology
M&O   management and operating
NBACC   National Biodefense Analysis and Countermeasures Center
NNSA   National Nuclear Security Administration
NSF   National Science Foundation
OMB   Office of Management and Budget
R&D   research and development
SEC   Securities and Exchange Commission
STE   Staffyears of Technical Effort

October 8, 2008

The Honorable John D. Dingell
Chairman
The Honorable Joe Barton
Ranking Member
Committee on Energy and Commerce
House of Representatives

The Honorable Bart T. Stupak
Chairman
The Honorable John M. Shimkus
Ranking Member
Subcommittee on Oversight and Investigations
Committee on Energy and Commerce
House of Representatives

In fiscal year 2006, the federal government spent $13 billion[1]—14 percent of all federal research and development expenditures—funding work at its 38 federally funded research and development centers (FFRDCs). These centers are agency-sponsored[2] entities that specialize in areas such as military space programs, nanotechnology, advanced microelectronics and semiconductors, nuclear warfare, biodefense countermeasures, and high- energy particle physics. Sponsoring agencies contract with nonprofit, university-affiliated, or private industry organizations to operate the FFRDCs. Based on your interest in how FFRDCs are managed, we identified (1) how federal agencies contract with organizations that operate FFRDCs and (2) the oversight processes agencies use to ensure that FFRDCs are effectively and efficiently managed.

We used a case study methodology to conduct our review. We chose three agencies with a long history of sponsoring FFRDCs—the departments of Defense (DOD), Energy[3] (DOE), and Health and Human Services (HHS)— as well as a fourth agency that has more recently established FFRDCs— the Department of Homeland Security (DHS). From the 29 FFRDCs that these four agencies sponsor, we selected a nongeneralizable sample of eight FFRDCs for in-depth review. We made our selections to achieve variation, both among the type of FFRDC (scientific laboratories versus other types) and the type of operating contractor (universities, nonprofits, and private industry). For each of the four federal agencies, we interviewed officials at the office that sponsors FFRDCs as well as those officials who have contract management or audit roles. We analyzed regulations, policies, guidance, contracts, sponsoring agreements, and other documentation. For the eight FFRDCs in our case study, we conducted site visits, interviewed key contractor personnel, and obtained information and documentation on how they met sponsoring agencies' research needs and adhere to requirements. For additional information on our scope and methodology, see appendix I.

We conducted this performance audit from October 2007 to October 2008, in accordance with generally accepted government auditing standards. Those standards require that we plan and perform the audit to obtain sufficient, appropriate evidence to provide a reasonable basis for our findings and conclusions based on our audit objectives. We believe that the evidence obtained provides a reasonable basis for our findings and conclusions based on our audit objectives.

RESULTS IN BRIEF

The federal agencies we reviewed use cost-reimbursement contracts with the organizations that operate their FFRDCs, and three of the four agencies generally use full and open competition to award these contracts. Only DOD has consistently awarded its FFRDC contracts on a sole-source basis, a practice that federal law and regulations permit if properly justified. The FFRDCs receive funding on a project-by-project basis from customers requiring the FFRDCs' research and development capabilities. In order to carry out these projects, FFRDCs frequently are provided with access to sensitive or proprietary data. For this reason, and because of the special relationship between sponsoring agencies and their FFRDCs, federal regulations require that FFRDC entities be free from organizational conflicts of interest. While the sponsoring agreements we reviewed address FFRDCs' organizational conflicts of interest, DOD and DOE also have policies that prescribe specific areas that FFRDC contractors must address to ensure their employees are free from personal conflicts of interest. In a May 2008 report, we recognized the importance of implementing such safeguards for certain contractor employees. Currently, although DHS's FFRDC contractors have their own internal policies that address employees' potential conflicts of interest, DHS and HHS policies do not specifically prescribe areas that FFRDC contractors must include to address these conflicts.

The four sponsoring agencies use various approaches in their oversight of FFRDC contractors. First, sponsors review and approve the work assigned to their FFRDCs to ensure it is within their purpose, mission, capacity, and special competency. In this process, DOD is the only agency that operates under congressionally imposed annual workload limits for its FFRDCs. In addition, agencies regularly assess the performance of their FFRDCs and contractors, including in some cases, performing audits of contractor costs, finances, and internal controls. Finally, in accordance with federal regulations, agencies conduct comprehensive reviews prior to renewing sponsoring agreements or contracts to assess the continued research need and the management and competencies of the FFRDCs. In conducting oversight, some agencies have adopted elements of the oversight practices used by other sponsoring agencies. For example, DHS mirrored most of DOD's FFRDC Management Plan—an internal DOD guidance document— and DHS officials told us they learned from DOE's experience in selecting and overseeing contractors for laboratory FFRDCs. In addition, HHS plans to implement certain DOE practices, including rewarding innovation and excellence in performance through incentive fees and award terms. While agency officials have noted potential benefits from sharing best practices, there is currently no formal cross-agency forum or other established mechanism for doing so.

To improve the effectiveness of FFRDC management, we are recommending that (1) DHS and HHS review and revise personal conflictof-interest policies to ensure they specifically address FFRDC employees in a position to make or influence research findings or agency decision making and (2) the four agencies we reviewed establish an ongoing forum to share best practices for FFRDC oversight. In commenting on a draft of this report, DHS and HHS concurred with our recommendation that they review and revise their conflict of interest policies. In addition, DOD, DOE, and DHS all concurred with our recommendation to establish a forum to share best practices, while HHS is considering participation in such a forum.

BACKGROUND

During World War II, the U.S. government partnered with academic scientists in ad-hoc laboratories and research groups to meet unique research and development (R&D) needs of the war effort. These efforts resulted in technologies such as the proximity fuse, advanced radar and sonar, and the atomic bomb. Those relationships were later re-structured into federal research centers to retain academic scientists in U.S. efforts to continue advancements in technology, and by the mid-1960's the term "federally funded research and development centers" was applied to these entities. Since that time, the U.S. government has continued to rely on FFRDCs to develop technologies in areas such as combating terrorism and cancer, addressing energy challenges, and tackling evolving challenges in air travel.[4] For example, one of DOE's laboratories was used to invent and develop the cyclotron, which is a particle accelerator that produces high energy beams, critical to the field of nuclear physics for the past several decades.

Today, FFRDCs support their sponsoring federal agencies in diverse fields of study. For example, DOE sponsors the most FFRDCs—16 in total—all of which are research laboratories that conduct work in such areas as nuclear weapons, renewable energy sources, and environmental management. DHS recently established two FFRDCs: one to develop countermeasures for biological warfare agents and the other to provide decision makers with advice and assistance in such areas as analysis of the vulnerabilities of the nation's critical infrastructures, standards for interoperability for field operators and first responders, and evaluating developing technologies for homeland security purposes.

FFRDCs are privately owned but government-funded entities that have long-term relationships with one or more federal agencies to perform research and development and related tasks. Even though they may be funded entirely, or nearly so, from the federal treasury, FFRDCs are regarded as contractors not federal agencies. In some cases, Congress has specifically authorized agencies to establish FFRDCs. For example, the 1991 appropriation for the Internal Revenue Service authorized the IRS to spend up to $15 million to establish an FFRDC as part of its tax systems modernization program.[5]

According to the Federal Acquisition Regulation (FAR), FFRDCs are intended to meet special long-term research or development needs that cannot be met as effectively by existing in-house or contractor resources. In sponsoring an FFRDC, agencies draw on academic and private sector resources to accomplish tasks that are integral to the mission and operation of the sponsoring agency. In order to discharge responsibilities to their sponsoring agencies, the FAR notes that FFRDCs have special access, beyond that which is common for normal contractual relationships, to government and supplier data—including sensitive and proprietary data—and other government resources. Furthermore, the FAR requires FFRDCs to operate in the public interest with objectivity and independence, to be free of organizational conflicts of interest, and to fully disclose their affairs to the sponsoring agencies.[6] FFRDCs may be operated by a university or consortium of universities; other nonprofit organizations; or a private industry contractor as an autonomous organization or a separate unit of a parent organization.

Agencies develop sponsoring agreements with FFRDCs to establish their research and development missions and prescribe how they will interact with the agency; the agencies then contract with organizations to operate the FFRDCs to accomplish those missions. At some agencies the sponsoring agreement is a separate document that is incorporated into the contract, and at other agencies the contract itself constitutes the sponsoring agreement. The sponsoring agreement and contract together identify the scope, purpose, and mission of the FFRDC and the responsibilities of the contractor in ensuring they are accomplished by the FFRDC.

Although the contract or sponsoring agreement may take various forms, the FAR requires FFRDC sponsoring agreements to contain certain key terms and conditions.[7] For example, the agreement term may not exceed 5 years, but can be periodically renewed in increments not to exceed 5 years. Sponsoring agreements must also contain prohibitions against the FFRDCs competing with non-FFRDCs in response to a federal agency request for proposals for other than the operation of an FFRDC. The agreement also must delineate whether and under what circumstances the FFRDC may accept work from other agencies. In addition, these agreements may identify cost elements requiring advance agreement if cost-type contracts are used and include considerations affecting negotiation of fees where fees are determined appropriate by sponsors.

The National Science Foundation (NSF), which keeps general statistics on FFRDCs, identifies the following types of FFRDCs:

Research and development (R&D) laboratories: fill voids where in-house and private sector R&D centers are unable to meet core agency needs. These FFRDCs are used to maintain long-term competency in sophisticated technology areas and develop and transfer important new technology to the private sector.

Study and analysis centers: used to provide independent analyses and advice in core areas important to their sponsors, including policy development, support for decision making, and identifying alternative approaches and new ideas on significant issues.

Systems engineering and integration centers: provide support for complex systems by assisting with the creation and choice of system concepts and architectures, the specification of technical system and subsystem requirements and interfaces, the development and acquisition of system hardware and software, the testing and verification of performance, the integration of new capabilities, and continuous improvement of system operations and logistics.

The NSF maintains a master list[8] of the current FFRDCs and collects funding data from their agency sponsors on an annual basis. According to NSF data, R&D funding for FFRDCs has risen steadily across the federal government, increasing 40 percent from fiscal year 1996 to 2005, from $6.9 billion to $9.7 billion. (See figure 1 below.) This does not represent the full amount of funding provided to FFRDCs by federal agencies, however, since it does not include non-R&D funding. Nevertheless, it is the only centrally reported information on federal funding for FFRDCs.

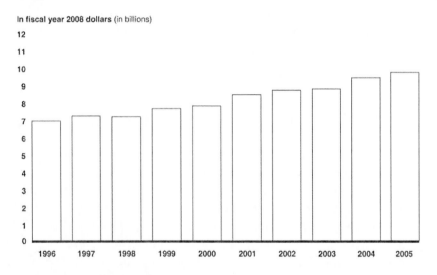

Source: GAO analysis of National Science Foundation data.

Figure 1. Federal R&D Funding for FFRDCs

For a list of the 38 FFRDCs currently sponsored by the U.S. government, see appendix II.

MOST AGENCIES COMPETE COST-REIMBURSEMENT CONTRACTS FOR OPERATING THEIR FFRDCS, BUT SOME DO NOT HAVE SPECIFIC PERSONAL CONFLICT-OF-INTEREST REQUIREMENTS

The four agencies we reviewed use cost-reimbursement contracts with the organizations that operate their FFRDCs, and three of these agencies generally use full and open competition in awarding these contracts. While the agencies require that their FFRDCs be free from organizational conflicts of interest in accordance with federal regulations, only DOD and DOE have agencywide requirements that prescribe specific areas that FFRDC contractors must address to ensure their employees are free from personal conflicts of interest. DHS and HHS policies do not specifically prescribe areas that contractors must include to address these conflicts.

Three Agencies Generally Compete FFRDC Contracts, While DOD Does Not

Federal law and regulations require federal contracts to be competed unless they fall under specific exceptions to full and open competition. One such exception is awarding contracts to establish or maintain an essential engineering, research, or development capability to be provided by an FFRDC.[9] While some agencies we reviewed awarded FFRDC contracts through other than full and open competition in the past, including sole-source contracts, three have generally used full and open competition in recent years.

Starting in the mid-1990's, DOE took steps to improve FFRDC laboratory contractors' performance with a series of contracting reforms, including increasing the use of competition in selecting contractors for its labs. Subsequent legislation[10] required DOE to compete the award and extension of contracts used at its labs, singling out the Ames Laboratory, Argonne National Laboratory, Lawrence Berkeley National Laboratory, Lawrence Livermore National Laboratory, and Los Alamos National Laboratory for mandatory competition because their contracts in effect at the time had been awarded more than 50 years ago. In addition, according to DOE officials, the Los Alamos contract was competed due to performance concerns with the contractor, and Argonne West's contract was competed to combine its research mission with that of the Idaho National Engineering and Environmental Laboratory to form the Idaho National Laboratory. DOE now routinely uses competitive procedures on contracts for its FFRDC laboratories unless a justification for the use of other than competitive procedures is approved by the Secretary of Energy. Of DOE's 16 FFRDCs, DOE has used full and open competition in the award of 13 contracts, is in the process of competing one contract, and plans to compete the remaining two contracts when their terms have been completed. For the 13 contracts that have been competed, in 2 cases the incumbent contractor received the new contract award, in 8 cases a new consortium or limited liability corporation was formed that included the incumbent contractor, and in 3 cases a different contractor was awarded the contract.

Other agencies also have used competitive procedures to award FFRDC contracts:

HHS has conducted full and open competition on the contract for its cancer research lab since its establishment in 1972,[11] resulting in some change in contractors over the years. Recently, however, HHS noncompetitively renewed the contract with the incumbent contractor. The last time it was competed, in 2001, HHS received no offers other than SAIC-Frederick, which has performed the contract satisfactorily since then. HHS publicly posted in FedBizOpps its intention to noncompetitively renew the operations and technical support contract with SAIC-Frederick for a potential 10-year period. Interested parties were allowed to submit capability statements, but despite some initial interest none were submitted.

DHS competed the initial contract awards for the start up of its two FFRDCs, with the award of the first contract in 2004. DHS plans to compete the award of the next studies and analyses FFRDC contract this year.

In contrast, DOD continues to award its FFRDC contracts on a sole-source basis under statutory exemptions to competition. In the early 1990s, a report by a Senate subcommittee[12] and a Defense Science Board task force both criticized DOD's management and use of its FFRDCs, including a lack of competition in contract award. This criticism mirrored an earlier GAO observation.[13] GAO subsequently noted in a 1996 report, however, that DOD had begun to strengthen its process for justifying its use of FFRDCs under sole-source contracts for specific purposes.[14] DOD plans to continue its sole-source contracting for the three FFRDC contracts that are due for renewal in 2008 and the six contracts to be renewed in 2010.

Agencies Use Cost- Reimbursement Contracts with Varying Types of Fee Structures, Primarily Funded through Program Offices

All of the FFRDC contracts we reviewed were cost-reimbursement contracts,[15] most of which provided for payments of fixed, award, or incentive fees to the contractor in addition to reimbursement of incurred costs. Fixed fees often are used when, according to the agencies we reviewed, the FFRDC will need working capital or other miscellaneous expense requirements that cannot be covered through reimbursing direct and indirect costs. Fixed fees generally account for a small percentage of the overall contract costs; for fiscal year 2007 fixed fees paid to the FFRDCs we reviewed vary from a low of about 0.1 percent to a high of 3 percent. Award or incentive fees, on the other hand, are intended to motivate contractors toward such areas as excellent technical performance and cost effective management.[16] These types of performance-based fees ranged from 1 to 7 percent at the agencies we reviewed.

Among agencies we reviewed, contract provisions on fees varied significantly:

Most DOD contracts are cost-plus-fixed-fee,[17] and DOD, as a general rule, does not provide award or incentive fees to its FFRDCs. DOD's FFRDC management plan—its internal guidance document for DOD entities that sponsor FFRDCs—limits fees to amounts needed to fund ordinary and necessary business expenses that may not be otherwise recoverable under the reimbursement rules that apply to these types of contracts. For example, the FFRDC operator may incur a one-time expense to buy an expensive piece of needed equipment, but the government's reimbursement rules require that this expense be recovered over several future years in accordance with an amortization schedule. DOD's management plan indicates that fees are necessary in such instances to enable the contractor to service the debt incurred to buy the equipment and maintain the cash flow needed for the contractor's business operations. DOD officials told us they scrutinize these fees carefully and do not always pay them. For example, the contract between DOD and the Massachusetts Institute of Technology (MIT), which operates the Lincoln Laboratory FFRDC, specifies that MIT will not receive such fees.

DOE and DHS use fixed fees, performance-based fees, and award terms, which can extend the length of the contract as a reward for good performance. For example, Sandia Corporation, a private company that operates Sandia National Laboratories, receives both a fixed fee and an incentive fee, which for fiscal year 2007 together amounted to about $23.2 million, an additional 1 percent beyond its estimated contract cost. In addition, Sandia Corporation has received award terms that have lengthened its contract by 10 years.

HHS provides only performance-based fees to the private company that operates its one FFRDC.

Rather than receiving direct appropriations, most FFRDCs are funded on a project-by-project basis by the customers, either within or outside of the sponsoring agency, that wish to use their services by using funds allocated to a program or office. FFRDC contracts generally specify a total estimated cost for work to be performed and provide for the issuance of modifications or orders for the performance of specific projects and tasks during the period of the contract.

Congressional appropriations conferees sometimes directed specific funding for some DHS and DOD FFRDCs in conference reports accompanying sponsoring agencies' appropriations. For example, although according to DOD officials, 97 percent of its FFRDC funding comes from program or office allocations to fund specific projects, half of its FFRDCs receive some directed amounts specified in connection with DOD's annual appropriations process. Specifically, for fiscal year 2008, the following DOD FFRDCs received conferee-directed funding in the DOD appropriations conference report: MIT Lincoln Laboratory Research Program, $30 million; the Software Engineering Institute, $26 million; the Center for Naval Analyses, $49 million; the RAND Project Air Force, $31 million;[18] and the Arroyo Center, $20 million. In addition, DOD officials noted that the congressional defense committees sometimes direct DOD's FFRDCs to perform specific studies for these committees through legislation or in committee reports. In fiscal year 2008, two DOD FFRDCs conducted 16 congressionally requested studies.

All Four Agencies Address Organizational Conflicts of Interest but Vary in Addressing Personal Conflicts of Interest of FFRDC Employees

As FFRDCs may have access to sensitive and proprietary information and because of the special relationship between sponsoring agencies and their FFRDCs, the FAR requires that FFRDC contractors be free from organizational conflicts of interest. In addition, we recently reported that, given the expanding roles that contractor employees play, government officials from the Office of Government Ethics and DOD believe that current requirements are inadequate to address potential personal conflicts of interest of contractor employees in positions to influence agency decisions.[19] While each agency we reviewed requires FFRDC operators to be free of organizational conflicts of interest, DOD and DOE prescribe specific areas that FFRDC contractors must address to ensure their employees are free from personal conflicts of interest.

The FAR states that an organizational conflict of interest exists when because of other interests or relationships, an entity is unable or potentially unable to render impartial assistance or advice to the government or the entity might have an unfair competitive advantage. Because sponsors rely on FFRDCs to give impartial, technically sound, objective assistance or advice, FFRDCs are required to conduct their business in a manner befitting their special relationship with the government, to operate in the public interest with objectivity and independence, to be free from organizational conflicts of interest, and to fully disclose their affairs to the sponsoring agency.[20] Each sponsoring agency we reviewed included conflict-of-interest clauses in its sponsoring agreements with contractors operating their FFRDCs. For example, a DHS FFRDC contract includes a clause that specifically prohibits contractors that have developed specifications or statements of work for solicitations from performing the work as either a prime or first-tier subcontractor.

In addition to organizational conflicts of interest requirements, DOD and DOE have specific requirements for their FFRDC contractors to guard against personal conflicts of interest of their employees. For purposes of this report, a personal conflict of interest may occur when an individual employed by an organization is in a position to materially influence an agency's recommendations and/or decisions and who—because of his or her personal activities, relationships, or financial interests—may either lack or appear to lack objectivity or appear to be unduly influenced by personal financial interests. In January 2007, the Under Secretary of Defense (Acquisition, Technology, and Logistics) implemented an updated standard conflict-of-interest policy for all of DOD's FFRDCs that requires FFRDC contractors to establish policies to address major areas of personal conflicts of interest such as gifts, outside activities, and financial interests. The updated policy and implementing procedures now are included in all DOD FFRDC sponsoring agreements and incorporated into the DOD FFRDC operating contracts. This action was prompted by public and congressional scrutiny of a perceived conflict of interest by the president of a DOD FFRDC who then voluntarily resigned.[21] As a result, DOD's Deputy General Counsel (Acquisition and Logistics) reviewed the conflict of interest policies and procedures in place at each of its FFRDCs and determined that although sponsoring agreements, contracts, and internal policies were adequate, they should be revised to better protect DOD from employee-related conflicts. DOD's revised policy states that conflicts of interest could diminish an FFRDC's objectivity and capacity to give impartial, technically sound, objective assistance or advice, which is essential to the research, particularly with regard to FFRDCs' access to sensitive information. Therefore, the policy provides that FFRDC conflict of interest policies address such issues as gifts and outside activities and requires an annual submission of statements of financial interests from all FFRDC personnel in a position to make or materially influence research findings or recommendations that might affect outside interests.

DOE's FFRDCs, which operate under management and operating (M&O)[22] contracts—a special FAR designation for government-owned, contractor- operated facilities such as DOE's—have additional provisions for addressing personal conflicts of interest. The provisions address such areas as reporting any outside employment that may constitute a personal conflict of interest.[23] In addition, the National Nuclear Security Administration (NNSA), which sponsors three of DOE's FFRDCs, is planning to implement additional requirements in its laboratory contracts later this year requiring contractors to disclose all employee personal conflict of interests, not just outside employment as is currently required. An NNSA procurement official noted that other personal conflict of interests may include any relationship of an employee, subcontractor employee, or consultant that may impair objectivity in performing contract work. NNSA officials stated that it plans to share the policy with the DOE policy office for potential application across the department.

Currently, DHS and HHS policies do not specifically prescribe areas that contractors must include to address employees personal conflicts. However, DHS officials stated that they provided guidance to the two contractors that operate DHS's FFRDCs to implement requirements to address some of their employees' personal conflicts with DHS's interests. In addition, both DHS and HHS FFRDC contractors provide that their staff avoid or disclose financial interests or outside activities that may conflict with the interests of the company. For example, the contractor operating the FFRDC for HHS requires about 20 percent of its employees to report activities that may constitute a conflict with the company's interests, but allows the bulk of its staff to self-determine when they need to report.

In May 2008, we reported that officials from the Office of Government Ethics expressed concerns that current federal requirements and policies are inadequate to prevent certain kinds of ethical violations on the part of contractor employees, particularly with regard to financial conflicts of interest, impaired impartiality, and misuse of information and authority. The acting director identified particular concerns with such conflicts of interest in the management and operations of large research facilities and laboratories. Our report noted that DOD ethics officials had generally the same concerns. Therefore, we recommended that DOD implement personal conflict-of-interest safeguards—similar to those for federal employees—for certain contractor employees. [24]

AGENCIES VARY IN FFRDC OVERSIGHT APPROACHES AND DO NOT REGULARLY SHARE BEST PRACTICES

Sponsoring agencies take various approaches in exercising oversight of their FFRDCs. The agencies determine appropriateness of work conducted by their FFRDCs; perform on-going and annual assessments of performance, costs and internal controls; and conduct comprehensive reviews prior to renewing sponsoring agreements. Each agency develops its own processes in these areas, and no formal interagency mechanisms exist to facilitate the sharing of FFRDC oversight best practices.

Agencies Approve Research Plans and Work Conducted at Their FFRDCs

To ensure work remains within each FFRDCs purpose, mission, scope of effort, and special competency, sponsoring agencies develop and approve annual research plans for the FFRDCs and review and approve FFRDC work assigned on a project-by-project basis. While the majority of each FFRDC's work is done for its sponsoring agency, FFRDCs may perform work for other institutions, subject to sponsoring agency approval. [25]

Officials at DOD, DOE, and DHS identified the processes they use to develop annual research plans that describe each FFRDC's research agenda. For example, DHS designates an executive agent to ensure that its FFRDC is used for the agency's intended purposes. [26] Each year DHS develops a research plan that is reviewed and approved by the executive agent, including any subsequent changes. DHS also uses an Advisory Group[27] to ensure that its FFRDCs produce work consistent with the sponsoring agreement. DOD has a similar mechanism for approving the annual research plan for its Lincoln Laboratory FFRDC. This FFRDC has a Joint Advisory Committee that annually reviews and approves the proposed research plan. Members of this committee include representatives from the various DOD services—e.g., Air Force, Army, and Navy—who are the users of the laboratory's R&D capabilities. Of the four agencies included in our review, only HHS does not create a separate annual research plan for its FFRDC. Instead, the work at HHS' FFRDC is guided by the National Cancer Institute's overall mission, which is described in its annual budgetary and periodic strategic planning documents.

In determining the proposed research plan, DOD must abide by congressionally set workload caps. These caps were imposed in the 1990's in response to concerns that DOD was inefficiently using its FFRDCs, and therefore, each fiscal year Congress sets an annual limitation on the Staffyears of Technical Effort (STE) that DOD FFRDCs can use to conduct work for the agency. The STE limitations aim to ensure that (1) work is appropriate and (2) limited resources are used for DOD's highest priorities. Congress also sets an additional workload cap for DOD's FFRDCs for certain intelligence programs.[28] Once DOD receives from Congress the annual total for STEs, then DOD's Office of the Undersecretary of Acquisition, Technology and Logistics allocates them across DOD's FFRDCs based on priorities set forth in the annual research plan developed by each FFRDC. DOD officials observed that while the overall DOD budget has increased about 40 percent since the early 1990s, the STE caps have remained steady, and therefore, DOD must turn aside or defer some FFRDC-appropriate work to subsequent years. Although the majority of work that DOD's FFRDCs conduct is subject to these limitations, the work that DOD FFRDCs conduct for non-DOD entities is not subject to these caps.

Each sponsoring agency also reviews and approves tasks for individual FFRDC projects to make sure that those tasks (1) are consistent with the core statement of the FFRDC and (2) would not constitute a "personal service"[29] or inherently governmental function.[30] Listed below are examples of procedures used by agencies included in our review to approve tasks for individual projects:

> DOD sponsors generally incorporate in their sponsoring agreement guidelines for performance of work by the FFRDC. The work is screened at various levels for appropriateness, beginning with FFRDC clients who request the work, then program and contract managers, and then it is reviewed and approved as well by the primary sponsor. In some cases, projects are entered into a computer-based tool, which the Air Force has developed to determine and develop its overall requirements for that year. The tool is intended to assist the Air Force in prioritizing requests for its FFRDC and in ensuring that work requested is in accordance with guidelines and that potential alternative sources have been considered.
> DOE FFRDCs must document all DOE-funded projects using work authorizations[31] to help ensure that the projects are consistent with DOE's budget execution and program evaluation requirements.[32] In addition, DOE uses an independent scientific peer-review approach—including faculty members and executives from other laboratories—at several of its FFRDC laboratories to ensure the work performed is appropriate for the FFRDC and scientifically sound. In some cases, DOE's Office of

Science holds scientific merit competitions between national laboratories (including FFRDCs), universities, and other research organizations for some R&D funding for specific projects.

HHS uses an automated "yellow task" system to determine if work is appropriate for its FFRDC, and several officials must approve requests for work, including the government contracting officer and overseeing project officer for the FFRDC, with reference to a set of criteria. This agency requires a concept review by advisory boards for the various HHS institutes to ensure the concept is appropriate for the FFRDC and meets its mission or special competency.

DHS requires certain officials at its sponsoring office to conduct a suitability review using established procedures for reviewing and approving DHS-sponsored tasks. This review is required under DHS's Management Directive for FFRDCs.

FFRDCs are required to have their sponsors review and approve any work they conduct for others, and the four agencies included in our review have policies and procedures to do so. FFRDCs may conduct work for others when required capabilities are not otherwise available from the private sector. This work for others can be done for federal agencies, private sector companies,[33] and local and state governments. The sponsoring agency of an FFRDC offers the work for others, with full costs charged to the requesting entity, to provide research and technical assistance to solve problems. At laboratory FFRDCs, work for others can include creating working models or prototypes. All work placed with the FFRDC must be within the purpose, mission, general scope of effort, or special competency of the FFRDC.[34]

Work for others is considered a technology transfer[35] mechanism, which helps in sharing knowledge and skills between the government and the private sector. Under work for others, according to DOD officials and federal regulation, the title to intellectual property generally belongs to the FFRDC conducting the work, and the government may obtain a nonexclusive, royalty-free license to such intellectual property or may choose to obtain the exclusive rights.[36] As required by FAR, sponsoring agreements or sponsoring agencies we reviewed identified the extent to which their FFRDCs may perform work for other than the sponsors (other federal agencies, state or local government, nonprofit or profit organizations, etc.) and the procedures that must be followed by the sponsoring agency and the FFRDC.[37] In addition, according to agency officials FFRDCs have a responsibility to steer inquiries about potential research for other entities to their primary sponsor's attention for approval. Agency officials stated that they work with their FFRDCs when such situations arise.

Table 1. Funding for FFRDC "Work for Others" (Fiscal Year 2001 to 2005)

Dollars in thousands					
Sponsoring agency and name of FFRDC	FY 2001	FY 2002	FY 2003	FY 2004	FY 2005[a]
DOE, Office of Science Ernest Orlando Lawrence Berkeley National Laboratory	$69,879	$67,053	$59,911	$76,360	$71,879
DOE, National Nuclear Security Administration Sandia National Laboratories	$114,390	$143,798	$130,614	$171,492	$270,438

HHS, National Cancer Institute National Cancer Institute at Frederick (NCI-F)	$30,810	$52,122	$119,490	$144,184	$105,559
DOD, Office of the Secretary of Defense C3I [Command, Control, Communications, and Intelligence] Center	$47,300	$69,800	$98,800	$134,000	$163,700
DOD, Office of the Secretary of Defense Institute for Defense Analyses (IDA) Studies and Analyses Center	$2,602	$5,712	$7,825	$22,504[b]	$6,547
DOD, Department of the Air Force MIT Lincoln Laboratory	$53,368	$51,604	$43,885	$65,161	$64,408
DHS, Office of Science and Technology Homeland Security Institute[c]				$0	$0
DHS, Office of Science and Technology National Biodefense Analysis and Countermeasures Center (NBACC)[d]					

Source: GAO Analysis of data provide by the National Science Foundation (NSF) and by listed agencies (where provided).

[a]Most recently available complete data.

[b]According to DOD, the fiscal year 2004 data for IDA includes $14.3 million from DHS for work regarding implementation of the Support Anti-terrorism by Fostering Effective Technologies Act of 2002 (the SAFETY Act).

[c]Homeland Security Institute (HSI), was funded as a new FFRDC in fiscal year 2004.

[d]National Biodefense Analysis and Countermeasures Center (NBACC), was funded as a new FFRDC in fiscal year 2007.

DOE's Office of Science established a "Work for Others Program" for all of its FFRDC laboratories. Under this program, the contractor of the FFRDC must draft, implement, and maintain formal policies, practices, and procedures, which must be submitted to the contracting officer for review and approval.[38] In addition, DOE may conduct periodic appraisals of the contractor's compliance with its Work for Others Program policies, practices, and procedures.[39] For DOE's National Nuclear Security Administration (NNSA), officials reported that the work for others process at the Sandia National Laboratories requires DOE approval before the Sandia Corporation develops the proposed statement of work, which is then sent to DOE's site office for review and approval.

For DHS, each FFRDC includes the work for others policy in its management plan. For example, one management plan states that the FFRDC may perform work for others and that such work is subject to review by the sponsoring agency for compliance with criteria mutually agreed upon by the sponsor and the FFRDC contractor. The DHS FFRDC laboratory director said he routinely approves any work-for-others requests but gives first priority to the DHS-sponsored work. The sponsor for this FFRDC also periodically assesses whether its work for others impairs its ability to perform work for its sponsor.

HHS and DOD also have work-for-others programs for the FFRDCs they sponsor. For example, at HHS's FFRDC the program is conducted under a bilateral contract between the entity that is requesting the work and the FFRDC to perform a defined scope of work for a defined cost. This agency developed a standard Work for Others Agreement for its FFRDC, the terms and conditions of which help ensure that the FFRDC complies with applicable laws, regulations, policies, and directives specified in its contract with the HHS.

Some agency sponsors report that work for others at their FFRDCs has grown in the past few years. For example, DOE officials said work for others at the Sandia National Laboratories related to nanotechnologies and cognitive sciences has grown in the last 3 years. As shown in table 1, the amount of work for others by FFRDCs since fiscal year 2001 has increased for many of the FFRDCs included in our review.

While funding for work for others has increased, some agencies in our review reported limiting the amount of work for others their FFRDCs conduct. For example, DOE's Office of Science annually approves overall work-for-others funding levels at its laboratories based on a request from the laboratory and recommendation from the responsible site office. Any work-for-others program that is above 20 percent of the laboratory's operating budget, or any request that represents a significant change from previous year's work-for-others program will be reviewed in depth before the approval is provided. Similarly, DOE officials limit commitments to conduct work for others at the National Renewable Energy Laboratory's to about 10 percent of the laboratory's total workload.

Agencies Assess FFRDCs' Performance, Costs, and Internal Controls

In addition to ensuring work is appropriate for their FFRDCs, the four sponsoring agencies in our case study regularly review the contractors' performance in operating the FFRDCs, including reviewing and approving costs incurred in operations and internal control mechanisms. Agency performance evaluations for FFRDC contractors vary, particularly between those that incorporate performance elements into their contracts and those that do not. Furthermore, contracting officers at each agency regularly review costs to ensure that they are appropriate, in some cases relying on audits of costs and internal controls to highlight any potential issues.

Agencies Review Performance of FFRDC and Operating Contractor

All four agencies conduct at least annual reviews of the performance of their FFRDCs and contractors. At three agencies, the outcomes of these reviews provide the basis for contractors to earn performance-based incentives or awards. Specifically, DOE, HHS, and DHS provide for award fees[40] to motivate contractors toward excellence in high performance, and contractors operating FFRDCs for DOE and DHS may earn additional contract extensions by exceeding performance expectations.

DOE uses a performance-based contracting approach with its FFRDCs, which includes several mechanisms to assess performance. First, DOE requires contractors to conduct annual self-assessments of their management and operational performance. Also, contracting officers conduct annual assessments of the performance of the FFRDC contractor, relying in part on user satisfaction surveys. All of this input contributes to each lab's annual assessment rating. For example, Sandia National Laboratories, operated by Sandia Corporation (a subsidiary of Lockheed Martin) received an overall rating of "outstanding" for fiscal year 2007 and was awarded 91 percent of its available award fee ($7.6 million of a possible total fee of $8.4 million). DOE noted that Sandia National Laboratories' scientific and engineering support of U.S. national security was an exceptional performance area. DOE publishes such "report cards" for its laboratories on the internet. DOE includes detailed performance requirements in each contract in a Performance Evaluation and Measurement Plan that is organized by goals, objectives, measures, and targets. The DOE Office of Science mandates that each of its ten FFRDC laboratories establish the same eight goals[41] in each FFRDC's contractual plan. For example, the Ernest Orlando Lawrence Berkeley National Laboratory, operated by the University of California, received high ratings in providing efficient and effective mission accomplishment and science and technology program management. These ratings resulted in an award of 94 percent or $4.2 million of the total available fee of $4.5 million.

HHS, which also uses performance-based contracting, has identified certain designated government personnel to be responsible for evaluation of the FFRDC contractor. This review process includes different levels of reviews, from coordinators who review performance evaluations to an FFRDC Performance Evaluation Board, which is responsible for assessing the contractor's overall performance. The board rates each area of evaluation based on an established Performance Rating System to determine the amount of the contractor's award fee. In fiscal year 2007, the National Cancer Institute at Frederick, operated by Science Applications International Corporation-Frederick (a subsidiary of Science Applications International Corporation), received 92 percent of its available award fee or $6.9 million of a possible $7.4 million.

Similar to the other agencies, DHS regularly conducts performance reviews throughout the life cycle of its FFRDC contract. This includes program reviews as described in the sponsoring agreement, midyear status reviews, technical progress reports, monthly and quarterly reports, and annual stakeholder surveys to ensure the FFRDC is meeting customer needs. DHS also drafts a multiyear improvement plan and collects performance metrics as evidence of the FFRDC's performance. For fiscal year 2007, Battelle National Biodefense Institute, operating the National Biodefense Analysis and Countermeasures Center, received 82 percent of its performance-based award fee amounting to $1.4 million. According to DHS officials, Analytic Services, Inc., which operates the Homeland Security Institute, received a fixed fee of about 2 percent or approximately $.68 million for fiscal year 2007.

DOD conducts annual performance reviews and other internal reviews, such as conducting periodic program management reviews and annual customer surveys to monitor the performance of its FFRDCs in meeting their customers' expectations. As part of this review process, major users are asked to provide their perspectives on such factors as the use and continuing need for the FFRDC, and how these users distinguish work to be performed by the FFRDC from work to be performed by others. According to DOD, these performance evaluations provide essential input to help it assess the effectiveness and efficiency of the FFRDC's operations. Typically the performance reviews obtain ratings from FFRDC users and sponsors on a variety of factors including the quality and value of the work conducted by the FFRDCs, as well as its ability to meet technical needs, provide timely and responsive service, and manage costs.[42]

Agencies Review Costs and Internal Controls

Federal regulations, policies, and contracts establish various cost, accounting, and auditing controls that agencies use to assess the adequacy of FFRDC management in ensuring cost-effective operations and ensure that costs of services being provided to the government are reasonable.[43] Sponsors of the FFRDCs we reviewed employ a variety of financial and auditing oversight mechanisms to review contractors' management controls, including incurred cost audits, general financial and operational audits, annual organizational audits, and audited financial statements. These mechanisms differ, depending on the agencies involved and the type of organization operating the FFRDCs.[44]

Under cost-reimbursement contracts, the costs incurred are subject to cost principles applicable to the type of entity operating the FFRDC.[45] Most FFRDC contracts we examined include a standard clause on allowable costs that limits contract costs to amounts that are reasonable and in compliance with applicable provisions of the FAR.[46] Under the FAR, contracting officers are responsible for authorizing cost-reimbursement payments and may request audits at their discretion before a payment is made. In addition, when an allowable cost clause is included in a contract, the FAR requires that an indirect cost rate proposal be submitted annually for audit.[47] At DOD, the Defense Contract Audit Agency (DCAA) generally performs both annual incurred cost audits and close-out audits for completed contracts and task orders at the end of an FFRDC's 5-year contract term. The audit results are included in the comprehensive review of DOD's continued need for its FFRDCs. DCAA also performs these types of audits for DHS's FFRDCs. At DOE, the Office of the Inspector General is responsible for incurred cost audits for major facilities contractors. At HHS, officials stated that while the contracting officer for its FFRDC regularly reviews the incurred costs, no audits of these costs have been performed.

Agencies and FFRDC contractors also conduct financial and operational audits[48] in addition to incurred cost audits. DOE relies primarily upon FFRDC contractors' annual internal audits[49] rather than on third-party monitoring through external audits. These internal audits are designed to implement DOE's Cooperative Audit Strategy—a program that partners DOE's Inspector General with contractors' internal audit groups to maximize the overall audit coverage of M&O contractors' operations and to fulfill the Inspector General's responsibility for auditing the costs incurred by major facilities contractors.[50] This cooperative audit strategy permits the Inspector General to make use of the work of contractors' internal audit organizations to perform operational and financial audits, including incurred cost audits, and to assess the adequacy of contractors' management control systems. DHS and DOD generally rely on audits performed by those agencies, a designated audit agency, or an accounting firm, though their FFRDC contractors usually perform some degree of internal audit or review function as part of their overall management activity.

In addition, all nonprofits and educational institutions that annually expend more than $500,000 in federal awards—including those that operate FFRDCs—are subject to the Single Audit Act[51] which requires annual audits of: (1) financial statements, (2) internal controls, and (3) compliance with laws and regulations. We have previously reported these audits constitute a key accountability mechanism for federal awards and generally are performed by independent auditors.[52] At DOD, for example, DCAA participates in single audits normally on a "coordinated basis"—at the election of the organization being audited— with the audited organization's independent public accountant. The financial statements, schedules, corrective action plan, and audit reports make up the single audit package, which the audited organization is responsible for submitting to a federal clearing house designated by OMB to receive, distribute, and retain. DOD's Office of Inspector General, for example, as a responsible federal agency, receives all single audit submissions for nonprofits and educational institutions that operate DOD's FFRDCs. These audit results are employed by DOD as partial evidence of its FFRDCs' cost- effectiveness and incorporated in the 5-year comprehensive reviews. These annual single audits for nonprofit and educational FFRDC contractors are a useful adjunct to other cost, accounting, and auditing controls discussed previously, designed to help determine contractor effectiveness, efficiency, and accountability in the management and operation of their FFRDCs.

Private contractors that publicly trade their securities on the exchanges— including those that operate FFRDCs[53]—are registered with the Securities and Exchange Commission (SEC) and are required to file audited financial statements with the SEC. These audited statements must be prepared in conformity with generally accepted accounting principles (GAAP) and securities laws and regulations, including Sarbanes-Oxley, that address governance, auditing, and financial reporting.[54] These financial statements are designed to disclose information for the benefit of the investing public, not to meet government agencies' information needs. Accordingly, SAIC and Lockheed—private contractors that manage National Cancer Institute at Frederick and Sandia National Laboratories respectively—prepare audited financial statements for their corporate entities, but do not separately report information on their individual FFRDCs' operations.

Finally, even though financial statements are not required by university and nonprofit sponsored FFRDCs, some of the FFRDCs in agencies we reviewed have audited financial statements prepared solely for their own operations. DOD's Aerospace and DHS's HSI and NBACC are examples. Most others' financial operations, however, are included in the audited financial statements of their parent organizations or operating contractor. Some, like MITRE, which manages not only DOD's C3I FFRDC but also two others (one for the Federal Aviation Administration and one for the Internal Revenue Service), provides supplemental schedules, with balance sheets, revenues and expenses, and sources and uses of funds for all three FFRDCs.[55] Others, like the Institute for Defense Analyses, which also operates two other FFRDCs in addition to the Studies and Analyses Center for DOD, provide only a consolidated corporate statement with no information on specific FFRDCs.

Agencies Periodically Rejustify Their Sponsorship of FFRDCs

The FAR requires that a comprehensive review be undertaken prior to extending a sponsoring agreement for an FFRDC. We found that the four agencies in our case study were conducting and documenting these reviews, but noted that implementation of this requirement by each agency is based on its own distinct management policies, procedures, and practices.

During the reviews prior to agreement renewal, sponsoring agencies should include the following five areas identified by the FAR

examination of the continued need for FFRDC to address its sponsor's technical needs and mission requirements;

consideration of alternative sources, if any, to meet those needs;

assessment of the FFRDC's efficiency and effectiveness in meeting the sponsor's needs, including objectivity, independence, quick response capability, currency in its field(s) of expertise, and familiarity with the sponsor;

assessment of the adequacy of FFRDC management in ensuring a cost- effective operation; and

determination that the original reason for establishing the FFRDC still exists and that the sponsoring agreement is in compliance with FAR requirements for such agreements.[56]

DOD sponsoring offices begin conducting detailed analyses for each of the five FAR review criteria approximately 1 to 2 years in advance of the renewal date. As DOD has received criticism in the past for its lack of competition in awarding FFRDC contracts, it now conducts detailed and lengthy comprehensive reviews prior to renewing FFRDC sponsoring agreements and contracts with incumbent providers. DOD's FFRDC Management Plan lays out procedures to help provide consistency and thoroughness in meeting FAR provisions for the comprehensive review process. DOD procedures require, and the comprehensive reviews we examined generally provided, detailed examinations of the mission and technical requirements for each FFRDC user, and explanations of why capabilities cannot be provided as effectively by other alternative sources. For example, DOD convened a high level, independent Technical Review Panel to review whether Lincoln Laboratory's research programs were within its mission as well as whether the research was effective, of high technical quality, and of critical importance to DOD. The panel—composed of a former Assistant Secretary of the Air Force, a former president of another FFRDC, former senior military officers, and a high level industry representative—found that no other organizations had the capacity to conduct a comparable research program. In addition, DOD sponsors use information from annual surveys of FFRDC users that address such performance areas as cost effectiveness and technical expertise. Determinations to continue or terminate the FFRDC agreement are made by the heads of sponsoring DOD components (e.g., the Secretary of the Army or Air Force) with review and concurrence by the Office of the Under Secretary of Defense for Acquisition, Technology, and Logistics.

DOE has a documented comprehensive review process that explicitly requires DOE sponsors to assess the use and continued need for the FFRDC before the term of the agreement has expired. DOE's process requires that the review be conducted at the same time as the review regarding the decision to extend (by option) or compete its FFRDC operating contract. According to DOE's regulation,[57] the option period for these contracts may not exceed 5 years and the total term of the contract, including any options exercised, may not exceed 10 years. DOE relies on information developed as part of its annual performance review assessments as well as information developed through the contractor's internal audit process to make this determination. The comprehensive review conducted prior to the most recent award of the contract to operate Sandia National Laboratories concluded that the FFRDC's overall performance for the preceding 6 years had been outstanding. The Secretary of Energy determined that the criteria for establishing the FFRDC continued to be satisfied and that the sponsoring agreement was in compliance with FAR provisions.

At DHS, we found that its guidance and process for the comprehensive review mirror many aspects of the DOD process. DHS has undertaken only one such review to date, which was completed in May 2008. As of the time we completed our work, DHS officials told us that the documentation supporting the agency's review had not yet been approved for release.

HHS—in contrast to the structured review processes of the other agencies—relies on the judgment of the sponsoring office's senior management team, which reviews the need for the continued sponsorship of the FFRDC and determines whether it meets the FAR requirements.

Agency officials stated that this review relies on a discussion of the FFRDC's ability to meet the agency's needs within the FAR criteria, but noted there are no formal procedures laid out for this process. The final determination is approved by the director of the National Cancer Institute and then the director of the National Institutes of Health.

No Formal Interagency Mechanisms Exist for Sharing of Best Practices for Overseeing FFRDCs

Some agencies have used the experiences of other agencies as a model for their own oversight of their FFRDCs. There is no formal mechanism, however, for sharing of best practices and lessons learned among sponsoring agencies.

DHS officials have adopted several of DOD's and DOE's policies and procedures for managing FFRDCs to help their newly created FFRDCs gain efficiencies. DHS mirrored most of DOD's FFRDC Management Plan, and officials have stated that the STE limitations for DOD could be a potentially useful tool for focusing FFRDCs on the most strategic and critical work for the agency. Also, DHS officials stated they have made use of DOE's experience in contracting for and overseeing the operation of its laboratories, such as including a DOE official in the DHS process to select a contractor to operate its laboratory FFRDC. In addition, HHS officials said they are incorporating the DOE Blue Ribbon Report recommendation to set aside a portion of the incentive fee paid on their FFRDC contract to reward scientific innovations or research. The idea for the new contract is to base 80 percent of the available award fee in a performance period on operations and use the final 20 percent to reward innovation. HHS also may adopt the technique used by DOE of providing for contract extensions on the basis of demonstrated exceptional performance.

To take advantage of others' experiences, some FFRDCs sponsored by particular agencies have formed informal groups to share information. For example, DOD's FFRDCs have formed informal groups at the functional level—Chief Financial Officers, Chief Technology Officers, and General Counsels—which meet periodically to share information on issues of common concern. In addition, the security personnel from the DOD FFRDC contractors meet once a year to discuss security and export control related issues. The contractor officials at Sandia National Laboratories said they share best practices for operating DOE's laboratory FFRDCs at forums such as the National Laboratory Improvement Council. This Council was also mentioned in a DOE review of management best practices for the national laboratories[58] as one of the few groups that deliberate a broader and more integrated agenda among laboratories.

Despite these instances of information sharing within agencies and the acknowledgment by some officials of potential benefits in such knowledge sharing, no formal mechanisms exist for sharing information across agencies that sponsor and oversee FFRDCs. We reported in 2005 that federal agencies often carry out related programs in a fragmented, uncoordinated way, resulting in a patchwork of programs that can waste scarce funds, confuse and frustrate program customers, and limit the overall effectiveness of the federal effort.[59] The report suggested frequent communication across agency boundaries can prevent misunderstandings, promote compatibility of standards, policies, and procedures, and enhance collaboration. For example, the Federal Laboratory Consortium for Technical Transfer was created to share information across national laboratories. This includes the FFRDC laboratories, but not the other types of FFRDCs. Some agency officials stated that there would be benefits to sharing such best practices.

CONCLUSIONS

All federal agencies that sponsor FFRDCs are subject to the same federal regulations, and each agency included in our review has developed its own processes and procedures to ensure compliance and conduct oversight of its FFRDCs. For the most part the differences in approaches are not of great consequence. In at least one key area, however, the different approaches have the potential to produce significantly different results. Specifically, while all FFRDCs are required to address organizational conflicts of interest, only DOD and DOE have requirements that their FFRDC contractors address specific areas of personal conflicts of interest of their employees. In light of the special relationship that FFRDCs have with their sponsoring agencies, which often involves access to sensitive or confidential information, it is critical not only that the FFRDC as an entity but also that employees of the entity in positions to make or influence research findings or agency decision making be free from conflicts. Lacking such safeguards, the FFRDC's objectivity and ability to provide impartial, technically sound, objective assistance or advice may be diminished. The two agencies with the most experience sponsoring FFRDCs have recognized this gap and have taken steps to address personal conflicts of interest. These steps are consistent with our recent recommendation to DOD that highlighted the need for personal conflictsof-interest safeguards for certain contractor employees. The other agencies included in our review of FFRDCs could benefit from additional protections in the area of personal conflicts of interest. Currently, although DHS and HHS have policies that generally require their FFRDC contractors to implement such safeguards, they lack the specificity needed to ensure their FFRDC contractors will consistently address employees' personal conflicts of interest.

Conflict-of-interest requirements is only one of several areas where agencies that sponsor FFRDCs can learn from each other. Other areas include the use of effective and efficient oversight mechanisms such as incentive and award fees, obtaining competition, and conducting comprehensive reviews. In the absence of established knowledge-sharing mechanisms, however, agencies may be missing opportunities to enhance their management and oversight practices. Sharing knowledge among agencies that sponsor FFRDCs, as has been done informally in some instances, could help to ensure that agencies are aware of all the various tools available to enhance their ability to effectively oversee their FFRDCs.

RECOMMENDATIONS FOR EXECUTIVE ACTION

To ensure that FFRDC employees operate in the government's best interest, we recommend

- that the Secretary of Homeland Security revise agency policies to address specific areas for potential personal conflicts of interest for FFRDC personnel in a position to make or materially influence research findings or agency decision making; and
- that the Secretary of Health and Human Services review agency policy regarding personal conflicts of interest for its sponsored FFRDC and revise as appropriate to ensure that this policy addresses all personnel in a position to make or materially influence research findings or agency decision making.

To improve the sharing of oversight best practices among agencies that sponsor the vast majority of the government's FFRDCs, we recommend that the Secretaries of Energy, Defense, Homeland Security, and Health and Human Services, which together sponsor the vast majority of the government's FFRDCs, take the lead in establishing an ongoing forum for government personnel from these and other agencies that sponsor FFRDCs to discuss their agencies' FFRDC policies and practices. Areas for knowledge sharing could include, for example, implementing personal conflicts of interest safeguards and processes for completing the justification reviews prior to renewing sponsoring agreements, among others.

AGENCY COMMENTS AND OUR EVALUATION

The Departments of Health and Human Services and Homeland Security concurred with our recommendation that they revise their conflict of interest policies. In addition, the departments of Defense, Energy, and Homeland Security all concurred with our recommendation to establish a forum to share best practices, while HHS is considering participation in such a forum. We received letters from Defense, Energy, and Health and Human Services, which are reprinted in appendixes III, IV, and V, respectively. In addition, the departments of Health and Human Services and Homeland Security provided technical comments, which we incorporated where appropriate.

As agreed with your office, unless you publicly announce the contents of this report earlier, we plan no further distribution of it until 30 days from the date of this report. We then will provide copies of this report to the Secretaries of Defense, Energy, Health and Human Services and Homeland Security and other interested parties.

William T. Woods

William Woods
Director
Acquisition and Sourcing Management

APPENDIX I. OBJECTIVES, SCOPE, AND METHODOLOGY

To conduct this review, we chose a nongeneralizable sample of four of the nine federal agencies that sponsor FFRDCs: the departments of Energy (DOE) and Defense (DOD) have the longest histories in sponsoring federally funded research and development centers (FFRDCs) and sponsor the most—16 and 10, respectively; the Department of Homeland Security (DHS) has the 2 most recently established FFRDCs; the Department of Health and Human Services (HHS) has 1 FFRDC laboratory. From the collective 29 FFRDCs that those four agencies sponsor, we selected a nongeneralizable sample of 8 FFRDCs that represented variation among the type of operating contractor, including some operated by universities, some by nonprofits, and some by private industry. Within DOD and DHS, we chose FFRDCs that represent the variation among types these two agencies sponsor, while DOE and HHS only sponsor laboratory type FFRDCs. See appendix II for the FFRDCs included in our case study.

To identify sponsors' contracting and oversight methods at the four agencies in our case study, we interviewed federal department officials at each office that sponsors FFRDCs as well as offices that have contractor management roles and audit roles: (1) DOE's Office of Science, National Nuclear Security Administration, Office of Energy Efficiency and Renewable Energy, Office of Environmental Management, Office of Nuclear Energy, and Office of Inspector General; (2) DOD's departments of the Navy, Air Force, and Army; Office of the Secretary of Defense; Office of Acquisition, Technology, and Logistics; Defense Contract Audit Agency; and the Defense Contract Management Agency;[60] (3) HHS's National Institutes of Health, National Cancer Institute, and National Institute of Allergy and Infectious Diseases; and (4) DHS's Directorate for Science and Technology. In addition, we obtained and analyzed federal and agency policies and guidance, contracts for the FFRDCs in our case studies and other supporting documentation such as performance and award fee plans, sponsoring agreements (when separate from contracts), and a variety of audits and reviews. While we did not assess the effectiveness of or deficiencies in specific agencies' controls, we reviewed agency documentation on incurred cost audits, general auditing controls, single audits, and audited financial statements. We also obtained and analyzed funding data from sponsoring agencies as well as from the National Science Foundation (NSF), which periodically collects and reports statistical information regarding FFRDCs, such as their sponsors, category types, contractors, and funding. While we did not independently verify the data for reliability, we reviewed the NSF's methodology and noted that it reports a 100 percent response rate, no item nonresponse, and no associated sampling errors.

For FFRDCs in our case study, we conducted on-site visits, interviewed key contractor administrative personnel, and obtained information and documentation on how they meet sponsoring agencies' research needs and adhere to policy guidance. We observed examples of the types of research the FFRDCs conduct for their sponsors and obtained and analyzed documentation such as contractor ethics guidance and policies, performance plans, and annual reports.

To obtain the perspective of the government contracting community, we met with high-level representatives of the Professional Services Council, a membership association for companies that provide services to the U.S. federal government.

APPENDIX II. LIST OF 38 FEDERALLY FUNDED RESEARCH AND DEVELOPMENT CENTERS

[Italics indicates the eight FFRDC case studies included in this review.]

Agency/ dept/office of primary sponsor	Name of FFRDC location	Contractor type of contractor	Type of FFRDC
Defense			
Department of the Air Force	Aerospace Center El Segundo, Calif.	Aerospace Corporation Nonprofit	Systems engineering and integration center
Department of the Army	Arroyo Center Santa Monica, Calif.	RAND Corp. Nonprofit	Studies and analyses center
Office of the Secretary of Defense	*C3I [Command, Control, Communications, and Intelligence] Center Bedford, Mass., and McLean, Va.*	*MITRE Corp.* *Nonprofit*	*Systems engineering and integration center*
Department of the Navy	Center for Naval Analyses Alexandria, Va.	CNA Corporation Nonprofit	Studies and analyses center
Office of the Secretary of Defense	*Institute for Defense Analyses Studies and Analyses Center Alexandria, Va.*	*Institute for Defense Analyses* *Nonprofit*	*Studies and analyses center*
National Security Agency	Institute for Defense Analyses Communications and Computing Center Alexandria, Va.	Institute for Defense Analyses Nonprofit	Research & development lab
Department of the Air Force	*Lincoln Laboratory Lexington, Mass.*	*Massachusetts Institute of Technology University*	*Research & development lab*
Office of the Secretary of Defense	National Defense Research Institute Santa Monica, Calif.	RAND Corp. Nonprofit	Studies and analyses center
Department of the Air Force	Project Air Force Santa Monica, Calif.	RAND Corp. Nonprofit	Studies and analyses center
Department of the Army	Software Engineering Institute Pittsburgh, Penn.	Carnegie Mellon University University	Research & development lab
Energy			
Office of Science	Ames Laboratory Ames, Iowa	Iowa State University of Science and Technology University	Research & development lab
Office of Science	Argonne National Laboratory Argonne, Ill.	University of Chicago University	Research & development lab

(Continued)

Agency/ dept/office of primary sponsor	Name of FFRDC location	Contractor type of contractor	Type of FFRDC
Office of Science	Brookhaven National Laboratory Upton, N.Y.	Brookhaven Science Associates, Inc. Nonprofit	Research & development lab
Office of Science	*Ernest Orlando Lawrence Berkeley National Laboratory Berkeley, Calif.*	*University of California University*	*Research & development lab*
Office of Science	Fermi National Accelerator Laboratory Batavia, III.	Universities Research Association, Inc. University	Research & development lab
Office of Nuclear Energy	Idaho National Laboratory Idaho Falls, Idaho	Battelle Energy Alliance, LLC Nonprofit	Research & development lab
National Nuclear Security Administration	Lawrence Livermore National Laboratory Livermore, Calif.	University of California University	Research & development lab
National Nuclear Security Administration	Los Alamos National Laboratory Los Alamos, NM	Los Alamos National Security, LLC Industry	Research & development lab
Office of Energy Efficiency and Renewable Energy	National Renewable Energy Laboratory Golden, Colo.	Midwest Research Institute; Battelle Memorial Institute; Bechtel National, Inc. Nonprofit	Research & development lab
Office of Science	Oak Ridge National Laboratory Oak Ridge, Tenn.	UT-Battelle, LLC Nonprofit	Research & development lab
Office of Science	Pacific Northwest National Laboratory Richland, Wash.	Battelle Memorial Institute Nonprofit	Research & development lab
Office of Science	Princeton Plasma Physics Laboratory Princeton, N.J.	Princeton University University	Research & development lab
National Nuclear Security Administration	*Sandia National Laboratories Albuquerque, NM*	*Sandia Corporation (subsidiary of Lockheed Martin Corp.) Industry*	*Research & development lab*
Office of Environmental Management	Savannah River National Laboratory Aiken, S.C.	Westinghouse Savannah River Co. Industry	Research & development lab
Office of Science	Stanford Linear Accelerator Center Stanford, Calif.	Leland Stanford, Jr., University University	Research & development lab

(Continued)

Agency/ dept/office of primary sponsor	Name of FFRDC location	Contractor type of contractor	Type of FFRDC
Office of Science	Thomas Jefferson National Accelerator Facility Newport News, Va.	Jefferson Science Associates, LLC University/Industry Partnership	Research & development lab
Health and Human Services			
National Institutes of Health, National Cancer Institute	*National Cancer Institute at Frederick Frederick, Md.*	*SAIC-Frederick (wholly owned subsidiary of Science Applications International Corp) Industry*	*Research & development lab*
Homeland Security			
Under Secretary for Science & Technology	*Homeland Security Institute Arlington, Va.*	*Analytic Services, Inc. Nonprofit*	*Studies and analyses center*
Under Secretary for Science & Technology	*National Biodefense Analysis & Countermeasures Center Frederick, Md.*	*Battelle National Biodefense Institute Nonprofit*	*Research & development lab*
National Aeronautics and Space Administration			
	Jet Propulsion Laboratory Pasadena, Calif.	California Institute of Technology University	Research & development lab
National Science Foundation			
	National Astronomy and Ionosphere Center Arecibo, P.R.	Cornell University University	Research & development lab
	National Center for Atmospheric Research Boulder, Colo.	University Corporation for Atmospheric Research University	Research & development lab
	National Optical Astronomy Observatories Tucson, Ariz.	Association of Universities for Research in Astronomy, Inc. University	Research & development lab
	National Radio Astronomy Observatory Charlottesville, Va.	Associated Universities, Inc. University	Research & development lab
	Science and Technology Policy Institute Washington, D.C.	Institute for Defense Analyses Nonprofit	Studies and analyses center
Nuclear Regulatory Commission			
	Center for Nuclear Waste Regulatory Analyses San Antonio, Tex.	Southwest Research Institute Nonprofit	Studies and analyses center

(Continued)

Agency/ dept/office of primary sponsor	Name of FFRDC location	Contractor type of contractor	Type of FFRDC
Transportation			
Federal Aviation Administration	Center for Advanced Aviation System Development McLean, Va.	MITRE Corp. Nonprofit	Research & development lab
Treasury			
Internal Revenue Service	Center for Enterprise Modernization McLean, Va.	MITRE Corp. Nonprofit	Systems engineering and integration center

Source: GAO

APPENDIX III. COMMENTS FROM THE DEPARTMENT OF DEFENSE

OFFICE OF THE UNDER SECRETARY OF DEFENSE
3000 DEFENSE PENTAGON
WASHINGTON, DC 20301-3000

ACQUISITION
TECHNOLOGY
AND LOGISTICS

SEP 29 2008

Mr. William Woods
Director, Acquisition and Sourcing Management
U.S. Government Accountability Office
441 G Street, N.W.
Washington, DC 20548

Dear Mr. Woods:

This is the Department of Defense (DoD) response to the GAO draft report, GAO-09-15, "FEDERAL RESEARCH: Opportunities Exist to Improve the Management and Oversight of Federally Funded Research and Development Centers," dated September 9, 2008, (GAO Code 120687).

The Department's comment to the report recommendation is enclosed. The Department appreciates the opportunity to comment on the draft report.

Sincerely,

Nancy L. Spruill
Director,
Acquisition Resources and Analysis

Enclosure:
As stated

GAO Draft Report Dated September 9, 2008
GAO-09-15 (GAO CODE 120687)

"FEDERAL RESEARCH: OPPORTUNITIES EXIST TO IMPROVE THE
MANAGEMENT AND OVERSIGHT OF FEDERALLY FUNDED RESEARCH AND
DEVELOPMENT CENTERS"

DEPARTMENT OF DEFENSE COMMENTS
TO THE GAO RECOMMENDATIONS

RECOMMENDATION: The GAO recommends that the Secretaries of Energy, Defense,
Homeland Security, and Health and Human Services, take the lead in establishing an ongoing
forum for government personnel from these and other agencies that sponsor Federally Funded
Research and Development Centers (FFRDCs) to discuss their FFRDC policies and practices.
(Page 33/GAO Draft Report)

DOD RESPONSE: Concur. The Department of Defense will work with the other agencies to
establish an ongoing forum for government personnel from all government agencies that sponsor
Federally Funded Research and Development Centers (FFRDCs) to discuss their FFRDC
policies and practices.

APPENDIX IV. COMMENTS FROM THE DEPARTMENT OF ENERGY

Department of Energy
Washington, DC 20585

October 1, 2008

William Woods
Director, Acquisition and Sourcing Management
U. S. Government Accountability Office
441 G Street, N.W.
Washington, DC 20548

Dear Mr. Woods:

This is the Department of Energy (DOE) response to the Government Accountability Office (GAO) Draft Report, GAO-09-15, "FEDERAL RESEARCH: Opportunities Exist to Improve the Management and Oversight of Federally Funded Research and Development Centers," dated October 2008 (GAO-Code 120687). We appreciate the opportunity to comment.

DOE concurs with the recommendation provided in this Draft Report as it relates to sharing best practices for Federally Funded Research and Development Center (FFRDC) oversight and the formation of a forum with the Department of Defense, Department of Homeland Security, and Department of Health and Human Services. The assembly of such a forum should be under the leadership of the Department of Defense, which represents the largest procuring agency and whose statutory exemption to competition is pivotal in any discussion on best practices and lessons learned.

My point of contact for this issue is Sandra Cover, who is available at (202) 287-1344.

Sincerely,

Edward R. Simpson
Director
Office of Procurement and
   Assistance Management

APPENDIX V. COMMENTS FROM THE DEPARTMENT OF HEALTH AND HUMAN SERVICES

DEPARTMENT OF HEALTH & HUMAN SERVICES   OFFICE OF THE SECRETARY

Assistant Secretary for Legislation
Washington, DC 20201

OCT   2 2008

William Woods, Director
Acquisition and Sourcing Management
Government Accountability Office
441 G Street NW
Washington, DC 20548

Dear Ms. Woods:

Enclosed are the Department's comments on the U.S. Government Accountability Office's (GAO) draft report entitled: "Federal Research: Opportunities Exist to Improve the Management and Oversight of Federally Funded Research and Development Centers" (GAO-09-15).

The Department appreciates the opportunity to review and comment on this report before its publication.

Sincerely,

Vincent J. Ventimiglia, Jr.
Assistant Secretary for Legislation

Attachment

**COMMENTS OF THE NATIONAL INSTITUTES OF HEALTH (NIH)
ON THE GOVERNMENT ACCOUNTABILITY OFFICE DRAFT REPORT, *OPPORTUNITIES
EXIST TO IMPROVE THE MANAGEMENT AND OVERSIGHT OF FEDERALLY FUNDED
RESEARCH AND DEVELOPMENT CENTERS (GAO-09-15)***

GAO RECOMMENDATION

The Secretary of Health and Human Services review its policy regarding personal
conflicts of interest for its sponsored FFRDC and revise as appropriate to ensure that it
addresses all personnel in a position to make or materially influence research findings or
agency decision making.

NIH RESPONSE

NIH concurs with the recommendation and is currently reviewing its options for revisions
to its conflict of interest policy. Although the GAO report states that HHS does not
require FFRDC contractors to implement personal conflict of interest policies, NIH R&D
contracts fall under the tenet of 45 CFR Part 94. NIH recently promulgated a standard
contract clause to reinforce compliance with 45 CFR Part 94, and the clause has been
included in the new FFRDC contract.

This regulation requires objectivity in research by establishing standards to ensure that
investigators (defined as the principal investigator and any other person who is
responsible for the design, conduct, or reporting of research funded under NIH contracts
and spouses and dependents of investigators) will not be biased by any conflicting
financial interest. Prior to expenditure of funds, and on an ongoing basis, an Institution,
including the FFRDC, must report to NIH the existence of any conflicting interests it has
found and provide assurance that the conflict has been managed, reduced, or eliminated
in accordance with the regulation. NIH is also drafting an Advance Notice of Proposed
Rulemaking (ANPRM) to seek comments from the public on whether the regulations
should be amended.

GAO RECOMMENDATION

The Secretaries of Energy, Defense, Homeland Security, and Health and Human
Services, which together sponsor the vast majority of the government's FFRDCs, take the
lead in establishing an ongoing forum for government personnel from these and other
agencies that sponsor FFRDCs to discuss their agencies' FFRDC policies and practices.

NIH RESPONSE

NIH is considering this recommendation, including aspects associated with the creation
of and participation in a forum to share best practices for FFRDC oversight.

Acknowledgments

In addition to the individuals named above, key contributors to this report were John Neumann, Assistant Director; Cheryl Williams, Assistant Director; Sharron Candon; Suzanne Sterling; Jacqueline Wade; and Peter Zwanzig.

End Notes

[1] Data from the National Science Foundation, *Science and Engineering Indicators* (2008)—the latest available.

[2] "Sponsor" means the executive agency that manages, administers, monitors, funds, and is responsible for the overall use of an FFRDC. Federal Acquisition Regulation (FAR) 35.017(b).

[3] References to DOE in this report include the National Nuclear Security Administration, a separately organized agency within DOE that is responsible for the management and security of the nation's nuclear weapons, nuclear nonproliferation, and naval reactor programs.

[4] For a brief overview of the evolution and legal framework applicable to FFRDCs, see GAO, *Principles of Federal Appropriations Law, vol. 4, 2nd ed.*, GAO-01-179SP (Washington, D.C.: March 2001), pp. 17-81 through 17-85.

[5] Pub. L. No. 101-509 (1990).

[6] FAR 35.017(a)(2).

[7] FAR 35.0 17-1, Sponsoring Agreements.

[8] http://www.nsf.gov/statistics (last accessed Oct. 3, 2008).

[9] See 10 U.S.C. § 2304(c)(3); 41 U.S.C. § 253(c)(3); FAR 6.302-3(a) (2)(ii).

[10] The Energy and Water Development Appropriations Act, 2004 (Pub. L. No. 108-137, § 301), requires DOE to compete its management and operations (M&O) contracts, the contract type DOE uses at its labs, unless the Secretary of Energy waives the requirement and notifies the Energy and Water Subcommittees 60 days prior to contract award.

[11] The lab was subsequently designated as an FFRDC in 1975.

[12] Subcommittee on Oversight of Government Management, Committee on Governmental Affairs, U.S. Senate. *Inadequate Federal Oversight of Federally Funded Research and Development Centers*, July 1992.

[13] GAO had reported in 1988, that full and open competition between FFRDCs and nonFFRDCs could provide some assurance that sponsors had selected the most effective source for the work. The report also stated, however, that exposing FFRDCs to marketplace competition could fundamentally alter the character of the special relationship between FFRDCs and their sponsors. GAO, *Competition: Issues on Establishing and Using Federally Funded Research and Development Centers,* GAO/NSIAD-88-22 (Washington, D.C.: March 1988).

[14] GAO, *Federally Funded R&D Centers: Issues Related to the Management of DOD- Sponsored Centers.* GAO/NSIAD-96-112 (Washington, D.C.: Aug. 6, 1996).

[15] Cost-reimbursement contracts—which the FAR generally considers to be the usually appropriate contract form for R&D—provide for payment of allowable direct and indirect incurred costs as prescribed in the contract. These contracts establish an estimate of total cost to obligate funds and establish a ceiling that the contractor may not exceed without contracting officer approval.

[16] See FAR subparts 16.3 and 16.4.

[17] According to FAR subpart 16.3, a cost-plus-fixed-fee contract is a cost-reimbursement contract that provides for payment to the contractor of a negotiated fee that is fixed at the inception of the contract. The fixed fee does not vary with actual cost, but may be adjusted as a result of changes in the work to be performed under the contract.

[18] This accounts for about 75 percent of Project Air Force's annual funding.

[19] GAO, *Defense Contracting: Additional Personal Conflict of Interest Safeguards Needed for Certain DOD Contractor Employees,* GAO-08-169 (Washington, D.C.: Mar. 7, 2008).

[20] FAR 35.017(a)(2); 35.017-2(h).

[21] In September 2006, the president and trustee of the Institute for Defense Analyses resigned before it was determined by DOD's Inspector General that his position on two defense subcontractors' corporate boards violated the FFRDC's conflicts-of-interest policy. In July 2006, his dual roles as FFRDC president and as a member of one of the defense subcontractor's board of directors drew public and congressional scrutiny regarding a business case for the Air Force on a multiyear procurement of the F-22 Raptor aircraft. Because this subcontractor manufactures a missile launcher for the F-22 aircraft's prime contractor, conflict of interest

concerns were raised that the FFRDC president stood to financially profit from a favorable multiyear procurement decision for the F-22.

[22] FAR 17.601 states: "Management and operating contract" means an agreement under which the government contracts for the operation, maintenance, or support, on its behalf, of a government-owned or -controlled research, development, special production, or testing establishment wholly or principally devoted to one or more major programs of the contracting federal agency.

[23] Department of Energy Acquisition Regulation 970.0371, Conduct of employees of DOE management and operating contractors.

[24] GAO-08- 169. This report identified some examples of how DOD FFRDC contractors that were implementing the new policy.

[25] FAR 35.017-3(a); 35.017(a)(2). An FFRDC may perform for other than the sponsoring agency (1) under the Economy Act, or other applicable legislation, when the work is not otherwise available from the private sector or (2) under a separate contract with the nonsponsoring agency, when permitted by the sponsor.

[26] The Homeland Security Act of 2002 included a provision to establish the Homeland Security Institute. Section 312 of the Act identifies specific types of duties or capabilities that may be requested to provide to DHS and the homeland security community.

[27] The Executive Agent designates membership and chairs the HSI Advisory Group, and designates replacements for HSI Advisory Group members.

[28] The National Intelligence Program and the Military Intelligence Program.

[29] As defined in the FAR 37.104, a personal services contract is characterized by the employer-employee relationship it creates between the government and the contractor's personnel. The government is normally required to obtain its employees by direct hire under competitive appointment or other procedures required by the civil service laws. Obtaining personal services by contract, rather than by direct hire, circumvents those laws unless Congress has specifically authorized acquisition of the services by contract. Agencies shall not award personal services contracts unless specifically authorized by statute (e.g., 5 U.S.C. 3109) to do so.

[30] FAR Part 2 definition of "inherently governmental functions": An inherently governmental function is a function that is so intimately related to the public interest as to mandate performance by government employees. These functions include those activities that require either the exercise of discretion in applying Government authority or the making of value judgments in making decisions for the government. Governmental functions normally fall into two categories: (1) the act of governing, i.e., the discretionary exercise of government authority, and (2) monetary transactions and entitlements.

[31] The decision to accept such work is to be in accordance with DOE's Work Authorization Order 412.1A.

[32] DOE field organizations (contracting officers) must receive a work authorization signed by the appropriate primary DOE Organization—organizations that direct work to be performed by site and facility management contractors and other contractors determined by the procurement executive. Primary DOE Organizations, including National Nuclear Security Administration (NNSA), must review and approve the work as acceptable for the contractor before obligating funds for the contract.

[33] DOD and DHS officials said their FFRDCs do not do "work for others" for private sector companies, and DOE officials said their FFRDCs generally conduct work only for federal agencies.

[34] FAR 17.504(e).

[35] Technology transfer can mean many things—technical assistance to solve a specific problem; use of unique facilities; access to patents and software; exchange of personnel; and cooperative research. Technology transfer mechanisms can include Cooperative Agreements, Cooperative Research and Development Agreements (CRADAs), Cost-Shared Contracts/Subcontracts, Licensing, and Work for Others.

[36] See generally FAR subparts 27.3 and 27.4.

[37] FAR 35.017(a)(2); 37.017-3(b).

[38] See DOE Order 481.1B, att. 1.

[39] DOE officials said that DOE programs and work for others customers both are charged an indirect cost rate that includes a Laboratory Directed Research Development component.

[40] In December 2005 and January 2007, we issued reports on the use of award and incentive fees at the Department of Defense and the National Aeronautics and Space Administration, respectively. GAO, *Defense Acquisitions: DOD Has Paid Billions in Award and Incentive Fees Regardless of Acquisition Outcomes*, GAO-06-66 (Washington, D.C.: Dec. 19, 2005) and *NASA Procurement: Use of Award Fees for Achieving Program Outcomes Should Be Improved*, GAO-07-58 (Washington, D.C.: Jan. 17, 2007).

[41] The performance-based approach focuses the evaluation of the contractor's performance against eight goals: (1) provide for efficient and effective mission accomplishment; (2) Provide for efficient and effective design, fabrication, construction and operations of research facilities; (3) provide effective and efficient science and technology program management; (4) provide competent leadership and stewardship; (5) sustain and enhance effectiveness of integrated safety, health, and environmental protection; (6) deliver efficient, effective, and responsive business systems and resources; (7) sustain excellence in operating, maintaining, and renewing the facility and infrastructure portfolio to meet laboratory needs; and (8) sustain and enhance the effectiveness of integrated safeguards, security, and emergency management systems.

[42] DOD generally does not provide award or incentive fees to its FFRDCs, which for our case study included the Institute for Defense Analyses, operating the Studies and Analysis Center; MITRE, operating the C3I systems engineering and integration center; and Massachusetts Institute of Technology operating the Lincoln Laboratory.

[43] FAR 35.017-2(e) requires that the FFRDC sponsor in establishing an FFRDC ensure that controls are established to ensure that the costs of the services being provided to the government are reasonable. FAR 35.017-4 requires that the review conducted prior to extending the FFRDC contract or agreement include an assessment of the adequacy of the FFRDC management in ensuring a cost-effective operation.

[44] Since this review of FFRDCs focuses only on broad processes employed in the management and operation of FFRDCs, we reviewed practices and procedures that agencies use but did not attempt to determine either the most effective agency cost, accounting, or auditing controls, or the effectiveness of or deficiencies in specific agencies' cost or internal controls at the agencies and FFRDCs we reviewed.

[45] FAR Part 31 specifies different cost principles on the allowabiity of various kinds of costs for different types of contractors: FAR 31.2 specifies allowable cost principles for commercial organizations; FAR 31.3, which incorporates OMB Circular No. A-21, applies to educational institutions; and FAR 31.7, which incorporates OMB Circular No. A-122, applies to nonprofit organizations. FAR 31.201-2(a) governing contracts with commercial firms states, for example, that the factors to be considered in determining whether a cost is allowable include: (1) reasonableness; (2) allocabiity; (3) standards promulgated by the Cost Accounting Standards Board, if applicable; otherwise GAAP; (4) the terms of the contract; and (5) any limitations set fort in subpart 31.2.

[46] FAR 52.216-7 "Allowable Cost and Payment" requires the government to pay a contractor, if requested, as work progresses, in amounts determined to be allowable by the contracting officer in accordance with the applicable cost principles identified above.

[47] FAR 42.705-1(b)(4); 42.705-2(b)(2).

[48] Financial audits address issues such as compliance with cost-accounting standards, compensation and labor cost reviews, and advance agreements on forward-pricing factors such as indirect cost rates and labor hour rates used in repetitive-pricing formulas, among many others. Operational audits include audits of accounting and information technology systems' internal controls; and reviews of integrated business processes, program administration, financial and business operations, and project execution.

[49] DOE generally requires M&O contractors, including the contractors for Sandia National Laboratory and the Ernest Orlando Lawrence Berkeley National Laboratory, to perform annual internal audits, under Department of Energy Acquisition Regulation § 970.5232-3 and standard contract clause I.103 (Accounts, Record, and Inspection–June 2007).

[50] The Cooperative Audit Strategy was first developed and implemented in 1992 and implemented in 2007 with respect to all M&O contractors, including FFRDCs.

[51] 31 U.S.C. 7501-7507. Office of Management and Budget (OMB) Circular A-133, "Audits of States, Local Governments, and Non-profit Organizations," implements the Single Audit Act and is applicable to all FFRDCs operated by an educational institution or non-profit organization, but not to those operated by commercial contractors. Audits are commonly referred to as "single audits" and are performed in accordance with Generally Accepted Government Auditing Standards (GAGAS). The Single Audit Act is designed to help federal agencies meet the need for oversight and uniformly structured audits of non-profit recipients that expend annually a total of $500,000 or more in federal awards. Rather than being a detailed review of individual programs, the single audit is an organization-wide financial statement audit that includes the audit of the Schedule of Federal Awards, and also focuses on internal control and the recipient's compliance with laws and regulations governing the receipt of federal financial awards. The federal agency that makes an award is responsible for overseeing whether the single audits are completed in a timely manner, while the award recipient is responsible for ensuring that a single audit is performed and submitted when due and for following up and taking corrective action on any audit findings.

[52] GAO, *Single Audit Quality: Actions Needed to Address Persistent Audit Quality Problems*, GAO-08-213T (Washington, D.C.: Oct. 25, 2007).

[53] According to the NSF Master List of FFRDCs, five FFRDCs (four at DOE and one at HHS) are operated by private companies.

[54] The Securities Exchange Act of 1934 as amended, including implementing regulations, requires publicly traded companies to make periodic filings with the Securities and Exchange Commission that disclose their financial status and changes in financial condition. These publicly traded companies are also subject to the Sarbanes-Oxley Act of 2002 requirements that include provisions for governance, auditing, and financial reporting.

[55] The supplemental information is prepared by MITRE's independent auditors and, while not formally audited, was subjected to the same auditing procedures as applied to the corporation's financial statements, and according to the auditor are "fairly stated in all material respects in relation to the financial statements taken as a whole."

[56] FAR 35.017-4(c).

[57] Department of Energy Acquisition Regulation § 970.1706-1.

[58] Department of Energy, *Report of the External Members Best Practices Working Group*, The Laboratory Operations Board, Management Best Practices for the National Laboratories, September 9, 2003.

[59] GAO, *Results-Oriented Government: Practices That Can Help Enhance and Sustain Collaboration among Federal Agencies*, GAO-06-15 (Washington, D.C.: Oct. 21, 2005).

[60] We did not meet with the National Security Agency since its FFRDC's work is classified, and it was not included in our case study.

In: Federal Role in Funding Research and Development   ISBN: 978-1-60741-486-5
Editor: Piper B. Collins   © 2010 Nova Science Publishers, Inc.

Chapter 7

RENEWABLE ENERGY R&D FUNDING HISTORY: A COMPARISON WITH FUNDING FOR NUCLEAR ENERGY, FOSSIL ENERGY, AND ENERGY EFFICIENCY R&D

Fred Sissine

SUMMARY

Energy research and development (R&D) intended to advance technology played an important role in the successful outcome of World War II. In the post-war era, the federal government conducted R&D on fossil fuel and nuclear energy sources to support peacetime economic growth. The energy crises of the 1970s spurred the government to broaden the focus to include renewable energy and energy efficiency. Over the 30-year period from the Department of Energy's inception at the beginning of fiscal Year (FY) 1978 through FY2007, federal spending for renewable energy R&D amounted to about 16% of the energy R&D total, compared with 15% for energy efficiency, 25% for fossil, and 41% for nuclear. For the 60-year period from 1948 through 2007, nearly 11% went to renewables, compared with 9% for efficiency, 25% for fossil, and 54% for nuclear.

INTRODUCTION

This report provides a cumulative history of Department of Energy (DOE) funding for renewable energy compared with funding for the other energy technologies — nuclear energy, fossil energy, and energy efficiency. Specifically, it provides a comparison that covers cumulative funding over the past 10 years (FY1998-FY2007), a second comparison that covers the 30-year period since DOE was established at the beginning of fiscal year 1978 (FY1978-FY2007), and a third comparison that covers a 60-year funding history (FY1948-FY2007).

GUIDE TO TABLES AND CHARTS

Table 1 shows the cumulative funding totals in real terms for the past 10 years (first column), 30 years (second column), and 60 years (third column). **Table 2** converts the data from **Table 1** into relative shares of spending for each technology, expressed as a percentage of total spending for each period.

Figure 1 displays the data from the first column of **Table 2** as a pie chart. That chart shows the relative shares of cumulative DOE spending for each technology over the 10 years from FY1998 through FY2007. **Figure 2** provides a similar chart for the period from FY1978 through FY2007. **Figure 3** shows a chart for FY1948 through FY2007.

BACKGROUND

The availability of energy — especially gasoline and other liquid fuels — played a critical role in World War II. Another energy-related factor was the application of research and development (R&D) to the atomic bomb and other military technologies. During the post World War II era, the federal government began to apply R&D to the peacetime development of energy sources to support economic growth. At that time, the primary R&D focus was on fossil fuels and new forms of energy derived from nuclear fission and nuclear fusion.

From FY1948 through FY1977 the federal government provided an extensive amount of R&D support for fossil energy and nuclear power technologies.[1] Total spending on fossil energy technologies over that period amounted to about $15.4 billion, in constant FY2008 dollars. The federal government spent about $46.4 billion (in constant FY2008 dollars) during that period for nuclear fission and nuclear fusion energy R&D.[2]

Table 1. DOE Energy Technology Cumulative Funding Totals (billions of 2008 dollars)

Technology	Period		
	FY1998-FY2007 (10 years)	FY1978-FY2007 (30 years)	FY1948-FY2007 (60 years)
Renewable Energy	$ 3.94	$ 15.43	$ 16.96
Energy Efficiency	6.02	14.18	14.32
Fossil Energy	5.36	24.22	39.60
Nuclear Energy	6.41	38.62	85.01
Electric Systems	0.93	2.85	3.02
Total	$22.66	$95.30	$158.91

Sources: *DOE Budget Authority History Table by Appropriation,* May 2007; *DOE Congressional Budget Requests* (several years); DOE (Pacific Northwest Laboratory), *An Analysis of Federal Incentives Used to Stimulate Energy Production,* 1980. Deflator Source: *The Budget for Fiscal Year 2009.* Historical Tables. Table 10.1. Gross Domestic Product and Deflators Used in the Historical Tables, 1940-2013. p. 194-195.

Table 2. DOE Energy Technology Share of Funding (percent; derived from Table 1)

Technology	Period		
	FY1998-FY2007 (10 years)	FY1978-FY2007 (30 years)	FY1948-FY2007 (60 years)
Renewable Energy	17.4%	16.2%	10.7%
Energy Efficiency	26.6%	14.9%	9.0%
Fossil Energy	23.7%	25.4%	24.9%
Nuclear Energy	28.3%	40.5%	53.5%
Electric Systems	4.1%	3.0%	1.9%
Total	100.0%	100.0%	100.0%

Sources: *DOE Budget Authority History Table by Appropriation,* May 2007; *DOE Congressional Budget Requests* (several years); DOE (Pacific Northwest Laboratory), *An Analysis of Federal Incentives Used to Stimulate Energy Production,* 1980; DOE Conservation and Renewable Energy Base Table. February 1990. Deflator Source: *The Budget for Fiscal Year 2009.* Historical Tables. Table 10.1. Gross Domestic Product and Deflators Used in the Historical Tables, 1940-2013. p. 194-195.

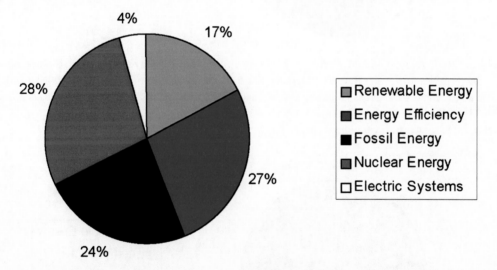

Sources: *DOE Budget Authority History Table by Appropriation*, May 2007; *DOE Congressional Budget Requests* (several years); Deflator Source: *The Budget for Fiscal Year 2009.* Historical Tables. Table 10.1. Gross Domestic Product and Deflators Used in the Historical Tables, 1940-20 13. p. 194-195.

Figure 1. DOE Energy Technology Share of Funding, FY1998-FY2007

The energy crises of the 1970s spurred the federal government to expand its R&D programs to include renewable (wind, solar, biomass, geothermal, hydro) energy and energy efficiency technologies. Modest efforts to support renewable energy and energy efficiency began during the early 1970s. From FY1973 through FY1977 the federal government spent about $1.5 billion (in constant FY2008 dollars) on renewable energy R&D, $140 million on energy efficiency R&D, and $170 million on electric systems R&D.[3]

The Department of Energy was established by law in 1977. All of the energy R&D programs — fossil, nuclear, renewable, and energy efficiency — were brought under its administration. DOE also undertook a small program in energy storage and electricity system R&D that supports the four main energy technology programs.[4] DOE's funding support for those technologies began in FY1978. Funding for all four of the main technologies skyrocketed initially, and then fell dramatically in the early 1980s.

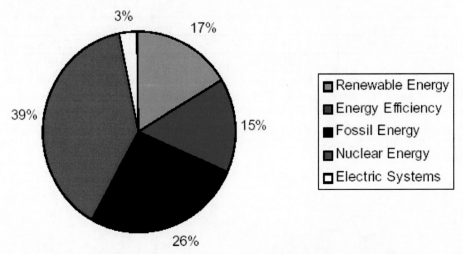

Sources: *DOE Budget Authority History Table by Appropriation*, May 2007; *DOE Congressional Budget Requests* (several years); Deflator Source: *The Budget for Fiscal Year 2009.* Historical Tables. Table 10.1. Gross Domestic Product and Deflators Used in the Historical Tables, 1940-20 13. p. 194-195.

Figure 2. DOE Energy Technology Share of Funding, FY1978-FY2007

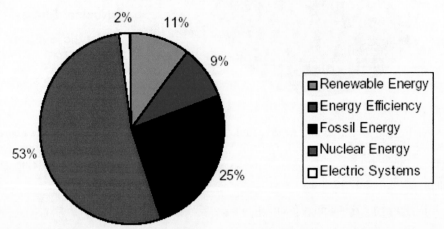

Sources: *DOE Budget Authority History Table by Appropriation*, May 2007; *DOE Congressional Budget Requests* (several years); DOE (Pacific Northwest Laboratory), *An Analysis of Federal Incentives Used to Stimulate Energy Production, 1980; DOE Conservation and Renewable Energy Base Table.* Feb. 1990. Deflator Source: *The Budget for Fiscal Year 2009.* Historical Tables. Table 10.1. p. 194-195.

Figure 3. DOE Energy Technology Share of Funding, FY1978-FY2007

End Notes

[1] DOE. Pacific Northwest Laboratory. *An Analysis of Federal Incentives Used to Stimulate Energy Production.* 1980. The spending for fossil energy included coal, oil, and natural gas technologies.

[2] DOE (Pacific Northwest Laboratory), *An Analysis of Federal Incentives Used to Stimulate Energy Production*, 1980.

[3] *DOE Conservation and Renewable Energy Base Table*. February 1990.

[4] This program includes R&D on advanced batteries to store electricity and transmission equipment to transfer electricity with less heat loss (i.e. at higher levels of energy efficiency).

CHAPTER SOURCES

The following chapters have been previously published:

Chapter 1 – This is an edited, excerpted and augmented edition of a United States Congressional Research Service publication, Report Order Code RL34645, dated September 24, 2008.

Chapter 2 – This is an edited, excerpted and augmented edition of a United States Congressional Research Service publication, Report Order Code RL33586, dated October 23, 2008.

Chapter 3 – This is an edited, excerpted and augmented edition of a United States Congressional Research Service publication, Report Order Code RL34435, dated September 26, 2008.

Chapter 4 – This is an edited, excerpted and augmented edition of a United States Congressional Research Service publication, Report Order Code RL34448, dated October 23, 2008.

Chapter 5 – This is an edited, excerpted and augmented edition of a United States Congressional Budget Office publication, Pub. No. 2927, dated June 2007.

Chapter 6 – This is an edited, excerpted and augmented edition of a United States Government Accountability Office (GAO), Report to Congressional Committees. Publication GAO-09-15, dated October 2008.

Chapter 7 – This is an edited, excerpted and augmented edition of a United States Congressional Research Service publication, Report Order Code RS22858, dated April 9, 2008.

INDEX

D

H

I

J

K

L